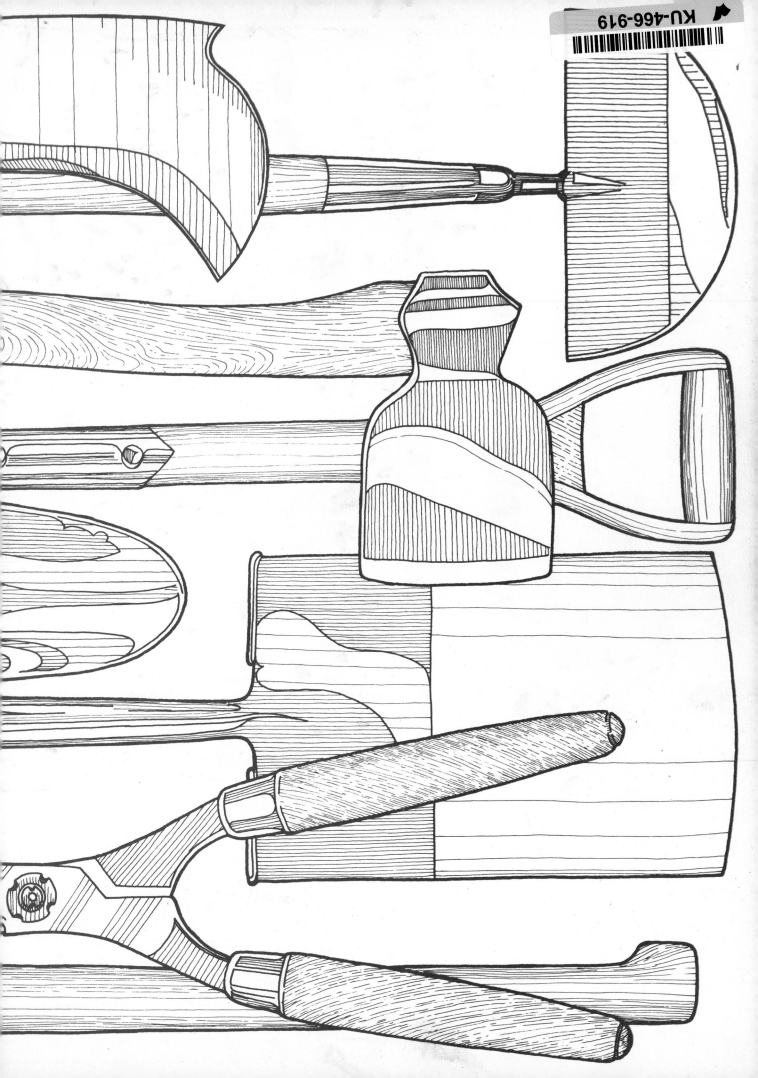

Gardening
for Beginners

Gardening for Beginners

Frances Hutchison

Marshall Cavendish London & New York

Editor: Rose-Marie Hillier

Published by
Marshall Cavendish Books Limited
58 Old Compton Street
London W1V 5PA

© Marshall Cavendish Limited 1976, 1978

First printed 1976
Reprinted 1978

ISBN 0 85685 157 4

Printed in Great Britain.

Title page: *Panther lily, Lilium pardalinum, is aflame with glorious colour.*

Page 4: *These freesias are bulbs with fragrant flowers ideal for cutting.*

Page 6: *Hibiscus 'Blue Bird' a cultivar of Hibiscus syriacus, syn. Althaea fruticosa.*

Page 8: *River-washed stones and concrete slabs make a delightful pathway through this garden.*

Introduction

There are a thousand ways to garden, which is perhaps why gardening is so absorbing and why a garden reflects something of its owner's personality. You can be a neat, weed-picking, orderly gardener, or a gardener who welcomes the nettles for the butterflies' sakes. Yet much the same things bind people to a love of gardening—the sight of a cherry tree breaking into blossom, the first crocus of the season bravely erect, a lone flower on a plant that has stayed obstinately poker-leaved for months, the changing yet familiar beauty of the seasons which speeds you through the months so fast.

So when you begin gardening you need to know yourself a little. If you have a very orderly laid-out landscaping plan, will you have the energy, the time and the patience to keep it up to scratch? There is nothing more disheartening than to know that you cannot keep up with the work. So aim to climb small mountains first; in gardening there will always be another peak ahead of you. That is its fascination—there is harder, more intriguing work to tackle as you grow more experienced.

To begin to garden is not difficult in any way. You could make do with a fork and spade, a packet of seeds and a patch of earth. And why not? There are no sacred paths to follow, gardening is a time to enjoy yourself, to enthuse, to cherish beliefs against a world of friendly advice and dire warnings. There will be disappointments, even disasters, but there are no greater triumphs of love and hope in any other pastime.

This book has many simple pieces of advice in it that you can follow when you want to. There are useful facts and a few more complicated explanations for those who want to add to their knowledge as they do more gardening.

There are some brief descriptions of how plants feed and grow, for if you have to use fertilizers or make a compost heap, you surely want a reason for doing it. There is a section on soil types, which is background information that you will find useful. Take it in when you are ready, do not feel it is all essential to know by heart before a shrub will wave a green and graceful finger at you or a flower will brave life on your border.

This book is here for you to enjoy along with your gardening, to give you fresh ideas. You can grow your own fruit and vegetables, and plan the most marvellous flower and shrub combinations. And when you have watched and worked through the seasons, you will go on to more and more exciting discoveries.

One thing is certain. Gardens of flowers grown by other people will not give you half the ecstatic pleasure that you will get from the smallest corner of plants you have grown yourself.

Contents

Planning the garden you want

You can spend many happy hours with paper and pencil poised over gardening catalogues, or sitting idly on a garden seat, deciding what you really want in the garden. Whether you have inherited your garden with your house or are beginning with a bare patch and an awesome pile of builders' rubble, you have to choose what you want to put into a garden and what you want to get out of it. It may be that you have the temperament to like a rather wild garden where animals and birds feel almost as much at home as you do. Or you may be gregarious, or have a romping family you would like to get outdoors all through the summer at least—and that is a good reason for an outdoor entertainment area and a barbecue. Or you may have a passion for alpines, those creeping, colourful perennials which can clothe a hillside garden with a patchwork quilt.

Then there are things that must go into a garden to make its organization easier—such as the utility area, tool-shed, compost heap or perhaps a greenhouse.

When you put a plant in the garden, label it unobtrusively, so that you know what is growing. It is incredibly easy to forget the names of plants you have put in. Alternatively, keep a rough diagram of the garden and mark in the plants on this; or keep notes in a 'gardener's diary'. You will be very glad later on to have easy reference

Below: *Dryopteris abbreviata, a fern, likes shade and moisture. Grows in a rocky crevice.*

Above: *An 18th century stone garden seat in an English garden.*

Below: *With native plants you can establish a wild garden.*

to the varieties you have chosen.

If you are designing your garden on paper, use the diagram to mark in the plants that are growing in the same way that any landscape garden plan is prepared by the professional.

It may not be the most romantic part of planning a garden but it is a good idea to start with the paths and where they will go. For path-paving materials and plantings, see later chapters in this book, but for path routes read on.

You need paved paths to all house doors, generally speaking and this alone can tax your imagination to stop them looking like the perimeter of a concentration camp. Then you need paths across the garden, a

path to a seat or two, a path to the utility area, and to the washing line. Paths can be straight but although it is the shortest route to your destination it probably is not the prettiest. You need a combination of artistry and practicality—try curving them a little.

If you live in a terrace house then the 'pocket-handkerchief' front garden and the path to the front door need to be considered as one space, with paving perhaps right up to the boundaries to create the illusion of greater space. This would need plants spilling over it and tubs of flowers and shrubs to soften the look. You could give a wide-paved path a special feeling with carefully-chosen plants and fill the rest of the garden

with a chamomile or ivy lawn surrounded by paving and planting pockets. On a large scale this sort of landscaping is expensive; in a terrace front garden it becomes economically viable. Choose small-scale plants such as the cushion and ground-covering plants in keeping with the size of the garden. Plants such as *Alyssum spinosum roseum* or *Dianthus neglectus* (one of the pinks), and the small winter-flowering cherry tree are ideal.

After paths, consider these alternatives.

A **labour-saving garden** is worth planning if you have limited time and if you

This water garden with fountains is elaborate but even a small pond can be fascinating.

are the sort of person who does not want to feel pressured into having a lot to do. It is in this initial thinking stage that you can save yourself later hard labour—by going for every idea that simplifies work and maintenance. Shrubs and trees are easier to look after than annuals; ground covers can save you weeding time and caring time; walls are more expensive to put up than hedges but they do not need clipping every year. Place paths and pavings carefully because where you pave you have to sweep, so route them away from debris-dropping trees. Avoid any beautiful plant so fussy that you have to slave over it.

Do you want **playing space** for young children? You want to watch toddlers, so give them play space of their own near the kitchen window and door. Give it boundaries so that wandering is strictly prohibited. Play space is not a static project, it should alter as children grow. Yesterday's sand pit is tomorrow's garden pool. For the very young—sand pit, small water containers and hose, space for a ball game and painting outdoors etc. For the next size up—swing, paved path for tricycle, paddling pool (to be supervized), solid, safe climbing structures. Leave a small garden bed for the child to grow plants. For older children, the garden might offer a barbecue, badminton and other sports and games; maybe even a swimming pool.

A **wild garden** within the main garden cuts down on work, reducing the amount of garden that needs a neat and trim look, and all the work that goes into it. Plan naturalized areas at the edge of the garden where it might run into a boundary, wood, field or ditch. Children love a wild, secret

Above: *Small sunny garden is mass-planted for colour. Greenhouse is behind fence.*

Below: *Raised beds of brick are softened by closely-planted rhododendrons.*

Below: *Fill a small tub with flowers for quick colour to brighten dull garden areas.*

place to visit in a garden and beasts, plants such as Japanese azaleas, lilies, ericas, and cotoneasters, and birds favour its screening and quiet.

A **bog garden** for intractably damp places. When you cannot beat nature join her! Team together for example, yellow arum lilies (zantedeschia) and the mauve-blue Japanese iris, or plant marsh marigolds, primulas and forget-me-nots, for this garden.

A **kitchen garden** will give you your own vegetables but it needs a place in the sun. If you can give it that and also a windbreak you are off to a good start.

If you are a bird-fancier? Then you might want a part of the garden with good cover for birds and with nesting boxes and bird table. Some even greater enthusiasts might want to plan an aviary.

A **paved terrace** for eating out or entertaining friends. This is more of a landscaping than a gardening project and an expensive one at that. You might be able to lay terrace paving yourself or save it as a later project, but consider it early so that you do not plant impossible things where the terrace might one day be. You want a terrace to be south or west-facing and wind-protected.

A **courtyard** suits a small garden because you can give it privacy and shelter and lovely walled backgrounds. It also suits a very large garden where you want to limit your intensive work to a small area and leave the rest of the garden informally planted. Courts can give charming vistas from house windows and ideally lead from French windows, extending useful living space. Come rain and snow and the living room will suffer, but in the bright sunny intervals so beloved by weather forecasters the family can go outside to enjoy themselves.

What do you see from windows? It cannot perhaps be a major consideration in garden design but it certainly is worth trying to give each window a special view of its own. However, if you happen to fall in love with a giant tree or a rampant plant, just outside the window is not the place to put it.

There is no point in making a beautiful garden if you cannot sit and enjoy it. Therefore **garden seats** should rank high in your garden plans. A hidden seat, for instance or perhaps a group where everyone can sit on a summer's evening. For a private seat, give the sitter something to contemplate— a small pool, a bird table, a rock garden.

Pools, ponds, springs, waterfalls, fountains—the soothing sound of water and the cool look of a pool are worth planning in any garden. From the smallest child upwards everyone finds fascination in water—but make sure the smallest child

cannot toddle to a pool on his own. Once established, pools need very little maintaining.

You cannot fit everything into the average-sized or small garden, and it is not only the size of the garden which limits your possibilities. It depends too, on the climate of the garden, and every garden also has its own microcosmic climate— places where it is damp, or shady, sunny or dry, sheltered or exposed. Half the fun and skill of gardening is to fit plants to the conditions that they enjoy and thrive in.

If you have a large garden, you can choose more space-taking ideas, such as the wild garden, kitchen garden, orchard, as well as having a more landscaped garden near the house. The approach to the large garden is to divide it into areas, or workable sections, with their own order and design. Areas can be separated by hedges, shrubbery, screen wall or fences, or the garden can merge attractively from lawn and borders to shrubbery and woodland, or pass through a pergola-lined walk to the main garden or orchard. The most simple large garden may have a minimum of organized flower beds and might rely more on large sweeps of grass, shrubbery, trees, bulbs and rhododendrons to create a woodland effect. Instead of the ornamental pond that a small garden might have, the large garden could have a natural-looking pond with scope for a variety of water-loving plants such as water lilies. If you do decide on a large-lawn effect, just keep to one or two special tree or shrub plantings in it to ease mowing.

Left: *This design, in plan form, gives an idea of what you might include in a small town garden (perhaps 15–20m long by 5–10m wide). There is plenty of space for outdoor relaxation and a small paved entertainment area has been included. Tubs with flowering annuals can be placed on the terrace for quick colour. The vegetable garden is hidden behind the hedge; utility area is suitably placed—a concrete slab path leads to this through a narrow lawn area.*

Right: *The larger garden (perhaps 50–60m long by 10–15m wide) could include a small orchard, greenhouse and utility area hidden behind a hedge that spans the complete width of the garden. A sand pit and play area for children have been included in this design— this can later be converted to an area for a small swimming pool, ball game field, or for building a landscaped rockery and fish pool. The area is bordered with shrubs including dwarf conifers. Both designs could be adapted to the dimensions of most properties and could include many more interesting aspects of gardening.*

The average garden has room for a small lawn area, flower beds, perhaps a tiny pool, or rockery and lots of shrubs and perhaps fruit trees trained to fences and walls. Keep away from choosing the very large, spreading trees. Priorities in the suburban garden are privacy-plantings, with evergreen shrubs and hedges, and the disguise by beautiful climbers of unattractive boundary fences if you have them. Give some space to pots that can be filled with whatever is currently in flower, and favour shrubs which will give spring or summer flowers and autumn colour. Choose evergreens with interesting shape and colour. Small plants like alpines and ground covers are attractive in corners.

In the small town or terrace house garden, scale down your plantings even further than for the average-sized garden. You might like to choose a special collection of ferns for a shady corner, a fountain or goldfish pool in the centre. The idea is that in such a small area you can landscape for luxurious and meticulous effects that the large garden owner has not the time to maintain. Design built-in seating, a rockery, easy-to-garden built-up beds, wall-to-wall paving—whatever suits you. Plant trees so that they do not block any sun. Choose some deciduous ones to let in more winter sunlight.

Give a tiny garden one focal point and build the garden design around it. If the soil is very poor, bring in some new loam, or plant in beds built up of peat blocks. Keep in mind some delicate plants do not like gritty town air. Successful plants in town gardens includes pieris, hydrangeas, ericas, geraniums, common jasmine, pyracantha, cotoneaster, lilac, clematis, some

of the climbing roses, laurels, and many of the leafy ground covers such as ivy.

Gardens in good shape
Once you have made up your mind about the kind of garden you want, you can start more detailed planning—the shapes of garden beds and lawn, where you will have some special feature. It is often the unexpected things in a garden that delight the eye and give it the personal touch.

Shrubs and trees are the background of a garden and perennials the mainstay of the flower beds. Both should be chosen to get interesting shapes and colour combinations in the garden, and to be on the right scale of size. A huge tree dwarfs a small garden, drains food from a large area, and casts shade where only certain plants will grow. A big shrub with a few small flowers beside it will look lopsided. To see the way to grade shrubs and flowers in size and combine, for contrasting texture and colour, visit private gardens on public show, the Royal Horticultural Society's garden at Wisley and the Northern Horticultural Society's garden at Harlow Car, Harrogate, Yorks, parks and botanical gardens. For example in Regent's Park in London, there is a lovely border every year of perennials and small shrubs which has been graded into waves of varying blues, rising in height to the back of the border.

Gentle curves—but not sharp ones—suit garden design better than severe straight lines, particularly if you have a rectangular suburban garden outlined in fencing.

The lawn earns its place in nearly every

Right: *For larger expanses of garden, introduce a focal point such as this tall urn.*

Below right: *In smaller areas you can landscape for meticulous effects.*

garden except the small, paved town garden. A lawn gives running space, entertainment space, perspective and distance to the garden layout and acts as a frame for the flower beds. There is nothing more serene-looking and orderly than an open sweep of lawn. It does not take a lot of work to maintain compared with the amount of the garden it usually takes up.

Now consider more detailed plantings—borders, rockery, a corner for cut flowers for the house, a herb garden and fruit trees.

Paper work saves you foot work
It is very much easier to work out a good garden design on paper than it is to work it out while you are in front of a half-dug garden bed or a lawn that is green in your imagination only.

A pencil and paper is the answer, preferably graph paper which has centimetre divisions marked on it, then you can make an accurate scale plan of the garden using a scale of, say, one centimetre to one metre. If you are using plain paper you can mark your own scale on it by dividing it into centimetre squares.

The measurements of the garden are marked on the paper first. (If you have a

Below: *Focal point for a small garden is a stone circular bed of yellow tulips.*

large garden you can reduce the scale, increase the amount of paper although it might be unwieldy, or divide the garden into sections for planning.) Then at the side of the plan it is useful to mark in aspects—north, south, east and west—and prevailing wind directions with notes as to whether there is shelter there or a howling gale. Mark in too, outside the plan perimeter, any distant views you want to preserve or frame, and if you live in the town or suburbs any view you would like to screen out.

Now mark in **existing physical features** of the garden—banks and dips, walls and fences, existing trees and shrubs you want to keep, any outhouses, etc. To mark in a plant, you draw a circle, taking up as much room on the map as the plant does in the garden.

Mark in of course the **outline of the house**. Very often a house is placed on a building site just as a plain rectangle but is angled in some way. If the site is wide then you might find you have interesting small areas of the garden flanking the house, that could be turned into special corners, such as a herb garden, or terrace, or court. Or you may have a narrow site and just room for paths between back and front gardens —and these have to be allowed for because easy movement from one part of the garden to another is essential.

Mark in **paths** you have that you want to or must keep. If your existing path is very straight, do not waste money by discarding it—you can add width with pebble stone strips along each side and break the straight line with cunning plantings that snake from one side to the other. You can do all sorts of things to distract the eye from the unattractive to the beautiful.

Now that you have marked down on your paper existing conditions in the garden, you can go ahead marking in the features you want.

In a suburban, rectangular garden, aim to break up straight boundaries with curved shapes of lawn and beds and groupings of shrubs and small trees.

Where you have changes of level in the garden you can plan a bank with lawn over it if the rise is gradual; steps and a sunken or raised section of garden; a rockery.

Near the house perimeter look for likely court or terrace areas—or a timber deck, if you want one; a place for a herb garden.

Where you have an existing large tree, you could pave around it and make a shady seat area. If it is further away from the house, could a group of shrubs or smaller trees be planted to make it a special point of interest?

Is there a bare wall of the house or garden where the silhouette of some really special tree could be shown alone to great

Above: *This is an informal type of garden with plants grouped in natural drifts.*   **Below:** *In the formal garden here miniature hedges enclose spring bedding plants.*

Imaginative use of timber beside a pool for decking, bridge and stepping stones.

advantage? This is what gardeners sometimes call a specimen tree and sometimes one is planted in the lawn to break its expanse.

Wherever you have hard surfaces in the garden, plan low-growing plants to soften the outlines of pavings, and climbers and creepers to clothe walls. In paved terraces or paths it is a good idea to leave a few pockets of earth between paving stones so that you can plant there.

Leave some interesting feature such as a bird bath or stone figurine for placing towards the bottom of the garden so that you make use of all available space, rather than crowding all the interest close to the house.

A front garden is often a public as well as a private space, so plan low-maintenance features there, with enough colour and charm to please the passers-by. For them, this part of the garden may well frame the house—so think of your garden planning here from the street view.

Do not plan too much to start with and do not plan fussy-shaped and lots of little garden beds. They are a trial to mark out and dig and a misery to take care of.

When marking out garden shapes . . .
You need some sharpened pegs or stakes, some garden twine for a line and a sharp spade. It helps if you can also make a garden square out of scrap timber. To do this cut three lengths, one 90cm (3ft) long, one 120cm (4ft) and one 150cm (5ft) and put together in a triangle, but if you have anything else about that will give you a clean 90-degree angle to work from, do not worry.

To make a diamond, measure out first two lines crossing at right angles—this will be the centre of the diamond. Then mea-sure out from the centre, half the width each way and half the length of the diamond each way—then these are the four diamond points.

For a circle, drive in a stake at the centre of the circle. Loop a length of twine (measuring the diameter of the circle you want) around the stake or peg and tie another peg to the other end of the twine—then just mark out the circumference of the circle.

Curved beds can be made by arranging a heavy rope or a hose in the outline you want.

Formal and informal gardens These adjectives refer to the shapes of garden beds. Formal refers to beds and borders of geometrical shapes, or patterns of plants set out geometrically. It does not matter whether the plants in these beds are of the same variety or not. Informal gardens are those of irregular lines, with the emphasis on natural-looking plantings.

Remodelling gardens

There are two kinds of gardens that need remodelling—one that has grown unhindered into a jungle, the second kind has never been much of a garden at all.

Sometimes in old gardens you see the results of early planting mistakes—the manageable 30cm (1ft) high shrub that grew into a door-blocking giant, or the random crowding of shrubs so that one shrub impeded another's growth. When planting out new gardens it is a great temptation to plant out too many plants because the spaces between the plants look a bit bare. In an old garden you can see what happens if you do.

In the neglected garden there has been order once—if you can discover what and where it was. If you have the patience—and gardeners should cultivate patience—wait through a year and see what happens at each season. You could be glad you did

not rush in to raze everything to the ground; beneath a carpet of weeds and behind unpruned branches you might find there was a reasoned, purposeful use of the land.

If you ignore what went before you, you might throw away the lessons learnt by the previous gardener and neglect his experience. A tree might have been planted as a vital windbreak, a shrub could be growing in a pocket of acid soil, plants might be lush because they are in a boggy area. If your predecessor found all this out by experience, what a pity it would be to repeat the same experiences for the same result.

Meanwhile clear the ground of debris. Inspect the land carefully, looking for rocks, logs, a caved-in pool, a forgotten rake, hidden plants.

Clear around trees and shrubs to save them from careless destruction. Having done so, cut the overgrown grass weeds in the general areas with a rotary mower suitable for use on rough ground. Set the blade high to avoid any obstructions you might have missed earlier.

The stubbly plot will now reveal some sort of pattern. You will see roughly what existed before. The passing year will tell you more, and you will have had time to live with the garden and work out your own patterns of activity in it. You will know then the problems facing you and the advantages you can make use of.

The garden that was never well-planned and planted in the first place may still have some good plants in it—so wait again through the seasons to see what comes up before drawing up a plan for a new garden.

To cover an ugly but useful shed—choose a rampant climber such as a vine like *Vitis coignetiae*, with leaves approx. 25cm (10in) across which turn to crimson and orange in the autumn. Other quick coverers are the common white jasmine and *Clematis montana* which will grow to a height of approx. 12m (40ft) and flowers in early summer. This has white flowers but the rubens variety has pink flowers and bronzy-purple leaves although it is a little slower growing.

To cover an old tree stump—plant the Russian vine *Polygonum* (*Bilderdyckia*) *baldschuanicum*. It bears panicles of white flowers flushed with pink profusely from July until autumn. It is very vigorous and will not suit a house wall.

If you want a quick-growing evergreen screen—try bamboos in a moist soil, such as *Sinarundin ria murieliae* (from 2·5m to 3·5m (8–12ft) or *S. nitida*, with slender purple-tinged canes and dainty leaves. In acid soil try a large rhododendron such as *R. auriculatum* which grows to around 4·5m (15ft) or more.

Learn the language of gardening
Choosing flowers

All the millions of plants that exist—from the tiniest moss to the towering metasequoia—are divided into a few simple categories that are easy to understand and make use of. You could say that gardeners divide flowers into perennials, annuals and bulbs. Then there are the shrubs—larger and woodier plants—and trees, larger still with a single main stem or trunk. These are general gardening terms—but plants are divided botanically in much more detail so that gardeners and botanists know exactly the plant they are dealing with. These botanical classifications are much more complicated and the beginner gardener only needs a general understanding of how each plant name is derived.

Each plant has a two-word name to identify it. This method of naming began in the 18th century when it was realized that many plants had definite similarities to each other, and that many more plants, forming larger groups, had distant links between them. Up until this time each separate plant, or species, had been considered a work of God unique from every other plant. But, having realized these relationships between plants, the famous Swedish naturalist Carl Von Linné and other botanists began an elaborate system of classification. It starts at a very broad

level of difference—between non-flowering plants such as fungi and ferns, and flowering plants—and descends into closer and closer relationships.

The plants the gardener grows are divided into large, loosely knit groups called 'families', sometimes wrongly called natural orders. They are then divided into smaller groups, each group being called a genus—this is the Latin word for birth and so the plural for genus is genera. The first name of any plant is the name of its genus, its closely related group. The second name of any plant is its own name, its specific name, that is, its species. Some of these specific names are descriptive, and these and the generic names are often in Latin or Greek—for it was important that naturalists and gardeners from every country could understand each other and also give the same name to the same plant. Often this did not happen in the past and there were confusing descriptions and names. Also many of the plant names are not true Greek or Latin words, they are Latinized forms of words from many languages and usually easily understood internationally.

A third name following the generic and specific name of a plant is the description of its variety. Varieties are divided into those of wild origin that breed true from

seed, and those that sported or mutated spontaneously in the wild or in cultivation and only persist when cultivated—and are therefore known as cultivars. Cultivars can also be man-produced hybrids or any plant that needs to be maintained in cultivation because it does not breed true or is sterile. It has been decided internationally to write the cultivar name beginning with a capital letter within single inverted commas, ie, *Salvia splendens* 'Blaze of Fire', meaning the Blaze of Fire cultivated variety of the scarlet sage. True varieties are, on the other hand, written in italics without capital letters in the same way that specific names are written.

A hybrid is a plant produced when two species are crossed. When you see a name such as *Forsythia x intermedia*, you know that this is a hybrid of forsythia, ie, a cross between species of forsythia.

The use of botanical names might sound a little complex but it is important to get a broad idea of what kind of clues plant names can give you. You will soon get used to sorting out the two names, genus and species, or the three-word names, genus, species and variety.

Small white flowers of the beautiful but rampant Cerastium tomentosum (snow-in-summer).

When choosing plants, arm yourself with some good books, nursery catalogues and a reliable encyclopedia; Sanders is just one. The main thing for the first-time gardener to do is to get to know what the individual flowers and plants look like. Check our gallery of pictures. Also make a note of everything you see that you like in other people's gardens, individual flowers or the way plants are teamed together, for photographs and words can never quite give you the effect of the living flowers, the shape of a bush and the texture of petals and leaves.

There are broad divisions that gardeners use among plants—the perennials, annuals, bulbs, shrubs and trees. What are these divisions and how are they used? It is a good idea to start with the perennials because these will give you the quickest permanent display in a new or remodelled garden.

There are three things about plants that should be noticed . . . their colours, shapes and textures.

Colour is fairly obvious but include in this the colour of leaves, the different greens—grey-green, yellow-green, silvery green—yellows, silver and bronze, reds and the grey-green-blue colour that gardeners call blue. Then there are the multi-colours of variegated plants. In flower colours too, differentiate between shades of pink and shades of red, and all the other shades of colours. Blue is used to describe plants with a bluish colour to their leaves, that is, blue-green or with a greyish-blue colour, or with a fine bluish bloom to the leaves. Sometimes the word glaucous is used to describe blue or green silvery bloom.

Variegated is usually part of a description about leaves and it means that the leaves of the plant have patches of one colour on another colour. It could be a variegated pelargonium, which has central yellow patches on a green leaf or scarlet leaves with green. There are dozens of variegated plants and they provide a lot of colour and character to foliage plantings. Yellow variegated ivy brightens up a wall in winter. Variegated plants have their place in the garden, giving variety and interest to shrub and evergreen backgrounds. They are very useful too in town gardens where too much shade prevents many flowers thriving.

Next there is the **shape** of a plant. Does it stand bolt upright, is it short and spreading, does it droop or weep, does it arch out in great canes?

All plants have character; some keep to themselves with compact, even growth, some are very neat and regular in growth, some prefer to be left alone. When choosing plants, keep the idea of their shape in mind because if you choose several very

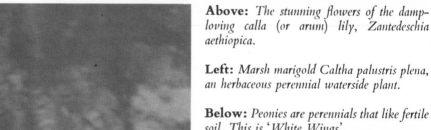

Above: *The stunning flowers of the damp-loving calla (or arum) lily, Zantedeschia aethiopica.*

Left: *Marsh marigold Caltha palustris plena, an herbaceous perennial waterside plant.*

Below: *Peonies are perennials that like fertile soil. This is 'White Wings'.*

Above: *Miscanthus sinensis foliis striatus has creamy white stripes on its leaves.*

Below: *The hairy leaves of the perennial, Stachys lanata, Lamb's ear, are distinctive.*

irregularly-shaped plants and put them all together, the general effect can be extremely untidy. The idea is to arrange an interplay of neat plants against arching plants or a low spreading plant against another with more upright growth.

Part of the plant shape is the silhouette. Some maples, for example, have the most striking layered silhouettes, which makes them ideal to plant against a bare wall on their own. Some weeping plants, trees and shrubs have soft and graceful silhouettes that are set off by a plain background. A plant like the New Zealand flax has swordlike leaves and a very spiky silhouette.

Weeping plants have a dropping, drooping form of growth—hanging downwards like the familiar weeping willow. There are several shrubs and trees in this group. Weeping plants need space so that their weeping habit can be clearly appreciated.

Finally, there is **texture** which from a gardening point of view is less to do with the actual texture of leaves than the texture of the plant as a whole—the effect it gives from a short distance away. It is the leaf size of the plant which most influences this more distant impression. A plant like a golden privet has a fine texture while a plane tree would have a more coarse and open texture. Leaf textures do affect the look of plants too; for example, the grey woolly foliage of Lamb's-ear or the shining, dark green leaves of a camellia. There are neat mounds or grassy tussocks, large sprays or gentle drifts.

Plants for damp places

Some plants like damp and shady places. You can plant them in damp spots on the banks of streams, or by any water or where bog conditions prevail.

Among the flowers that will thrive are primulas, astilbes, *Iris sibirica* and *Iris kaempferi*, the Japanese water iris with its spectacular flat blooms. The mauve-blue of these is sometimes teamed perfectly with yellow lilies. Then there are kingcups (*Caltha palustris*) and the globe flower (*Trollius* species). See also chapter on rock pools and bog plants.

The perennials

A **perennial** is a plant that does not die after flowering and which grows for more than two years. Although strictly speaking, you could say that shrubs and trees are perennial, the word is usually used to describe the hardy herbaceous plants that are grown in garden beds, rockeries and borders. Lupins, for example, have a life of about five or six years. The herbaceous peonies and the oriental poppy both have far longer lives.

Perennials are the backbone of flower beds and borders and cover a huge number of flowers that give a year after year breath-taking display for very little work. Primroses, cowslips, violets, poppies, larkspurs and lupins, pinks and columbine and the Christmas rose are all perennials and decidedly individual in their style and beauty.

The vast majority of perennials are quite tough and able to survive the continual bleak winters, hence their description, hardy. Some, like Michaelmas or shasta daisies would quickly take root and establish themselves even if left lying on the soil surface, so planting is easy for these and many others.

You can plant your perennials from seed and they will flower a few months or a year or more after planting or, you can buy them as container-grown plants from the nursery and enjoy their character and charm earlier. It saves you too from a garden bed that is all bare earth and latent promise.

A great many perennials can be planted

Above: *Rudbeckia 'Goldsturm', a large-flowered perennial for a sunny border.*

Right: *Perennial Shelford hybrid Eremurus grows from 1–2m, flowers in June and likes the sun.*

Below: *Monkshood, Aconitum carmichaelii, is tolerant of shade, beautiful but poisonous.*

Below: *Erigeron 'Merstham Glory' is a semi-double flower with delicate blooms.*

Below: *Pansies are mainly used for summer colour. Many have attractive markings.*

Above: *Flowers of Anemone narcissiflora, an herbaceous plant for open woodland planting.*

Below: *Aim for border contrasts. Try yellow Ligularia przewalskii and purple lupins.*

Above: *Achillea filipendulina 'Gold Plate' grows to 2m and is a hardy border perennial.*

Below: *Vividly-coloured delphiniums grow in a stately fashion and are ideal for border cultivation.*

from September to March, which gives you plenty of time to prepare a loamy, well-fed soil for them. The plants will be living in the same place for years so the bed must be made with plenty of nutrients and humus. (See later for complete details.) However, check individual planting times for the perennials you choose. Autumn planting gives perennials a long time to root strongly before the heat of summer. But if the soil is cold and wet in your area then no plant will want to chance its life in it.

Many people start their collection of perennial plants with gifts from friends who have been dividing up old clumps. Every few years perennial clumps get large and unwieldy in the border, outgrowing their neighbours. or fading away in the centre of the clump and shooting from outside. It is the younger more vigorous outside shoots that are worth planting. Plant them with the new season's dormant shoots a few centimetres below soil level.

If you plant seeds of perennials, you must plant them in a seed box in sheltered, warm conditions, then prick out, ie transplant carefully to a larger and deeper seed box when the seedlings are big enough to handle (see chapter 'How to Plant Properly'), and finally transplant into the garden from April onwards.

Or you can plant straight outdoors from April onwards into a seed bed and then transplant. For some of the more popular perennials you can now buy pelleted seed, ie, seed with a coating around it. Pelleted seeds are sown singly directly outdoors and can produce stronger seedlings and faster flowers.

May or June are good months to sow perennial seeds in boxes or a seed bed. As with all seed planting, you must prepare the bed with a very fine soil surface. You can sow doronicum, aquilegia, anchusa, *Campanula pyramidalis* and *C. persicifolia*, border carnations, shasta daisy, delphiniums, oriental poppies, lupins, double and single pyrethrum, coreopsis, hollyhock ('Triumph Supreme' is highly rust resistant), Michaelmas daisy, heuchera and geum. Some are not quick to germinate so be patient—aquilegia can take up to six months—but this is a very cheap way to stock up for beds and borders.

Whichever you use, seedlings or plants, keep in mind that staking and tying the taller plants in a border because they need support, can be a tedious business. So look for varieties of perennials that are compact and sturdy.

Among the perennials there are the herbaceous plants:

The **herbaceous plant** is one where the top growth is not woody, the whole plant dying down in winter, and being newly

Left: *Tall-growing perennial grass Miscan-thus sacchariflorus has smooth, shiny leaves. It is hardy and needs no special conditions.*

Below left: *Variegated Hosta fortunei albo picta gives foliage contrast. It likes plenty of moisture and is hardy.*

Right: *Dianthus 'Red Robin' has brilliant colour. Most dianthus are perennial but some are annuals or biennials.*

Below: *The oriental poppy, Papaver orientale, is a perennial with many forms. Grows in the sun and reaches a height of about 1m.*

resurrected in spring. Although this is the strict definition, you sometimes find the word herbaceous used generally for most plants in the border—non-woody, a little woody, alpine and shrubby.

The **herbaceous border** was originally a long bed given over to a riotous show of summer-long colour—supplied by perennials that died down at the end of the summer and lay dormant during the winter. During the winter the herbaceous border offered no more than the promise of next summer's glory. This was possible to tolerate in a large garden but not in a small garden, and so the herbaceous border began to be infiltrated by other plants such as bulbs, corms, shrubs, creepers and alpines and perennials that obstinately stayed on top during the winter, some even being evergreen. The idea now for most gardeners is to have a perennial border that gives interest and colour for the longest time possible. Included in the woody in-betweens often seen in borders and sometimes called a sub-shrub, are the plumbago-flowered *Ceratostigma willmottianum*, *Caryopteris x clandonensis* and Russian sage, *Perovskia atriplicifolia*. Sub-shrubs are actually plants where the lower-part is woody and the upper shoots are soft.

Planning and planting the herbaceous border

As most herbaceous borders have a mixture of perennials, woody and otherwise, bulbs, shrubs and even sometimes a background hedge, it is a good idea to check the shrubs section of this chapter before you complete your final border plan. However many lovely border effects are achieved by the inspired combinations of perennials—and having seen here what some individual perennials are like, it is now important to see how breath-taking they can look together. A border is enormous fun to plan and you will probably make some mistakes in choice. Be light-hearted—you can only learn from your mistakes. A plant might thrive in itself and yet look wrong against the plants beside it; for the beginner it is an experimental but rewarding time.

Begin with the thought of your background planting, whether it is to be a hedge or an informal grouping of shrubs and small trees, or a wall or fence. You can of course have a border set in the lawn as an island bed or have it running up the centre of a driveway if you have one. As a beginner you might find it complicates the planning of effects, and the grading of harmonious heights, so experiment and see.

If you have a wall or fence at the back of the border, certain plants might need extra staking and tying. In rough weather strong gusts of wind develop at the wall base which can topple the flowers unless they

Above: A gay border is worth the planning and soil preparation which goes into it.

Below: Eranthis x tubergenii has longer-lasting flowers than the common winter aconite.

Above: Tagetes erecta is a full-flowered marigold. Sow from seed.

Below: Geranium pratense grows in lovely clumps a metre high and flowers in summer.

are well-secured.

A hedge on the other hand can rob the border plants, unless you leave at least a 60cm (2ft) gap between it and the back rows. If the hedge is already established, dig out a trench about 30cm (1ft) from the base of the hedge when it is dormant and chop back all the fibrous roots with a sharp spade. Then plant your border. Yew is a good plant for a background hedge. It is slow-growing, compact and needs only an annual trim. Privet on the other hand is likely to take over.

One good point to remember is that the border will not look its best if you inter-mingle border plants right the way through. Plant fairly large clumps of the same variety of plant together so that their colour and character can make an impact.

The clumps should not be too evenly-shaped and one clump should drift naturally into the next, shading or contrasting the colour. For your first border, do not use too many hectic colours. Occasionally gar-deners plant borders of one colour only which can be very attractive, but the mixed-colour border looks quite delight-ful. Some gardeners think that the strong colours should go towards the centre of the border, and pale and pastel colours towards the end, for a comfortable balance, but it is purely personal taste.

You can plan many borders with a few nursery catalogues and paper and pencil. In the border described below the paler shades are at each end, with the brighter, more vivid colours in the centre.

The pure whites of *Phlox paniculata alba*, *Achillea ptarmica* 'The Pearl', and *Gypso-phila* 'Bristol Fairy' melt almost imper-ceptibly into the cool primrose yellows of *Achillea taygetea* and *Verbascum bombyci-ferum* (syn: *broussa*), flanked by the deeper yellows of *Hemerocallis* 'Hyperion', one of the best of the free-flowering day lilies, and *Lysimachia punctata*, the yellow loose-strife.

The middle of the border glows with scarlet *Lychnis chalcedonica*, *Lobelia fulgens*, *Potentilla* 'Gibson's Scarlet', and the garnet-red *Astilbe* 'Fanal'. Once past the centre the border progresses to white once more through the blues of delphiniums, and sea holly (*Eryngium maritimum*) whose leaves, as well as the flowers, are metallic blue, then the stately *Echinops ritro*, with thistle-like dark green foliage and drumstick flower heads of steely blue. Other suitable blue perennials include the attractive indigo-blue monkshood, *Aconitum* 'Bres-singham Spire' and the curious balloon flower *Platycodon grandiflorum*.

These followed by the soft pinks of *Geranium endressii*, *Sidalcea* 'Sussex Beauty', the long-flowering *Veronica spicata*—'Pavane' and 'Minuet' are both good varieties—and the later-blooming ice plant, *Sedum spectabile* 'Brilliant'.

And so back to white again, this time represented by Japanese anemones, *Anemone x hybrida* 'Honorine Jobert'. *Lysimachia clethroides*, *Potentilla alba* and a good garden form of the sweetly scented meadow sweet, *Filipendula ulmaria* 'Plena'.

Preparing the ground

A good time of the year to prepare the ground for a border or flower bed is late summer or early autumn. This will give the winter frosts a chance to break up heavy clods of earth to a finer planting texture. This is most important if your soil is clay.

You need a sunny site where the plants will not suffer from shade or any drips from overhanging trees. Most of the widely-grown perennials are sun-lovers so that a position facing south or west is best. When you read that a plant likes a south wall, it means a wall facing south, which in England is towards the sun and warmth.

Preparing the bed for the perennial border requires conscientiousness because the more thorough your work the more successful will be the result. Whether you have a predominantly clay soil, or have tamed it into a loamy texture, you will need plenty of humus in the soil to hold food for the plants. (See chapter on soil types, manures, etc.)

Dig over the ground thoroughly. Be careful not to bring the subsoil to the topsoil position because it has less bacteria life, decayed leaves, worms and plants' foods, etc, than the topsoil. Leaf mould, manure and compost can be added to the topsoil. Before embarking on garden-bed preparing, read the chapters 'A Down to earth Start' and 'How To Plant Properly'.

The vast majority of popular perennials and herbaceous perennials will thrive in most types of soil although they might vary in height and vigour. They will be in the bed undisturbed for at least a few years however, which is why the bed should be well-supplied with plant food.

It is vital to remove any vestige of perennial weeds in the border site; this can be a little difficult. Ground elder, couch grass and bindweed are three villains. In autumn and early spring give the border a thorough forking-over, removing and burning perennial weeds, not risking the worst in any compost heap. If some clumps of perennials have got weeds growing in them, dig them out, clean them and return them, first splitting the root clumps into extra plants if you want them. If you re-plant immediately the plants will not suffer.

When friends give you plants for your border, check before planting them that they are free of weeds. Most likely they

Planning the border. **Left:** *Irregularly-shaped groups of plants are laid out.* **Below left:** *These are then planted firmly with good soil around the roots.* **Below:** *Firm the soil by treading close to the plant, pushing the soil downwards and inwards towards the plant.* **Bottom:** *After cutting back the top growth of border plants in the autumn, the border is forked over between the plants. If the border is not on view from the house, tidying can be left until spring so that dead leaves and stems can protect the crowns of plants in severe winter weather. During winter, plan new borders to include interesting colour combinations. Peonies and grey-leaved border plants can be planted in the spring.*

will have done it for you.

A few weeks before the border is planted, give a booster supply of fertilizer. Organic ones such as bonemeal and fish manure are slow-acting and give good results applied at a rate of 50–75g (approx 2–3oz) to the square metre. Or use a good general fertilizer, following the manufacturer's directions. With any of these, rake it into soil or fork lightly in. Repeat each spring.

The Californian tree poppy, Romneya coulteri, is a perennial with large, delicately-petalled flowers.

A selection of herbaceous plants

Name	Height in metres	Colour	Season
Acanthus	1·2–1·5m	lilac-pink	July–Aug
Achillea spp & vars	30cm–1·2m	white, yellow	June–Aug
Alchemilla	30–45cm	yellow-green	June–July
Anaphalis	30–60cm	white	July–Sept
Aquilegia hybs	30–90cm	various	May–June
Armeria	30cm	pinks	June–July
Artemisia	90cm–1·5m	grey foliage	Aug–Sept
Aster spp & vars	30cm–1·5m	various	Aug–Oct
Astrantia	60–90cm	green-pink	June
Bergenia	30–45cm	pinks, white	March–April
Campanula	30cm–1·2m	blues, white	June–Aug
Centaurea	60cm–1·5m	blues, yellow	June–Oct
Cimicifuga	60cm–1·2m	creamy-white	July–Sept
Coreopsis	60–90cm	golden-yellow	June–Sept
Corydalis	30cm	yellow	May–Oct
Delphinium	90cm–2·5m	blues, mauves	June–July
Dianthus	15–45cm	various	May–June
Dicentra	30–60cm	pink	April–May
Doronicum	30–75cm	yellow	March–April
Echinacea	60–90cm	purple-red	Aug–Sept
Echinops	60cm–1·5m	steely blue	July–Aug
Erigeron hybs	30·60cm	blue, pink	June–Sept
Eryngium	60cm–1·2m	glaucous blue	July–Aug
Euphorbia	30–90cm	yellow	April–June
Gaillardia hybs	60cm	yellow, orange	July–Aug
Galega	60cm–1·2m	mauve	June–July
Gentiana	30–60cm	blues and yellows	July–Aug
Geranium	30–75cm	pinks, mauves	June–July
Helenium	90cm–1·5m	yellows, copper	July–Sept
Hemerocallis	60–90cm	yellow, orange	July–Sept
Heuchera hybs	30–75cm	pinks, reds	May–Aug
Iris	30cm–1·5m	various	May–June
Kniphofia	45–90cm	yellow, orange	July–Sept
Lupin hybs	60cm–1·2m	various	June
Lythrum	60cm–1·2m	purple-red	June–Sept
Lysimachia	60cm–1·2m	yellow, white	July–Sept
Macleaya	1·5–2·5m	apricot pink	July–Sept
Malva	60cm–1·2m	mauves, pinks	July
Monarda	60cm–1·2m	various	June–Aug
Nepeta	30–60cm	blue	May–Sept
Paeonia spp & hybs	60cm–1·2m	pink, red, white	May–June
Phlox	60cm–1·2m	various	July–Sept
Pyrethrum	30cm–90cm	various	May–June
Salvia spp	60cm–1·5m	mauves	June–Sept
Sidalcea hybs	30–90cm	pinks	June–Aug
Verbascum	90cm–2·5m	yellow, pink	July–Oct
Veronica spp & vars	30–90cm	blues, mauves	July–Oct

Above: *Romantically named Adonis vernalis, this perennial has large spring flowers. Likes a fairly rich soil.*

Above: *There are many hybrids of verbascum. It has woolly foliage and is commonly called blanketweed.*

Above: *Agapanthus is a fine border or tub plant which needs a warm or sheltered climate. Commonly called the African lily.*

Above: *The Shirley poppy, an annual with a good range of colours. It flowers in summer.*

Below: *Sweet Pea 'Bijou' only grows to half a metre and carries a good flower crop.*

Below right: *'Torch' is a variety of the dahlia-like tithonias which are half-hardy annuals.*

The annuals

An **annual** has a life span of a year or less, growing up, flowering, setting seed and dying in a round of the seasons. Their glory over, they are pulled up and taken to the compost heap where their decay will help next year's flowers. Some can be left to set seed.

While you are busy putting in permanent plants in the garden, you will find that the area of earth between young plants looks big and bare. Annuals will fill these dull places with luxuriant growth and colour, making a young garden look older and well-established. Annuals demonstrate more than most plants the miracle of growth—going from seed to full flower in one summer. They can be used to hide the withering top growth of the spring season's bulbs, they will cascade down any garden barrel, urn or pot, fill a window box or terrace bed, and give abundant life to the darkest corner of the garden. Added to all that, they are fairly easy to grow.

If you have an old garden that you are reorganizing or you are waiting through the summer to see what comes up, then use annuals to ensure some summer display. Fill pots with them along paths and on the terrace if you have one; put them in wherever the earth is cleared and empty. If you are slowly pruning back old trees or shrubs, you might find some places near them where you have brought back sunlight. Feed the soil well and it will help the shrubs and the flowers.

There are **hardy** annuals which will stand the cold and **half-hardy** annuals which can only be planted when all danger of frost is past.

Hardy annuals are sown in the spring to bloom in the summer or some of them can be sown the previous late summer, to over-winter in the garden bed, and produce their flowers earlier than they would have done with a spring sowing.

A few of the plants that can be sown the late summer before are sweet peas, silene, poppies, larkspurs, cornflowers, candytuft, clarkia, calendula, godetia, alyssum and agrostemma. Larkspur make very good bushy plants if sown in August or September of the year before and protected with a cloche or twiggy sticks in severe weather. This early sowing does expose the plants to more risk so have plenty of hardy annuals ready too for spring sowing. Thin out the seedlings once but leave the final thinning out until the following spring.

Hardy annuals sown in spring can be planted where they will bloom, in a well-drained soil well-raked over. Wait for favourable weather and prepare the ground well. Some damp horticultural peat added to the top 5 or 7·5cm (2 or 3ins) of soil will help to condition the soil and make it crumbly so that frail young roots can push down comfortably into it. (See chapter on sowing seed.)

Among the hardy annuals you can sow in spring are the above ones already listed for late summer sowing, and many more—annual chrysanthemums, sweet sultan, delphinium, eschscholzia, including the Californian poppy. Gypsophila, sunflowers and limnanthes (the plant likes a moist, sunny place and attracts bees), forget-me-not and sweet peas all seed freely.

Many annuals will not take transplanting so that it is not only easier but also essential that they are planted where they will grow. Sprinkle the seed very lightly in a shallow drill or scatter at a depth of about 1–1·5cm ($\frac{1}{4}$–$\frac{1}{2}$in). Cover with a fine layer of earth and pat down gently. As soon as the seedlings are big enough to handle, thin them out to give them room to root and to grow. Seedlings must never be allowed to dry out so water often with a fine spray.

Half-hardy annuals are sown under glass (cloche, frame or greenhouse) and planted in the summer in late May or in early June, if you want them to flower as early as possible. Or you can sow them straight into the ground in May or June and have them flowering later in the season.

A lot of the half-hardy annuals are used as bedding plants—a gardening method whereby you raise plants in seed boxes and pots under glass and 'bed' them out in a garden bed for either a dazzling spring or summer show. This is often done in large parks and gardens, but is time-consuming and expensive for the small garden owner to have to prepare a special bed and plant it just for a season. Instead, the half-hardy annuals and other greenhouse-raised plants are used to boost the more permanent perennial displays in the garden.

In Victorian bedding-out schemes, pots of half-hardy annuals and other plants were often buried up to their necks in the bed—giving the effect that they were planted but with the advantage that the pots could be moved. This is still a good idea in the small garden if you want quick colour somewhere specific.

In cloches, cold frames and greenhouses you can sow alyssum, nemesia, stocks, schizanthus, asters, *Mesembryanthemum criniflorum*, French and African marigolds, petunias, zinnias, *Phlox drummondii* and cosmeas, from about March and April depending on how much warmth you can provide for the seeds—they need about 13°C to 16°C to germinate. Once the seeds are big enough to handle, prick out (transplant) into larger seed boxes or peat pots. Gradually harden them off by exposing them to more ventilation and lower temperatures before planting in the garden or removing cloches in about May or June.

You can keep the flowering season of your annuals prolonged by snipping off the withered flowers and making sure that no flower fades on the plant. A plant life cycle has its priorities. When flowers stay on a plant and form seed pods then the plant devotes its attention to seed production and stops flower production. By preventing seed pods forming, you encourage the plant to continue its flowering programme.

If you want to collect your annual's ripe seed to keep and plant the next year, let the pods ripen thoroughly on one or two plants and harvest the seeds when they are ready to drop. Keep them safe in a dry, cool place.

Annuals in pots
You can sow annuals straight into pots, urns and barrels in the spring and summer —nasturtiums will romp happily over the rim and also provide lovely orange flowers and peppery leaves for your summer salads. Alyssum, candytuft, Virginian stock,

Left: *A pompon chrysanthemum 'Carrissima'. This group consists of small-flowered varieties that bear plenty of flowers.*

Below left: *Nemesia, a half-hardy annual, brightens the border with its many-coloured varieties. Plant in a sunny position.*

Right: *Eschscholzia californica, a hardy annual for a sunny, well-drained bed. Sow seeds in spring where plants are to flower.*

Below: *Flowers of Petunia 'Moonglow' are yellow, an uncommon colour for petunias. Petunias are half-hardy, ie, will not stand frost.*

Bottom left: *The lupin, 'Harvester', has long spikes of soft apricot flowers.*

forget-me-not and arctotis are other possibilities for pot growing.

Annuals in borders and beds
It is easier to plant annuals together with perennials and shrubs in beds and borders unless the garden has one or two small beds near a terrace, or just outside the living room window, in which case they could be filled with annuals only without too much work. Choose contrasting colours like yellow and blue or blue and white, or just have these small beds massed with one plant, perhaps changing the type each season. The beds really must be very small unless you have plenty of time to spend on experimenting with all sorts of flower combinations. The important thing is to take into account the height of various plants. Check whether the height of plants used together blends harmoniously. Or if you are planting just one annual variety in a small bed—is the height of the plant right for easy viewing from path, window or terrace?

When trying out bed and border combinations keep a yearly diary and note the results you have with various plants so that each year you start out wiser than the year before.

Flowers for cutting
It is all very well to grow superb flowers in the garden but it is hard to cut them off in their prime to stock the vases in the house, and you may find that the blooms you do take leave a definite gap in the flower beds.

The cutting garden flowers should be based on perennials that will give you the least amount of work and which are known to cut and last well. Choose a sunny spot in the kitchen garden or near the vegetable plot or in some inconspicuous place. Firstly, check the list of perennials for cutting given in the chart.

Above: *The half-hardy annual, Ageratum houstonianum is used for summer planting.*

Above: *Nasturtiums growing in a concrete pot for quick colour. Are also good wall covers and rockery plants.*

Above: *Calendulas, sometimes called pot marigolds, are hardy annuals growing to 30cm.*　　**Below:** *Clarkia, a group of hardy annuals from North America has a good colour range.*

Above: *Virginian stock is a simple annual to grow. Botanical name is Malcolmia maritima.*

Below: *Cladanthus arabicus is a western Mediterranean plant.*

Above: *Papaver somniferum, the opium poppy is a hardy annual with single or double flowers.*

Left: *Antirrhinum majus 'Fiery Red' is one of the familiar snapdragons. Treat as half-hardy.*

Below: *Nemesia strumosa, a half-hardy annual. Plant out in the early summer.*

Left: *Various colours of the Chinese aster, Callistephus chinensis, a half-hardy annual.*

Below: *One of the many bedding lobelias, 'Emperor William'.*

31

Gallery of biennials

The biennial completes its life cycle within two years and within this group of plants are the Canterbury bells, foxgloves, wall-flowers and hollyhocks. The latter is not strictly biennial but often treated as such. They spend the first year growing sturdy and reserving their strength to produce beautiful, delicate and abundant flowers in the second year. Biennials need time and patience for their cultivation, but they have all the sweet romance of the cottage garden.

You can sow biennials in the April of the first year in cloche, frame or green-house or outside in a seed bed from May onwards. Do not delay because they need plenty of time in their first year. In October or November they are strong enough to go out to the garden bed where they are to flower the following year. During their moving be careful not to disturb or damage the roots.

When biennials grow tall and begin to flower they may need some support. A stake driven in behind them away from their roots will do; tie the plant loosely to it. As the flowers fade, cut them off. Since they only flower for a season let them flower for as long as possible.

Above: *Wallflowers have fragrant flowers attractive to bees. Plant in pots, beds or wall crevices. Sow seed in late spring.*

Right: *Foxgloves (digitalis) are excellent woodland plants, useful for wild gardens as well as borders. Plant in drifts in rich moist soil.*

Below: *Lobelia cardinalis, the Cardinal flower, reaches 1m and has deep red flowers. Usually needs protection against any frost.*

Left: *Cineraria hybrida grandiflora is typical of cineraria hybrids. Treat as half-hardy.*

Below: *The stocks are useful summer-flowering plants and are deliciously scented.*

Monthly calendar
JANUARY
Sow for summer colour; take root cuttings to fill gaps in perennial borders.
FEBRUARY
Take cuttings of delphiniums and dahlias. Clear established borders; fork in dressing between plants. Harden protected flowers. Plan the sowing of everlastings.
MARCH
Plant hardy perennials in new border; in established border, lift and divide plants that require this. Put in edging plants (primulas, pansies, etc). Use gay, winter-flowering heathers to complement the small spring flowers in your indoor flower arrangements. Sow exotic foliage plants (eg *Atriplex hortensis*, ricinus, perilla) under glass.
APRIL
Plant out dahlia tubers. Sow hardy annuals. Feed plants with liquid fertilizer. Weed, dig, mulch established borders.

MAY
Stake plants. Feed delphiniums and phlox weekly with diluted liquid manure. Plant out hardened off chrysanthemums. Cut irises for indoors. Sow biennials and perennials for next year's flower arrangements.
JUNE
Remove any tulips to make room for half-hardy bedding plants. Fork fertilizer into soil before planting. Destroy decaying petals.
JULY
Support annuals with twiggy sticks. Water gladioli well. Remove flowers from delphiniums, lupins and peonies as they fade. Pick everlasting flowers (not wet) for drying.
AUGUST
Stake dahlias. Sow calendula, godetia, candytuft, cornflowers, sweet sultan, lark-spur, echium, alyssum and agrostemma for early summer bloom. Cut gladioli for

flower arrangements. Give cut hollyhocks and clematis hot water treatment.
SEPTEMBER
Cut back frost-blackened dahlia tops to within a few centimetres of ground. Lift, clean and store tubers. Clear ground, prepare and plant spring and early summer biennials. Make sure foliage for flower arrangements is cut at the right moment.
OCTOBER
Lift and divide herbaceous border plants (if need be). Label plants with height and colour before lifting. Polythene bag 'sleeves' will protect branches laden with berries (they will then stay plump till Christmas).
NOVEMBER
Cut down top growth of later-flowering perennials. Weed and fork between plants.
DECEMBER
Prepare new borders, deep dig and manure ground ready for spring planting. Protect delphiniums and lupins against slugs.

A selection of half-hardy annuals

Ageratum	Ageratum, Floss Flower	15–45	blue
Amaranthus caudatus	Love-lies-bleeding	60	reddish-purple
Antirrhinum	Snapdragon	23–90	various
Arctotis hybrids	African Daisy	30–45	various
Begonia semperflorens	Begonia	15–23	white, pink, crimson
Brachycome iberidifolia	Swan River Daisy	38	white, pink, blue
Callistephus	Annual or China Aster	23–75	various
Celosia cristata	Cockscomb	30–45	yellow, scarlet
*Cobaea scandens	Cups and Saucers	cl	purple and green
Cosmos bipinnatus	—	90–120	various
Cosmos sulphureus	—	45	orange
Dimorphotheca aurantiaca	Cape Marigold, Star of the Veldt	30–45	orange, buff, salmon white
Eccremocarpus scaber	Chilean Glory Flower	cl	orange-scarlet
Ipomoea purpurea	Morning Glory	cl	various
Kochia scoparia trichophila	Summer Cypress	30–90	foliage scarlet in autumn
Limonium bonduellii	Annual Statice	30–45	yellow
Limonium suworowii	Annual Statice	45–60	bright rose-pink
Lobelia erinus	Lobelia	15	blue, red, white
Matthiola incana	Ten-week Stock	30–38	various
Mesembryanthemum criniflorum	Livingstone Daisy	tr	various
Mimulus tigrinus	Annual Musk	30	various
Nemesia strumosa	—	23–30	various
Nicotiana	Flowering Tobacco	38–90	white, reds
Petunia	Petunia	23–45	various
Phlox drummondii	Annual Phlox	23–30	various
Portulaca grandiflora	Sun Plant	7·5	various
Rudbeckia Tetra Gloriosa	Gloriosa Daisy	75	various
Salpiglossis sinuata	Salpiglossis	30–75	various
Salvia splendens	Scarlet Salvia	23–38	scarlet
Tagetes	French and African Marigolds	15–90	various
Ursinia	—	23–45	various
Venidio-arctotis	—	45–60	various
Venidium fastuosum	—	75	various
Verbena hybrids	—	30	various
Zinnia	Zinnia	23–75	various

A selection of annuals for the greenhouse

Ageratum	Ageratum, Floss Flower	15–45	blue
Alonsoa	Mask Flower	30–60	scarlet, pink
Calendula officinalis	Pot Marigold	60	orange, yellow
Celosia cristata	Cockscomb	30–45	yellow, scarlet
Clarkia elegans	Clarkia	45–60	various
Exacum affine	—	30–50	violet, blue
Felicia bergeriana	Kingfisher Daisy	15–23	blue and yellow
Impatiens balsamina	Balsam	60	rose, scarlet, white
Ipomoea purpurea	Morning Glory	cl	various
Mimulus tigrinus	Annual Musk	30	various
Nemesia strumosa	Nemesia	23–30	various
Nicotiana affinis	Flowering Tobacco	38–90	white, reds
Primula malacoides		30–45	mauves, pinks
Salpiglossis sinuata	Salpiglossis	30–75	various
Schizanthus	Poor Man's Orchid, Butterfly Flower		various
Senecio croentus (cineraria)	Cineraria	30–50 45–60	various

Annuals for cutting

Amaranthus caudatus	Love-lies-bleeding	60	reddish-purople
Arctotis hybrids	African Daisy	30–45	various
Calendula officinalis	Pot Marigold	60	orange yellow
Callistephus	Annual or China Aster	23–75	various
Centaurea cyanus	Cornflower	30–75	various
Chrysanthemum carinatum	Tricoloured Chrysanthemum	60	various
Chrysanthemum coronarium	Crown Daisy	30–60	various
Clarkia elegans	Clarkia	45–60	various
Cosmos bipinnatus	Cosmos	30–90	various
Cosmos sulphureus	Cosmos	45	orange
Delphinium ajacis	Larkspur	60–90	various
Dimorphotheca	Cape Marigold	30–45	orange, salmon
Gypsophila elegans	Annual Gypsophila	45	white, pink, carmine
Helichrysum bracteatum	Everlasting	60	various
Lathyrus odoratus	Sweet Pea	cl	various
Matthiola	Stocks	30–38	various
Limonium	Annual Statice	30–60	various
Moluccella laevis	Bells of Ireland	45–75	green and white
Nigella damascena	Love-in-a-mist	45	blue
Phlox drummondii	Annual Phlox	23–30	various
Scabiosa atropurpurea	Pincushion Flower, Sweet Scabious	45–70	various
Tagetes	African and French Marigolds	15–90	various
Tropaeolum majus	Nasturtium	15 & tr	oranges, yellow, red
Zinnia elegans	Zinnia	23–75	various

A recommended list of bulbs

Early Spring (February–March)

Botanical Name	Common Name
Camassia	Quamash
Chionodoxa	Glory of the Snow
Crocus	Crocus
Eranthis	Winter Aconite
Galanthus	Snowdrop
Ipheion uniflorum	
Iris reticulata	Iris
Iris danfordiae	
Leucojum vernum	Spring Snowflake
Narcissus cyclamineus	
Scilla sibirica	Siberian Squill
Tulipa	Tulip
(Species tulips)	
T. kaufmanniana	
T. fosteriana	
T. greigii	

Mid-season (March–April)

Botanical Name	Common Name
Hyacinthus	Hyacinths
Muscari	Grape Hyacinth
Narcissus	Daffodil
Trumpet	
Narcissus	Daffodil
Medium Cupped	
Tulipa	Tulip
Single Early	
Tulipa	Tulip
Double Early	
Triumph	
Mendel	

Late (April–May)

Botanical Name	Common Name
Iris (Dutch)	Iris
Narcissus	Daffodil
Short Cupped	
Scilla campanulata	Spanish Squill
Tulipa	Tulip
Lily-flowered	
Double Late	
Paeony-flowered	
Tulipa	Tulip
Darwin Hybrid	
Parrot	
Cottage	
Darwin	

Summer (June–September)

Botanical Name	Common Name
Acidanthera	Abyssinian Wildflower
Anemone	Windflower
Begonia	Begonia
Brodiaea	
Crinum	Cape Lily
Crocosmia	
Dahlia	Dahlia
Freesia	Freesia
Galtonia	Spire Lily
Gladiolus	Gladiolus
Iris	Iris
English	
Spanish	
Ismene	
Leucojum aestivum	Summer Snowflake
Lilium	Lily
Montbretia	Montbretia
Ornithogalum thyrsoides	Chincherinchee
Ranunculus	
Sparaxis	African Harlequin Flower
Tigridia	Shell Flower
Vallota speciosa	Scarborough Lily
Zantedeschia	Arum Lily

Autumn (September–November)

Botanical Name	Common Name
Crocus (some)	Crocus
Colchicum	Autumn Crocus

cl = climbing tr = trailing * = perennials usually treated as annuals

| Sternbergia | Winter Daffodil |
| *Zephyranthes candida* | Flower of the West Wind |

Bulbs for naturalizing

Anemone blanda	
Camassia	Quamash
Colchicum	Autumn Crocus
Crocus	Crocus
spring and	
autumn-flowering	
Endymion nonscriptus	Bluebell
Eranthis	Winter Aconite
Erythronium dens-canis	Dog's Tooth Violet
Fritillaria meleagris	Chequered Lily
Galanthus	Snowdrop
Leujocum	Snowflake
Muscari	Grape Hyacinth
Narcissus	Daffodil
Ornithogalum umbellatum	Star of Bethlehem
Puschkinia libanotica	Striped Squill
Scilla sibirica	Siberian Squill

Bulbs for cut flowers

Alstroemeria	Peruvian Lily
Anemone	Windflower
De Caen	
St. Brigid, etc.	
Convallaria majalis	Lily-of-the-Valley
Crocus chrysanthus	Crocus
Dahlia	Dahlia
Freesia	Freesia
Gladiolus	Gladiolus
Iris	Iris
Dutch	
Iris	Iris
Spanish	
English	
Lilium	Lily
Montbretia	Montbretia
Muscari	Grape Hyacinth
Narcissus triandrus	
N. cyclamineus	
N. jonquilla	
Doubles	
Trumpet	
Small Cupped	
N. poeticus	
Ornithogalum umbellatum	Star of Bethlehem
arabicum pyramidale	
Ranunculus	
Scilla	Squill
Tulipa	Tulip
Taller Species	
all tall-stemmed	
garden tulips	
Tritonia	
Ixia	African Corn Lily

Bulbs for indoor cultivation

Chionodoxa sardensis	
Crocus	Crocus
Eranthis cilicica	
Freesia	Freesia
Hyacinthus	Hyacinths
Prepared	
Early Romans	
Iris reticulata	Iris
I. danfordiae	
I. histriodes major	
Narcissus	Daffodil
types and varieties as	
listed for cut flowers	
Scilla sibirica	Siberian Squill
Tulipa	Tulip
Single early	
Double Early	

A selection of hardy annuals

Botanical Name	Common Name	Height cm	Colour
Althaea	Annual Hollyhock	120–150	various
Anagallis linifolia	Pimpernel	60	blue, red
Argemone	Prickly Poppy	60	yellow, orange, white
Calendula officinalis	Pot Marigold	60	orange, yellow
Centaurea cyanus	Cornflower	30–60	various
Centaurea moschata	Sweet Sultan	30–38	various
Chrysanthemum carinatum	Tricoloured Chrysanthemum	60	various
Chrysanthemum coronarium	Crown Daisy	30–60	various
Clarkia elegans	Clarkia	45–60	various
Collinsia	—	30–38	various
Convolvulus tricolor	Annual Convolvulus	30–70	various
Delphinium ajacis	Larkspur	60–90	pink, red, blue, white
Dianthus sinensis	Indian Pink	15–23	various
Eschscholzia	Californian Poppy	30	various
Gilia × hybrids	—	8–15	various
Godetia	Godetia	15–75	pink, crimson, white
Gypsophila elegans	Annual Gypsophila	45	white, pink, carmine
Helianthus annuus	Sunflower	90–240	yellow, bronze, brown
Helipterum	Everlasting	30	white, pink, yellow
Lathyrus odoratus	Sweet Pea	cl	various
Laverata trimestris	Mallow	60–90	white, pink
Leptosyne stillmanii	—	45	golden-yellow
Limnanthes douglasii	Butter and Eggs	15	white and yellow
Linaria maroccana	Annual Toadflax	23–38	various
Linum grandiflorum	Annual Flax	28–45	red, blue, pink, white
Lobularia	Sweet Alyssum	10–30	white, pink, lilac
Lupinus hartwegii	Annual Lupin	30–90	various
Malcolmia maritima	Virginia Stock	15–30	various
Malope grandiflorum	Mallow	60–90	pink, crimson, white
Matthiola bicornis	Night-scented Stock	30	lilac
Mentzelia lindleyi	Blazing Star	45	yellow
Nemophila menziesii	Baby Blue-eyes	tr	blue
Nigella damascena	Love-in-the-mist	45	blue, pink, white
Papaver rhoeas	Shirley Poppy	45–60	various
Papaver somniferum	Opium Poppy	45–90	various
Phacelia campanularia	—	23	blue
Reseda odorata	Mignonette	30–45	red, yellow, white
Rhodanthe manglesii	Everlasting	30	rose and white
Salvia horminum	—	45	blue
Saponaria vaccaria	Annual Soapwort	28	pink, white
Scabiosa atropurpurea	Sweet Scabious	45–90	various
Silene pendula	Annual Catchfly	15	various
Thelesperma burridgeanum	—	45	yellow, red-brown
Tropaeolum majus	Nasturtium	15 & tr	oranges, yellow, red
Tropaeolum peregrinum	Canary Creeper	cl	yellow
Viscaria oculata	Catchfly	15–30	various

Hardy annuals to sow in the autumn

Calendula officinalis	Pot Marigold	60	orange yellow
Centaurea cyanus	Cornflower	30–75	various
Cladanthus arabicus	—	75	yellow
Clarkia elegans	Clarkia	45–60	various
Delphinium ajacis	Larkspur	60–90	pink, red, blue, white
Eschscholzia	Californian Poppy	30	various
Godetia	Godetia	15–75	pink, crimson, white
Gypsophila elegans	Annual Gypsophila	45	white, pink, carmine
Iberis	Candytuft	15–38	various
Lathyrus odoratus	Sweet Pea	cl	various
Limnanthes douglasii	Butter and Eggs	15	white and yellow
Lobularia maritima	Sweet Alyssum	30	white, pink, lilac
Lychnis githago	Corn-cockle	60–90	pale lilac
(syn *Agrostemma githago*)			
Malcolmia maritima	Virginia Stock	15–30	various
Nigella damascena	Love-in-a-mist	45	blue, pink, white
Oenthera biennis	Evening Primrose	75	yellow
Papaver rhoeas	Shirley Poppy	45–60	various
Saponaria vaccaria	Annual Soapwort	75	pink, white
Scabiosa atropurpurea	Sweet Scabious	45–90	various
Specularia speculumveneris	Venus's Looking Glass	25	blue
Viscaria	Catchfly	15–30	various

Perennials for cutting

Name	Height in metres	Colour	Season
Acanthus mollis	1·2–1·5m	lilac-pink	July–Aug
Achillea 'Moonshine'	60cm	sulphur-yellow	June–July
Alchemilla mollis	1–1·5m	yellowish-green	June–July
Anaphalis triplinervis	23 cm	white 'everlasting'	July–Aug
Aquilegia hybrids	up to 1m	various	May–June
Aster (perennial)	up to 2m	white, pinks, purples	Aug–Oct
Astrantia	60–90cm	greenish-white, pink	June
Coreopsis grandiflora	60–90cm	golden-yellow	June–Sep
Dianthus	15–30cm	various	May–June
Heuchera spp & varieties	60cm	pinks, reds	June–July
Iris germanica	up to 1m	various	May–June
Phlox decussata	up to 1m	various	July–Sep
Pyrethrum cultivars	60cm	various	May–June
Trollius	60cm	yellow, gold	May–June

Bulbs, corms and tubers

The first of the spring bulbs appear when winter aconite and the snowdrops push their fresh green shoots through the bare wintry earth. More of their kind follow—the wild hyacinth or bluebell, so intensely blue, more sweet-smelling, heavy-headed hyacinths, daffodils, the stiff-necked tulip and the irises.

The terms bulbs, corms and tubers are rather prosaic for such beautiful flowers and there is quite a lot of confusion for beginners about which is which. They all have one characteristic in common—they are reserves of food for the growing plant. When the flowering of the plant finishes the reserves are at their lowest point—and so it is essential to remove the flowers when they are dead to stop energy going into seed-setting, and to leave the leaves of the plant growing as long as possible so that the underground food reserves are re-stocked from them.

Bulbs are made up of bulb scales borne on a main stem; **corms** have no scales but are shortened, swollen stems; **tubers** can be swollen stems or swollen roots such as the stem tuber of a potato or a Jerusalem artichoke, and the fat root tubers of dahlias.

Usually soon after these plants have finished flowering, next year's flower is being formed in miniature underground. When the leaves wither and fade, so do usually the roots, and the whole plant enters a period of rest during which it can be moved or stored, for it is ready for next year's flowering.

Bulbous plants are generous to the gardener and will grow anywhere. They can be moved around, and lifted after flowering and withering to give extra space in the bed. They will pack together in bowls or pots too, and still flower profusely.

Bulbs grow offsets, that is, new bulbs, so that the gardener who plants half a dozen daffodils together one year, will find several years later that he has many more than he started with, all growing in a natural drift that is far prettier than his original group. Places to plant bulbs can include a grassy bank, beneath the trees, throughout the wild garden or along the village roadside. The only care you have to take is not to cut the grass until the bulb leaves have turned yellow or withered.

Corms replace themselves annually. After having grown leaves and flowers each corm shrivels away and a new corm or, sometimes several, form while the leaves and flowers of the old corm are still growing.

Stem tubers will have many buds on them, like the eyes of the potato; root tubers have buds on the short piece of stem attached to their upper end.

There are other thickened stems grow-

Left: *Bearded irises grow from rhizomes, and have tufts of coloured hairs on the falls (lower petals). You will find numerous forms listed.*

Below: *Crocus tomasinianus, from the area of Dalmatia and Serbia, flowers in early spring. The corm is almost round and a few centimetres wide. This is an easy species to naturalize.*

Right: *Tulips, hyacinths and narcissi are massed together to give a dazzling display. Spring-flowering bulbs are the mainstay of most spring bedding schemes.*

Below right: *Bulbs and corms are storage organs which enable many plants to over-winter in or out of the ground. A bulb has fleshy or scaly leaves whereas a corm is a solid, swollen stem base without scales.*

Above: '*Beersheba*' *is one of the most popular white daffodils. It has a long trumpet. There is a massive family of daffodils (narcissi) to choose from.*

Below: *A longitudinal section through a hyacinth bulb showing it at an early stage of growth.*

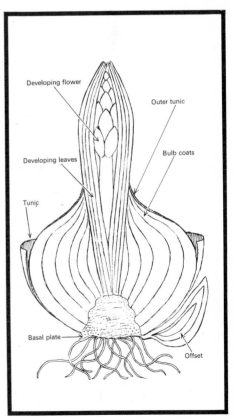

Developing flower

Outer tunic

Developing leaves

Bulb coats

Tunic

Basal plate

Offset

ing horizontally below ground called **rhizomes** from which plants grow and multiply. There are thin, rapidly-growing rhizomes that weeds have (such as ground elder), and fleshier ones (such as those of mint or lily-of-the-valley); or the short stumpy rhizomes of the flag iris, for example.

Planting bulbs

It is important to get good quality bulbs which are free from disease from the nursery and it is best to plant them straight away if you can. If you have to keep them a little while, store them in a cool, dark, well-ventilated place.

Among the bulbs you look for, keep in mind winter aconite, snowdrops, scilla, the autumn crocus, the little wild wood anemone, *Anemone blanda*, the wild hyacinth or English bluebell, *Endymion non-scriptus*, the grape hyacinths, muscari, narcissi, from trumpeted daffodils to white star-like flowers, and lilies and irises of many kinds.

Plant spring-flowering bulbs from early September to mid-December.

Daffodils should be planted before the end of October.

Autumn-flowering bulbs (crocus and colchicum) are planted in August.

Summer-flowering bulbs are planted in March and April.

Lilies can be planted in November and December as well as in early spring.

Iris are either bulb or rhizome plants. The bulbs are planted in September and the rhizomes in autumn or early spring.

Bulbs are usually planted with the pointed end uppermost and tubers horizontally. The right end of an anemone might be hard to sort out but look for signs of an old stem or roots.

Spring-flowering bulbs such as hyacinths, daffodils and tulips are planted about 15cm (6in) deep or 5–10cm (2–4ins) for most small and spring flowering bulbs.

On the whole bulbs like an open, porous soil and plenty of water when growing but little when dormant. Therefore well-drained soil is needed. Many bulbs do not mind some shade, in fact it will often prolong their flowering. You can mulch bulbs in the summer but do not manure them in any way whereby their roots will contact it. A slow-acting fertilizer is better. An annual application of bonemeal will keep bulbs healthy.

Bulbs can also give pleasure indoors. In January you can bring in hyacinths when the buds are well out of the neck of the bulbs. Brought in too soon, the flower will be short-stemmed among the leaves. When you first bring them in from a plunge bed where they have wintered, covered in earth, bring to a temperature of about 10C (50F) and then day by day

Above: *Narcissus odorus, the campernelle, bears up to four flowers on a stem in spring.*

Below: *Fritillaria meleagris, snake's head, with pendulous chequered flowers, quite hardy.*

Above: *One of the Lilium x maculatum forms with upright orange flowers.*

Below: *The large flowers of Darwin tulip 'London' give brilliant dashes of colour.*

Below: *Snowdrop, Galanthus nivalis, grows under shrubs, in the lawn or rock garden.*

Below: *'Caribbean', a 'blue' cultivar of gladiolus. Gladioli grow from corms.*

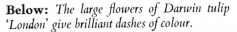

Above: *Many splendid hybrid hyacinths have been raised for bedding purposes from the common hyacinth, H. orientalis.*

increase this to 16C (60F). That should be the maximum temperature, for you are only trying to give them the warmth of a good spring day. Do not place the bulbs over or near a radiator, but on or near a window sill because they need light.

The shoot of narcissi should be about 10cm (4in) long when you bring them indoors. If the bulbs are 'double nosed' some of the shoots will not have flowers within them—so nip these off so that the plant can concentrate on shoots that have flowers. When the flower is almost ready, spray the buds lightly with water twice a day, but stop once the petals are open.

Tulips and the little bulbs like crocuses and snowdrops, take longer to mature and should not be brought in as early as January. They are brought indoors when the flower bud is showing colour and is about to break from its sheath.

For growing daffodils indoors you can use any container at least 7·5cm (3in) deep (a plastic lining will stop special china being stained). Put in the bottom of the bowl some pieces of charcoal which, with broken crock will cover the drainage holes, if there are any. Cover with a good potting compost if the bulbs are to be planted out in the garden later (for flowering the following spring). Set medium-sized bulbs in upright position, allowing a little space between each. Pack compost around each bulb to within 2·5cm (1in) of the container rim. Top could be finished with smooth pebbles.

39

The panther lily, Lilium pardalinum, has long recurved orange-pink flowers, likes moist but well-drained soil. Up to 20 flowers per stem.

Monthly Calendar

JANUARY
Start to bring plunged or covered hyacinths and narcissi indoors. Keep moist.

FEBRUARY
Move overcrowded snowdrops. Plant corms of *Anemone coronaria*, ranunculus tubers, *Camassia quamash*.

MARCH
Plant gladioli corms and hardy oxalis species.

APRIL
Cut off dead flower stems from narcissi. Hand weed tulip beds. Sow lily seeds; complete lily bulb planting. Lightly top dress gladioli at the end of the month.

MAY
Lift lily bulbs from garden for tub decoration. Lift tulips when finished; heel-in for bulbs to ripen.

JUNE
Lift overcrowded bulbs; dry off in boxes. Drench gladioli during dry weather.

JULY
Lift and dry off tulip bulbs. Complete bulb order for autumn planting.

AUGUST
Plant narcissi. Prepare bulbs for indoor winter flowering.

SEPTEMBER
Plant spring-flowering bulbs, with the exception of tulips.

OCTOBER
Lift half-hardy summer-flowering bulbs; clean and store. Cut down gladioli foliage as it turns yellow. Lift, clean, store corms.

NOVEMBER
Plant tulips. Do not shallow-plant.

DECEMBER
If lily bulbs received this month are shrivelled, pack in damp peat for a week or two. Dust corms in store with insecticide.

Learn the language of gardening
Choosing shrubs, trees & climbers

Shrubs and trees make up the main background of the garden, provide its skyline and record the seasons with spring blossom, summer leafiness or the change to autumn colour and leaf fall. Not all shrubs are bare in winter, some stay green, or bear berries, some even flower, but their importance lies more in the shape and outline they give to a garden, so that its views stretch upwards, and out and back.

A **shrub** has many woody stems branching from its base. A **tree** is also a woody plant but it has a single main stem or trunk and grows above 4–5m (12–15ft).

Trees and shrubs can be deciduous or evergreen. **Deciduous** means that the leaves last for one growing season and then fall to the ground. When the leaves have fallen at winter time the branches of the tree or shrub are bare. **Evergreen** shrubs and trees hold their leaves throughout the

winter and never have bare branches. They do not hold their leaves forever although they might appear to. The leaves are shed —not dramatically and completely every winter—but gradually throughout the entire year. The leaf cycle from bud to ground fall takes several years and the tree always has some active leaves. These can be grey, silver or gold as well as green.

When it comes to choosing shrubs and trees it is important to choose the right size otherwise you are either going to have to spend endless time trimming and pruning to keep the size down or you will have a huge tree where you do not want it, and perhaps later have to obtain the services of an expert to have it cut down. Although nursery catalogues and gardening books

A border of mixed shrubs chosen for their flower and foliage colours.

give average sizes, you cannot be sure that in your garden conditions, trees and shrubs will not vary from those specified. Allow for some adjustment in planning and do not crowd the garden to begin with.

It is a good idea too to try and balance out spring blossom, spring and summer flowers, autumn colour, seeds and seedpods, winter berries, the pussy-willow buds, the catkins. All these portray the seasons more vividly, and provide branches for indoor decoration.

Shrubs
One of the pleasant things about shrubs is that they live on in the garden, giving very little trouble and needing very little care. All that you have to do is to plant them with thoughtfulness, see that they are thriving and prune some of them from time to time. If the garden was all flowers

and no shrubs your first year of gardening would probably be your last, for a garden full of flowers does take considerable energy. A garden of shrubs takes far less.

Shrubs are among the most beautiful plants, providing intermediate height necessary between the trees and the garden beds. Many of them grow very well under trees, whereas many flowers do not.

Choose your shrubs with a balance between deciduous and evergreen—placing the evergreen where you want year-round screening or privacy, or a background to a more showy plant. Check too which deciduous shrubs are handsome when they are bare. Some look beautiful, some look bereft. Some have interesting coloured stems or bark and others are overcoat grey.

Make sure the conditions are right for each plant. Some shrubs like rather acid, leaf-mould filled or peaty soil and to give them anything else will cause you nothing but disappointment when they fail to flourish. Vary your choice of shrubs but suit the ones you choose to the existing conditions. Again, check with the local nurseryman and your neighbours: all gardeners love to give advice.

Do not forget the scale of plants, letting heights grade harmoniously. Vary shapes, so that a shrub with a very special weeping or arching habit is clearly seen against a plainer background and has room to develop its growth habit without crowding. Remember that colours should vary too, to help outline one plant against another; a lighter green against a dark green, a blue-leaved shrub against green ones, and cheerful yellow leaves to give the effect of sun when there is none.

Some shrubs need pruning after flowering, others need pruning in the dormant period just before spring growth, and others need no pruning at all. Check the chapter on pruning for more about pruning shrubs.

Many evergreen shrubs do not need pruning. *Berberis x stenophilla* with its sprays of golden-orange flowers and *Berberis darwinii*, with miniature holly-like leaves and orange flowers which appear in April and May, do not need pruning if they are grown as individual shrubs. As hedges, prune them after flowering to keep the hedge outline. *Mahonia aquifolium* and *Mahonia japonica* are two lovely flowering evergreens which need no pruning. Neither does *Garrya elliptica* which has long silvery-green catkins in February.

Deciduous winter-flowering shrubs which do not need pruning are chimonanthus and *Hamamelis mollis* (witch hazel) which has yellow, spicily-scented flowers and autumn-tinted foliage, and the lovely viburnums. This is a delightful family of deciduous and evergreen shrubs, giving

Above: *The bottle-brush, Callistemon citrinus splendens, evergreen shrub, needs full sun.*

Below: *Common dogwood, Cornus sanguinea, shrub to 2m, leaves colour in autumn.*

Below: *The yellow-fruited Pyracantha stalantioides, a good choice for town gardens.*

Below: *Fuchsia 'Beauty of Bath' has semi-double flowers in white and pink.*

Above: *Hamamelis mollis pallida, a sulphur-yellow form of the Chinese witch hazel.*

Above: *A very popular barberry is Berberis darwinii. It has holly-like leaves.*

Below: *Double-flowered form of the fragrant Gardenia jasminoides. Needs a warm climate.*

flowers, fruits or vibrant autumn tints.

Shrubs are bought from the nursery usually either with a hessian wrap around both the roots and earth—called a balled root—or in a container. It is important not to disturb roots, and to get the balled plant into the earth as fast as you can. Containers can wait longer if the plant has room and is kept moist and comfortable. Container plants have the best start because they can be planted in the garden with minimum disturbance to the roots. If a plant comes in a metal container, cut down the side with metal cutters to free it. See the planting chapter for more detailed instructions.

Keep young shrubs well-watered in dry weather, making sure the water thoroughly soaks in and is not just a light sprinkle on the surface. You can mulch over moist soil in summer to stop it drying out. Use an organic or inorganic fertilizer once a year.

Generally speaking, shrubs do not get very many pests and diseases, and if one plant is persistently troubled it might be better to take it out than persevere with hopeful remedies. Sometimes aphids will suck the sap or caterpillars will eat holes in the leaves, but at times it is better to leave a chain of life from the microscopic insects to the birds, rather than to constantly use strong chemical sprays.

Below: *The leaves of Mahonia bealei colour well in autumn.*

Above: *Kalmia latifolia, a summer-flowering (waxy pink) evergreen shrub.*

Above: *Evergreen shrub, Skimmia rubella, useful for winter effect on a chalky soil.*

Above: *Jasminum nudiflorum flowers on bare wood in winter. Is a deciduous, hardy shrubby climber.*

Below: *Black berries of the common privet, Ligustrum vulgare, form when it is not clipped. It will grow into a hedge in shade.*

Above: *The fruits and flowers of Hypericum elatum 'Elstead' in late summer.*

Below: *Evergreen shrub Rhododendron 'China'. Check many more in nursery lists.*

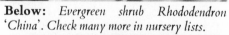

Above: *The Knaphill strain of azalea. This is 'Daybreak' with flame-coloured flowers.*

Above: *Hardy evergreen Viburnum x burk-woodii has scented flowers, in early spring.*

Above: *The berries of Vaccinium glauca are covered with blue-grey bloom.*

Above: *Viburnum opulus fructo-luteo, yellow fruited form of guelder rose or snowball tree.*

Above: *Viburnum betulifolium, shrub to 4m has shiny red berries into the winter.*

Right: *Hydrangeas produce deep but subtle blue flowers in acid soils, pale pink flowers in lime or chalky soils.*

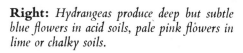

45

Gallery of shrubs

Strong, narrow upright lines
Berberis thunbergii 'Erecta'
Prunus 'Amanogawa'
P. X hillieri 'Spire'
P. 'Umineko'
Sorbus 'Joseph Rock'
S. aucuparia 'Fastigiata'
Ulmus sarniensis 'Aurea'
Malus 'Van Eseltine'

Conifers
Juniperus virginiana 'Skyrocket'
J. communis 'Hibernica'

Rounded compact growth
Acer palmatum 'Dissectum'
A. p. 'Dissectum Atropurpureum'
Ceanothus papillosus roweanus
Choisya ternata
Cistus in variety
Cotinus coggygria 'Royal Purple'
Cytisus praecox
Hebe albicans
H. 'Marjorie'
Lavandula 'Hidcote'
Philadelphus 'Manteau d'Hermine'
Potentilla 'Elizabeth'
P. fruticosa 'Tangerine'
Rhododendron 'Britannia'
Santolina chamaecyparissus
Senecio greyi

Conifers
Chamaecyparis lawsoniana 'Forsteckensis'
C. l. 'Gimbornii'
C. pisifera 'Filifera Aurea'
C. p. 'Boulevard' ('Cyanoviridis')
Cryptomeria japonica 'Elegans Nana'

Arching and pendulous branches
Berberis X stenophylla
Betula pendula 'Youngii'
Cytisus scoparius in variety
C. monspessulanus
Buddleia alternifolia
Genista cinerea
G. aetnensis
G. lydia
Potentilla fruticosa 'Primrose Beauty'
Rose species, particularly Rosa hugonis (or 'Canary Bird'), californica 'Flore Plena', willmottiae
Salix purpurea 'Pendula'
S. caprea 'Pendula'

Conifers
Juniperus X media 'Globosa Cinerea'
J. X m. 'Hetzii'
Podocarpus salignus
Taxus baccata 'Dovastonii Aurea'
T. b. 'Semperaurea'
Tsuga canadensis 'Bennett'

Horizontal growth or prostrate habit
C. horizontalis 'Variegatus'
C. 'Skogholm'
C. microphyllus cochleatus
Cytisus scoparius 'Prostratus' (maritimus)
Potentilla fruticosa 'Longacre Variety'
Rosa 'Max Graff'
R. 'Raubritter'
R. X paulii

Conifers
Juniperus sabina 'Tamariscifolia'
J. X media 'Pfitzerana Glauca'
J. X m. 'Pfitzerana Aurea'
J. horizontalis 'Bar Harbor'
J. communis 'Depressa Aurea'
J. c. 'Effusa'
Picea abies 'Pseudoprostrata'
Tsuga canadensis 'Prostrata'

Flowering shrubs
Abutilon megapotamicum
A. vitifolium

Camellia japonica, C. recticulata, C. sasanqua, C. X williamsii
Campsis radicans (climber)
Cantua buxifolia
Carpenteria californica
Cistus ladanifer, C. palhinhae, C. X purpureus
Clematis X jackmanii, C. macropetala, C. tangutica, C. viticella (all climbers)
Cornus florida, C. nuttallii
Crinodendron hookerianum
Desfontainea spinosa
Eucryphia X nymansensis
Fuchsia hybrids (many vars.)
Hibiscus sinosyriacus
Hydrangea macrophylla (many vars.)
Hypericum 'Hidcote', H. 'Rowallane'
Kalmia latifolia
Magnolia denudata, M. grandiflora, M. sinensis, M. X soulangiana, M. wilsonii.
Michelia doltsopa
Paeonia suffruticosa (many vars.)
Philesia magellanica
Punica granatum
Rhododendron albrechtii, R. campanulatum, R. cinnabarinum, R. griffithianum, R. nuttallii, R. sinogrande, R. thomsonii
Rubus X tridel
Styrax obassia

For autumn berries
Aucuba japonica
Berberis X rubrostilla and other deciduous species
Clerodendrum trichotomum
Coriaria terminalis
C. t. 'Xanthocarpa'
Cotoneaster conspicuus 'Decorus'
C. c. X watereri 'Cornubia'
C. c. 'Highlight'
Euonymus europaeus and 'Red Cascade'
Hippophae rhamnoides
Ilex aquifolium 'J. C. Van Tol'
I. a. 'Amber' and many others
Pyracantha rogersiana
P. r. 'Flava'
Rosa moyesii 'Geranium'
Skimmia japonica (female)
Stranvaesia davidiana

For autumn colour foliage
Acer palmatum 'Osakazuki'
Amelanchier florida
Berberis thunbergii
B. wilsoniae
Cotinus americanus
Disanthus cercidifolius
Euonymus alatus
Hydrangea quercifolia
Rhododendron (azalea) molle (japonicum), Knaphill and Ghent hybrids
Rhus typhina
Rosa nitida
Stephanandra incisa
Viburnum plicatum (tomentosum) 'Mariesii'

Climbers
Parthenocissus tricuspidata 'Veitchii'
Vitis amurensis
V. 'Brandt'
V. coignetiae and others

Variegated leaves
Abutilon megapotamicum 'Variegatum'
A. X milleri
Aralia elata 'Aureovariegata'
Berberis thunbergii 'Rose Glow'
Cornus alba 'Elegantissima'
C. alternifolia 'Argentea'
C. controversa 'Variegata'
C. mas 'Variegata'
Coronilla glauce 'Variegata'
Cotoneaster horizontalis 'Variegata'
Daphne odora 'Aureomarginata'
Elaeagnus pungens 'Maculata'
Euonymus 'Silver Queen'
Fuchsia magellanica 'Versicolor'
Hebe X andersonii 'Variegata'
Hydrangea macrophylla 'Maculata'
Hypericum moserianum 'Tricolor'
Ilex aquifolium (variegated forms)
Kerria japonica 'Variegata'
Pachysandra terminalis 'Variegata'

Pieris japonica 'Variegata'
Pittosporum 'Silver Queen'
Salvia officinalis 'Icterina'
S. o. 'Tricolor'
Weigela praecox 'Variegata'

Grey or silver foliage
Artemisia arborescens
Atriplex halimus
Ballota pseudodictamnus
Calluna vulgaris 'Silver Queen'
Caryopteris X clandonensis
Cistus 'Silver Pink'
C. pulverulentus
Convolvulus cneorum
Cytisus battandieri
Dorycnium hirsutum
Elaeagnus angustifolia
Feijoa sellowiana
Halimium atriplicifolium
Hebe albicans
H. colensoi 'Glauca'
H. pinguifolia 'Pagei'
Lavandula spica
Leptospermum cunninghamii
L. lanigerum
Olearia X scilloniensis
Salix lanata
S. repens 'Argentea'
Senecio greyi
Teucrium fruticans
Potentilla fruticosa mandshurica
P. f. 'Vilmoriniana'
Santolina neapolitana
S. chamaecyparissus

Conifers
Chamaecyparis lawsoniana 'Fletcheri'
C. l. 'Chilworth Silver'
C. l. 'Pembury Blue'
C. pisifera 'Boulevard'
Cupressus cashmeriana
C. glabra 'Pyramidalis'
Juniperus chinensis 'Obelisk'
J. 'Grey Owl'
J. X media 'Pfitzerana Glauca'
J. sabina 'Hicksii'
J. squamata 'Meyeri'
J. horizontalis 'Wiltonii' ('Blue Rug')

Golden and yellow foliage
Acer japonicum 'Aureum'
Berberis thunbergii 'Aurea'
Calluna vulgaris 'Aurea'
C. v. 'Joy Vanstone'
C. v. 'Serlei Aurea' and others
Hedera helix 'Buttercup' (climber)
Lonicera nitida 'Baggesen's Gold'
Philadelphus coronarius 'Aureus'
Physocarpus opulifolius 'Luteus'
Ribes sanguineum 'Brocklebankii'
Sambucus racemosa 'Plumosa Aurea'
Weigela X 'Looymansii Aurea'

Conifers
Chamaecyparis lawsoniana 'Lanei'
C. l. 'Lutea Nana'
C. l. 'Winston Churchill'
C. obtusa 'Crippsii'
C. o. 'Tetragona Aurea'
C. pisifera 'Filifera Aurea'
Juniperus X media 'Pfitzerana Aurea'
Taxus baccata 'Standishii'
Thuja occidentalis 'Rheingold'

Red or purple
Acer palmatum 'Dissectum Atropurpureum'
Berberis X ottawensis 'Purpurea'
B. thunbergii 'Atropurpurea'
B. t. 'Atropurpurea Nana'
Brachyglottis repanda 'Purpurea'
Corylus maxima 'Purpurea'
Cotinus coggygria 'Royal Purple'
Photinia glabra 'Rubens' (red young leaves)
P. fraseri 'Robusta' (red young leaves)
Pieris formosa forrestii 'Wakehurst' (red young leaves)
Prunus spinosa 'Purpurea'
Rosa rubrifolia
Weigela florida 'Foliis Purpureis'
Parthenocissus henryana (climber)
Vitis vinifera 'Purpurea' (climber)

Shrubs for shady sites
Aucuba japonica
Buxus sempervirens
Camellia japonica in variety
Danae racemosa
E. fortunei and cultivars
Fatshedera lizei
Fatsia japonica
Hypericum calycinum
Ilex aquifolium in variety
Mahonia aquifolium 'Atropurpurea'
Prunus laurocerasus 'Otto Luyken'
Rhododendron in great variety (acid soil)
Ruscus aculeatus
Skimmia japonica
Symphoricarps—all species

For winter display—flowers and stems
Abeliophyllum distichum
Acer davidii
A. palmatum 'Senkaki'
A. pensylvanicum
Arbutus X andrachnoides
A. unedo
Betula ermanii
B. papyrifera
Camellia japonica
C. saluenensis
C. sasanqua
C. X williamsii
Chimonanthus praecox
Clematis calycina
Cornus alba 'Sibirica'
Cornus mas
C. stolonifera 'Flaviramea'
Corylus avellana 'Contorta'
Daphne laureola
D. mezereum
Edgworthia papyrifera
Erica arborea alpina
E. carnea
E. X. darleyensis
E. mediterranea (erigena)
Forsythia giraldiana
Garrya elliptica
Hamamelis X intermedia
H. japonica
H. mollis
Jasminum nudiflorum
Lonicera fragrantissima
L. X standishii
Mahonia bealei
M. lomariifolia
Parottia persica
Prunus davidiana
P. maackii
P. serrula
P. serrulata semperflorens
P. subhirtella 'Autumnalis'
Rhododendron arboreum
R. barbatum
R. 'Christmas Cheer'
R. 'Cornubia'
R. mucronulatum
R. X nobleanum
R. X praecox
R. stewartianum
Rosa omeiensis
R. pteracantha
Salix alba 'Chermesina'
S. caprea
S. daphnoides
S. matsudana 'Tortuosa'
Sarcococca hookeriana digyna
S. humilis
S. ruscifolia
Stachyurus praecox
Viburnum X bodnantense
V. farreri
V. grandiflorum
V. tinus

Above: *Chamaecyparis obtusa.*
Below: *Hibiscus syriacus 'Coeleste'.*

Roses

Roses are among the most beautiful and best-known flowering shrubs. There were wild roses—called species roses—in Asia, China, Japan, North America, Europe and Britain and from these all our bewildering and fascinating array of new and old roses have been developed. Some roses cross-pollinated and seeded hybrids in the wild; others were produced by rose growers who for more than four centuries have been documenting their results, although until the 18th century the deliberate crossing or hybridizing of plants was not generally understood.

An enormous step forward in the development of roses was when it was found that hybrids from the long-flowering China rose produced roses also with the long-flowering habit—roses that would flower twice in one season or throughout the season. They were called perpetual-blooming roses and the long-flowering habit is in many modern roses.

Roses fall mainly into these groups—hybrid tea, floribunda and shrub roses, miniatures and climbers.

The **hybrid tea roses** are all descendants of the tea-scented rose which was a wild hybrid rose of China, but it is really the work of the rose growers who hybridize and select the best seedlings over the years which have produced the hybrid tea as we know it—a rose with elegant long buds, and flowers with petals exquisitely curved around a high centre. The hybrid teas vary greatly. Some are fragrant, some not, some have single flowers, many are full or very full, but all flower over long periods because their ancestors from China had the perpetual or ever-blooming habit. A boost to the popularity of hybrid teas came with 'Ophelia' in 1912, and another when a young French hybridist François Meilland raised a seedling he called after his mother Mme Antoine Meilland. The second world war intervened and the Americans launched the rose at the end of it as 'Peace'.

The main species **shrub roses** were the white rose, *Rosa alba*, and the red rose or French rose, *R. gallica*, both of which had been grown in Britain from at least Saxon times, the cabbage rose, *R. centifolia*, the damask rose, *R. damascena* and the musk rose, *R. moschata*. The musk rose was of Asian origin, coming to Europe in the 16th century. It is fragrant and free-flowering but rather tender. On the whole these old-fashioned roses make large rather untidy shrubs for a small garden, but try 'Felicité Parmentier', a sweet-scented alba, 'Madame Hardy', a variety of the damask rose, or *Rosa mundi* (syn. *Rosa gallica versicolor*), the earliest of the striped roses, the 16th century 'Apothecary's rose'.

The moss rose was a mutation of the

Above left: *Peat can be used as a summer mulch around rose bushes to conserve moisture. Spread on after the soil has been well watered.*

Above: *Peat being worked into the soil before planting roses. Planting can be done from autumn to early spring.*

Left: *In early summer a mulch of manure is applied to established roses. This follows a spring application of fertilizer.*

Below: *'Lady Seton' is a hybrid tea rose with the typical conical-shaped centre.*

Above: *Rosa moyesii grows to a large shrub and has lovely lantern-shaped hips.*

Left: *The pink and white Rosa gallica versicolor, better known as Rosa mundi.*

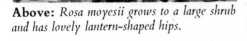

cabbage rose and the Old Pink Moss has lovely mid-pink blooms and the characteristic moss-like growth on buds. It sported or mutated again and again producing the *R. centifolia muscosa*. In the 19th century, with the introduction of the China and tea-scented roses, hybridizing went ahead with the appearance of the Noisettes, now mostly gone, the Bourbon roses (which only flower once a year although related to the China rose), the hybrid perpetuals and the hybrid teas.

Last century the Japanese rose was introduced, *R. rugosa* and *Rosa moyesii*, a native of Western China and one of the most beautiful of the species roses.

Among the species roses too, is the sweet brier (*R. eglanteria*; syn. *R. rubiginosa*), an English native rose, loved for its fragrant foliage, lovely hips and free flowers, and also hybridized last century to produce among others the varieties 'Lord Penzance' and 'Lady Penzance'.

Among the hybrid tea crosses was one that produced what is sometimes called the hybrid musk, but which has little to do with the musk rose since it was so far back in its ancestry. The China rose and the musk rose were crossed to produce 'Champney's Pink Cluster' which in turn produced a noisette rose which many generations later produced a hybrid musk. The hybrid musks are like tall versions of the floribundas—roses which produce clusters of flowers.

A very beautiful form of the early Austrian brier (a native of the Near East) is *Rosa foetida bicolor* which has grown for about 300 years and is ancestor to the flame, orange and bi-colour hybrid tea roses.

The next groups are the **polyanthas** and **floribundas.** The first polyanthas were raised from a cross of *Rosa multiflora*, a wild, white rambler rose, and probably one of the China roses, the result being a rose plant that was a perpetual-flowering dwarf. These were crossed with single and semi-double hybrid tea roses to produce the hybrid polyanthas—small, long-flowering, vigorous roses. These were then crossed with hybrid teas, hybrid musks and other roses, producing many variations which looked very different from the original polyanthas and so became a new cross—floribundas. The floribundas are vigorous, bear flowers in large trusses or clusters in which many open at the same time, and bloom over a long period. Some have flowers shaped conically like the hybrid teas. The floribundas are probably almost equalling the hybrid teas in popularity and are still being crossed extensively for more cultivars. Try 'City of Belfast', a bright orange floribunda growing to about 60cm (2ft); or 'Stephen Langdon', a hybrid tea type of floribunda; rosy pink 'Sunday

Above: *Miniature roses can be grown in pots, rock gardens. This is 'Baby Masquerade'.*

Below: *Hybrid tea rose 'Super Star' keeps its colour well and is one of the best scarlets.*

Below: *One of the old Pemberton hybrid musk roses, 'Penelope', forms a good hedge. Some roses make good boundary hedges because of their thorns.*

Above: *Rosa filipes, a vigorous climber with greyish foliage and white flowers, borne in trusses. Its vigorous cultivars will climb over trees and walls.*

Above: *This is 'Alberic Barbier' grown as a standard. A standard is trained with a long stem.*

Below: *The deep pink double flowers of Rosa californica plena flower profusely.*

Times', or 'Masquerade' which changes colour as it grows, from yellow buds to yellow flower, then to pink flower and darkening at last to red. 'Iceberg' is a lovely white, and yellow 'Arthur Bell' is fragrant.

Roses like well-drained, well-aerated soil and at least 30cm (1ft) in depth of it. The soil should have plenty of humus-forming material. Put on a fertilizer of bonemeal or meat and bonemeal after pruning the roses on the rose bed at the rate of about two handfuls a square metre. In about April, follow with a complete rose fertilizer such as Tonk's formula and in May or when buds are opening, feed again or use a 5cm (2in) mulch over moist soil of leaf mould or compost.

Tonk's formula can be bought ready-made and is 12 parts of superphosphate of lime, 10 parts of nitrate of potash, 8 parts of sulphate of lime, 2 parts sulphate of magnesia and 1 part sulphate of iron.

For climbing roses and ramblers, see page 63.

The all-shrub border

A border of nothing but shrubs can give you spring or autumn displays, flowers for the house, and a very low-maintenance sweep of garden that you can leave almost entirely alone except for occasional pruning and tidying up.

The front of this border would have the low plants and ground covers, such as dwarf broom (*Cytisus x beanii* or Bean's broom) which grows to 30cm (1ft), many of the ericas or heaths that will take very general conditions and flower at all times of the year (some have leaves that turn coppery in the winter), and the low-growing cotoneaster. There are also dwarf conifers, many fuchsias that like some shade, a treasure house of azaleas, camellias, rhododendrons (azaleas belong to this family) and the variegated shrubs such as golden holly or *Elaeagnus pungens* 'Maculata' which has little bell-shaped flowers.

At the back of the border choose the trees and taller shrubs—a Killarney strawberry tree for example, magnolias, prunus, conifers and maples.

You need evergreens in the border to stop it looking too bare in the winter. The ericas and conifers have been mentioned but the winter-flowering *Erica carnea* puts on a lovely show in the off-season. Among the cotoneasters and barberries there are good evergreen shrubs too—*C. lactea*, the prostrate *C. dammeri*, the grey-foliaged *C. franchetii* and *Berberis darwinii* and *B. gagnepainii*.

Shrubs in pots

Shrubs can look marvellous in terrace pots. It is generally said that one of the advantages of large pots filled with shrubs is their

Above: *A weeping standard rose makes a fine specimen bush for planting in a lawn.*

Right: *The blooms of Rosa primula grow on a widely-spreading shrub.*

Below: *'Louise Odier', a bourbon rose, has the old-fashioned style of flower.*

Below right: *'Silver Lining' has a two-toned silvery look. It is a hybrid tea.*

portability, but they are often too heavy to move. But plants soften the look of terrace pavings and walls; you can give them exactly the soil requirements they need and cherish them from day to day. Keep a potted plant well watered for it will dry out faster than one in a bed, and feed the plant with liquid manure during the main growing season.

Gallery of trees

Trees have to be very carefully chosen. You cannot move trees about like perennials, or prune them like shrubs. They are a permanent fixture just as they grow. You can get them cut down if they are hopelessly large and taking all the space, food and light around them—but that can be upsetting. There are plenty of moderate-sized trees, lovely in growth, flower or fruit, that will fit into the moderate-sized garden.

There are two main types of trees.

Conifers have linear or needle-type leaves like the pines and cedars. The fruit is a cone of tough scales which encloses the seed. The structure of the wood is distinctive, which has given rise to the popular, although not always accurate term, softwood. All conifers are evergreen, except for a few which include the lovely ginkgo (which has fan-shaped leaves), larch, and the useful swamp cypress.

Broad-leaved trees are like oaks and elms —they have veined leaves and are mostly deciduous. The seed production and carrying of the pollen is different from the conifers. So is their timber structure, which is popularly called hardwood, although not without exception harder than the softwoods.

Check the conditions for the trees you choose. Most trees like to grow on an acid or neutral soil but if you have a soil with lime then you must choose trees which will stand it. The Cornish elm and the tulip tree will tolerate lime, so will apples, pears, rowans, crataegus, alders, the Chinese maples, prunus (cherries, plums, peaches, almonds), the horse chestnuts and buck eyes, the arbutus, the common box, hornbeams, the catalpa, *Davidia*, the dove tree, beeches, ashes, holly, walnut, laburnum, oaks, rhus, willows, the common elder, cedars, cypresses and yews. If you live on chalk hills such as the Chilterns or the South Downs you still have plenty of choice. These trees will also grow in non-alkaline conditions.

In wet parts of the garden you can plant alders, willows or the swamp cypress.

Check the shape of your trees so that you give height to the garden where you need it or place a silhouette where it can be really appreciated; or put an evergreen where you want a background or a screen. Give trees a chance to be seen, do not crowd them together or place them too close to buildings where later they might have to be lopped. Keep them well away from drains, house foundations and gutters.

Above: *Picea breweriana, Brewer's weeping spruce, reaches to about 16m when mature.*

Left: *Ulmus procera 'Vanhouttei' is a golden-leaved form of the common English elm.*

A tree has its own natural symmetry which lopping and shaping alter. Lopping is disastrous especially for conifers, because they cannot fill the gap with new growth.

To give the garden as much sun as you can, plant large trees and any trees for shade on the northern side so that their shadows do not fall across the garden too much. However, if you live in a built-up area, consider your neighbour's garden as well!

Evergreen and ever useful

Evergreens give very good value in the winter, when the grey, green or glaucous-blue foliage, shining berries and attractive flowers give life to the garden scene. Use shrubs as well as trees; with plants like the ericas or heath in flower, it is possible to soften bare winter masonry with leafy growth or flank the now-muted garden beds with wide green conifers. On the horizons of the garden the columnar shapes of conifers give interesting winter perspectives. All conifers need space, light and air around them if they are to keep green branches down to the ground.

One of the most handsome evergreens that enjoys growing alone beside a wall (it enjoys wall protection), or in the lawn, is the *Magnolia grandiflora*, with its thick, glossy, large leaves and creamy white-scented giant flowers measuring up to 20cm (8in) or more. It can take years to flower but when it does in July to September it is a sight worth waiting for. The cultivated variety 'Exmouth' has attractive cinnamon felting on the undersides of the leaves and flowers when younger.

The Killarney strawberry tree (*Arbutus unedo*) is often grown alone as a terrace tree or even a tub tree. Its interesting bent branches give it a rather fascinating silhou-

Below: *Pinus pumila, the dwarf stone pine is shrubby and grows to about 2·5m.*

Above: *The turkey oak, Quercus cerris, large erect tree grows to 40m with acorns 3cm long.*

Below: *Acacia 'Claire de Lune', evergreen and spring-flowering. Known as wattle (or mimosa).*

Below: *Leaves of this holly, Ilex aquifolium 'Golden King' are yellow-edged.*

ette and its colouring is good too: dark green leaves, white flowers something like lily-of-the-valley, and small scarlet fruits like strawberries. These are just edible but very sharp. Fruit and blossom are often on the tree at the same time. These trees can grow to 10m (approx 30ft) or more. Equally fine is the hybrid *A. x andrachnoides* which has mahogany-red bark, grey-green foliage and vivid orange fruits.

For winter colour, consider the plants that bear berries. The pyracantha or fire-thorns are small trees that are hardy and evergreen and provide vivid berries. They do not mind some shade but will not be transplanted. There are several cotoneasters that produce berries throughout the winter. *Pernettya mucronata* is a hardy shrub that produces berries through the winter to spring.

Spring blossom

Peach, plum, cherry, apricot and almond blossom—the prunus family, is the main-stay of spring. You can have fruiting forms or purely ornamental trees. Prunus comes from the old Latin word for plum and there are so many garden trees of this genus that you would have to search through catalogues and check with your nurseryman to get exactly what you want. You can have single-flowering trees with delicate starry blossoms, trees thick with a froth of flowers or weeping forms bowed down with blossom. Some flower very early and some later, some are particularly

Above: *An Acer dissectum, the Japanese maple contrasts its fiery autumn colouring against the yellows of Ginkgo biloba, maiden-hair tree.*

Below: *Deciduous Cotinus coggygria has brilliant autumn colouring. It grows to about 5m and has fruiting panicles. (syn. Rhus cotinus).*

Below: *Magnolia x soulangeana rustica rubra is a deciduous tree growing to about 6m.*

Above: *A variety of Prunus serrulata, the Japanese flowering cherry.*

Below: *Creamy-white bracts of Davidia involucrata, the dove or handkerchief tree.*

Above: *Tsuga mertensiana, the mountain hemlock, is a large conifer liking good rainfall.*

Below: *Showing the fine lines of the dove tree which grows from 15–20m.*

Below: *The long cones of the Norway spruce, Picea abies. Tree grows to 33m.*

Above: *Eucalyptus gunnii, the cider gum, is hardy and evergreen like all gums.*

Above: *Fastigiate (upright growing) flowering cherry, Prunus 'Amanogawa'.*

Above: *Lacy leaves of Rhus typhina laciniata, stag's horn sumach; deciduous tree.*

Above: *The red bark of Arbutus x andrachnoides, one form of the strawberry tree. Is a hardy, evergreen and small tree which flowers in late autumn or spring.*

Left: *Liquidambar styraciflua, or sweet gum, is a hardy, deciduous tree with splendid autumn colour. It grows, pyramid-shaped, to about 30m and likes moist, well-drained soil.*

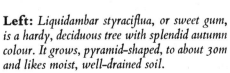
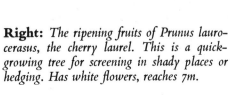

Right: *The ripening fruits of Prunus laurocerasus, the cherry laurel. This is a quick-growing tree for screening in shady places or hedging. Has white flowers, reaches 7m.*

57

scented. Plums are often grown for their leaf colours of rusty red, purple or bronze.

Most prunus are deciduous and part of their stunning display results from the leaves hardly being out when the blossom is crowding on the branches. However, the Portuguese laurel, with hawthorn-scented flowers is evergreen, so is the cherry laurel.

The Japanese have been growing cherries for centuries and many of their varieties are now grown here. Like all prunus they like open, sunny positions, well-drained, fertile soil and are planted in the dormant season. They really do not need pruning and many stay quite small; they are suitable for the average-sized garden. *Prunus yedoensis*, the Yoshino cherry, has distinct, almond-scented pale pink flowers that wreath the arched branches. It will eventually grow to around 10m (30ft). Cheal's weeping cherry ('Kiku-shidare Zakura') has pendulous branches and clusters of bright pink double flowers. Another lovely weeping tree is *P. subhirtella* 'Pendula' with single pink flowers in spring, but there is an autumn or winter flowering cultivar. The best of the late-flowering cherries is probably 'Shimidsu Sakura', with large white blossoms opening from pink-tinted buds. It is a small tree that would fit into any garden.

Flowering peaches are small trees with blossom in pink, white or red, and include *P. davidiana*, the Chinese peach, a slender upright tree. There is also a white cultivar of *P. persica*, 'Iceberg', a peach with lovely double, pure white blossoms.

The almonds, *Prunus amygdalus*, have pink or white blossoms and *P. amygdalus* 'Macrocarpa' bears the best nuts. It grows 3–6m (10–20ft).

In the flowering apricots, *Prunus mume*, there are lovely small trees too, with delicate pale pink or white flowers.

Among the other early-flowering trees is *Parrotia persica*, with dull scarlet tassels borne at the end of winter. *Salix caprea* has early catkins and even earlier are the catkins of the violet-willow, *Salix daphnoides*.

The crab apples all flower in spring and they are small or moderately-sized trees, even sometimes large bushes. They are extremely hardy and produce regular blossoms and fruit. Given enough space they can be left unpruned except for removing damaged branches. Grow *Malus prunifolia* for fruit or *M. x robusta*, and *M. spectabilis* for flowers.

Halesia carolina, the snowdrop tree,

Above right: *The tulip tree, Liriodendron tulipifera, has sweetly scented flowers.*

Right: *Eugenia myrtifolia, an Australian fruiting myrtle which bears red fruits. It is not suitable for cold climates.*

Above: *Sea lavender, Limonium latifolium, flowers in summer and is ideal for coastal areas.*

Left: *Jacaranda acutifolia, has mauve-blue flowers and needs a warm climate.*

Below: *The distinctive narrow shapes of the Lombardy poplar, Populus italica.*

flowers in spring with white bell-shaped flowers. It is deciduous.

Although there are many beautiful ornamental flowering trees, also plant fruit-producing ones so that your garden combines beauty with usefulness.

Autumn colour

Some of the trees that generously blossom in spring will colour in autumn too, such as the Japanese cherry *Prunus sargentii* or *P.* 'Kanzan'. The rowans which first give flowers then berries can also colour brilliantly in red and gold before their leaves fall. A good choice is *Sorbus matsumurana*. There are rowans with yellow instead of scarlet fruits. One cultivated variety is 'Joseph Rock', also good for its autumn tints. There is also the Chinese rowan or mountain ash.

The fiery splendour of the Japanese maple, *Acer palmatum dissectum*, and its feathery, fiery comrade *Acer palmatum* 'Osakazuki', are hard to surpass, but nearly all the maple family with their deep-cut leaves—scarlet or yellow in autumn and rich green in spring—are a pleasure to grow. The Japanese varieties need protection from spring frosts or hard winds. There are also maples which have decorative snake-bark, and ones which have coloured leaves, such as the box elder, *Acer negundo*, which can be variegated, or the cherry plums and their hybrids which have copper leaves, such as *Prunus x blireana*.

The *Parrotia persica*, already mentioned for spring tassels, turns to a red and golden cascade when the autumn arrives.

Ghent and Exbury strains of deciduous azaleas turn to vivid orange and flame. Their spring display is just as splendid. Then there is the *Ginkgo biloba*, the maidenhair tree, which takes on a golden yellow. The dogwoods such as *Cornus florida* 'Rubra' are worth planting and the swamp cypress, lover of damp places, will turn to bronze.

Shrubs and trees for salt-wind exposed gardens

A salt-laden wind will only be tolerated by plants that are hardy and able to stand salt air and exposed conditions. Sea buckthorn, *Hippophae rhamnoides*, which has fine grey-green foliage makes a good windbreak and so do the deceptively delicate-looking plumes of tamarisk. If you use male and female plants of the sea buckthorn you will get plenty of orange berries.

Atriplex halimus (tree purslane) is an evergreen with silver-grey foliage which makes a good seaside hedge. Plant in winter; trim in early spring.

Box (*Buxus sempervirens*) is an old favourite with good reason. It does well in any soil, particularly likes chalk soils and

Above: *Euphorbia pulcherrima*, the poinsettia, has showy bracts and is a warm-climate plant.

Right: *Eryngium maritimum*, sea holly, a hardy perennial growing to half a metre.

Below: *Eugenia maire*, a New Zealand myrtle, has white flowers followed by red fruits. It has a smooth white bark.

does not mind the sea. Trim in summer or if cutting back hard, in spring. There is an edging box, about 1m (3ft) in height whereas the common box grows up to 6m (18ft).

Here is a list of plants adapted to seaside environment:

Calluna vulgaris and cultivars (acid soil)
Cistus species
Cornus alba and cultivars
C. stolonifera 'Flaviramea'
Cotinus coggygria
Cytisus scoparius
Elaeagnus X ebbingei
Escallonia macrantha
Genista hispanica
Halimium ocymoides
Hebe—most species and hybrids
Helianthemum—all species
Hippophae rhamnoides
Hydrangea macrophylla Hortensia and Lacecap
Ilex aquifolium and cultivars
Lavandula species
Olearia X haastii, O. nummularifolia, O. macrodonta
Osmarea burkwoodii
Philadelphus—most species and hybrids
Phillyrea decora
Pittosporum tenuifolium, P. crassifolium
Prunus spinosa 'Purpurea'
Rosa species and cultivars
Santolina species
Senecio greyi
Spartium junceum
Tamarix, all species

Conifers

Cupressus macrocarpa, C. glabra 'Pyramidalis'
Juniperus communis, J. c. 'Hibernica', J. X media 'Pfitzerana', J. chinensis, J. horizontalis
Pinus contorta, P. mugo, P. nigra, P. n. 'Maritima', P. pinaster, P. radiata, P. sylvestris
Taxus baccata

Climbers

True climbers do their own clinging to supports, either by tendrils, such as clematis uses, or twining stems, such as the honeysuckle has. Or there are those that hold on with sucker pads, like the Virginia creeper whose tenacious grip advances across the wall or support. Then there are the clingers that use aerial roots, like the ivies.

Besides these natural climbers, there are many more shrubby plants which can be trained against walls and over supports with a little judicious pruning and tying, such as the climbing roses and ceanothus, the Californian lilacs with vivid blue flowers, which like a warm wall.

With all these groups to choose from you have plenty of variety for wall, fence or pergola cover.

If you are planting climbers against the house walls where they are seen from the windows, keep in mind their round-the-year appeal rather than their summer or spring glory.

Climbers on house walls do not really harm them but they do provide nesting sites for birds, and to some extent insulate the house, and protect the walls from weathering. Clip back from windows and check suckers or aerial roots creeping their way into sill mortar.

Climbers can be used to cover netting or many other indifferent boundary markers.

Above: *Young's weeping birch, Betula pendula youngii, is a small deciduous tree.* **Below:** *Tamarisk is a good hedge or screen plant for a seaside garden.*

They will turn an open support into a privacy screen. They will hide old stumps or dead trees, they will romp over ugly sheds or trellises behind which can be hidden a utility area, the clothes line or the dust bins.

Tendril and twining plants need grips to hang on to—pergola posts, wire or timber archways, wire fencing, trellis and other lath supports. If the latter is used in front of walls or fences they must be spaced about five centimetres away to allow entwining. Vine eyes which are screwed into the jointing of walls or into wooden posts will hold climbing wires or there are straining bolts which can be tightened to take up slack wire. There are individual ties, lead-headed nails, for tying in long woody growths.

Give climbers rich, good earth, though it is seldom found against wall foundations or fence posts where builders tend to bury rubble. Plant them at least 15cm (6in) from the wall base. An annual mulch helps to keep plants moist in the summer.

Akebia quinata is an evergreen twining climber that will grow large to about 10m (30ft) and produce scented, dark purple flowers in April.

There are evergreen clematis, for example, *C. armandii*, which has white flowers in April and *C. balearica*, a smaller climber with yellowish-white flowers produced earlier, sometimes in February. The first will grow to 8m (25ft) but can be kept in bounds by cutting out some of the old growth after flowers fade. The midrib of each compound leaf of clematis acts as a tendril, curling around the nearest support. The clematis family is a large one, with deciduous climbers, and there are many varieties to choose from. They like a soil rich in decayed manure so mulch liberally with compost or manure every spring. They also like cool roots but heads in the sun.

The passion flower (*Passiflora caerulea*) is a slightly tender climber with strange and exotic flowers in pale pink or white and purple. It likes a south or south-west wall and is pruned in February by shortening the small shoots. It needs plenty of water in dry weather and good feeding.

Wisteria sinensis is hardy and grows in any fertile soil. Its mauve hanging clusters are more prolific if you shorten young shoots not needed for extension between January and March. If you are growing wisteria naturally over a tree, do not prune it at all. You can get pale rose, blue, white or violet species of wisteria.

Among the jasmines, there is winter jasmine that can be trained to a bare wall and provides the sunniest yellow flowers on bare stems in the depths of the dormant months: or common jasmine (*Jasminum*

Above: *Lonicera japonica halliana, a honeysuckle with fragrant white to yellow flowers.*

Below: *Parthenocissus henryana, a fine self-clinging climber that is deciduous.*

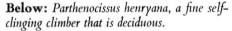

Below: *Scarlet pelargonium climbs over painted dowel supports.*

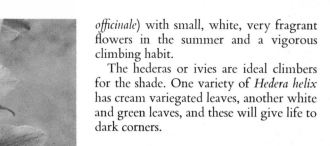

Above: *Climbing rose 'Mermaid' has huge fragrant flowers and glossy leaves. Is vigorous.*

Right: *Clematis patens 'Nelly Moser' is a large-flowered cultivar blooming in early summer.*

Below: *Climbing rose 'Chaplin's Pink Companion' trained along a pergola.*

officinale) with small, white, very fragrant flowers in the summer and a vigorous climbing habit.

The hederas or ivies are ideal climbers for the shade. One variety of *Hedera helix* has cream variegated leaves, another white and green leaves, and these will give life to dark corners.

Rambling and climbing roses

The rambling roses are all climbers, some climbing better than others, but not all the climbing roses are ramblers. The ramblers are all of one type of climber, distinguished by their supple canes, relatively small blooms in clusters, and their flowering once-a-year on new wood (stems) formed the previous season.

The climbing roses have stiffer growth and usually larger blooms carried on laterals grown in the current year. The first climbers were among the hybrid Noisette roses, descendants of the cross between the musk rose and the pink China, but the China roses also produced some climbers when they sported, or mutated. However, the hybrid teas have contributed most to modern climbing roses, many of them producing climbing sports, and also many of these being perpetual-flowering. There are also some climbers grown from floribundas.

Climbers are much easier to look after than ramblers since the rambler has to be pruned back hard every year, cutting away all of one year's growth as soon as it has flowered, whereas the climber is pruned only to remove diseased, damaged and old growth.

'Albertine' is a pretty copper-salmon rambler that is fragrant and free-flowering. Or there is 'Felicité et Perpetue', a vigorous graceful creamy-white rambler with shining dark leaves. The latter's parentage is *R. sempervirens* which occurs wild in southern Europe. The former's parentage is *R. wichuraiana* which many ramblers have in their ancestry. This is an old far-eastern species rose named after its German discoverer.

Among the lovelier climbers is 'Mermaid', an amber and yellow rose which is a slow starter but worth waiting for. The flowers are single and the leaves dark glossy green. 'Maigold' is a modern hybrid sometimes classed as a shrub but can be classed as a climber of about 2–3m (7–10ft) high. The new long-flowering climbers, sometimes referred to as ever-blooming, include 'New Dawn', a blush-pink hybrid tea climber with a sweet perfume, and 'Aloha', a hybrid of the former with large flowers of dark and light rose. Try 'Etoile de Hollande', a climbing sport, and 'Zephirine Drouhin', a Bourbon type rose sometimes called the thornless rose.

Morning glory or ipomoea is a twiner that can be used for quick screening, but it is half-hardy.

Below left: *Lonicera x americana, a honey-suckle hybrid with long yellow and pink flowers.*

Below: *Parthenocissus quinquefolia, the Vir-ginia creeper, a deciduous tendril climber.*

More shrubs to choose from:

Actinidia chinensis
A. kolomikta
Akebia quinata
Aristolochia sipho
Azara microphylla
Billardiera longiflora
Buddleia colvilei
B. crispa
Callistemon salignus
C. speciosus
Camellia japonica in variety
C. reticulata in variety
C. sasanqua in variety
C. X williamsii in variety
Campsis (Tecoma) grandiflora
C. (Tecoma) radicans
Carpenteria californica
Ceanothus all kinds particularly:
Ceanothus 'Burkwoodii'
C. 'Delight'
C. dentatus
C. 'Gloire de Versailles'
C. thrysiflorus
Celastrus orbiculatus
Clematis—most species and hybrids
Clianthus puniceus
Coronilla glauca
Cotoneaster franchetii sternianus
C. horizontalis
C. lacteus
Crinodendron hookerianum
Cytisus battandieri
Daphne odora
Fremontodendron (Fremontia) californicum
Eriobotrya japonica
Forsythia suspensa atrocaulis
Garrya elliptica
Grevillea rosmarinifolia
G. sulphurea
Hedera canariensis 'Variegata'
H. colchica 'Dentata Variegata'
H. helix in variety
Humulus lupulus 'Aureus'
Hydrangea petiolaris
Jasminum officinalis
J. nudiflorum
Kerria japonica 'Pleniflora'
Lonicera americana
L. caprifolium
L. 'Dropmore Scarlet'
L. japonica 'Aureoreticulata'
L. japonica 'Repens'
L. tellemanniana
Parthenocissus tricuspidata 'Veitchii'
Passiflora caerulea
Piptanthus laburnifolius
Pyracantha—all species including crenulata rogersiana and coccinea 'Lalandei'
Climbing roses—many, and in particular Climbing rose 'Allen Chandler'
C. r. 'Madame Gregoire Straechelin'
C. r. 'Gloire de Dijon'
C. r. 'Hamburger Phoenix'
C. r. 'The New Dawn'
C. r. 'Leverkusen'
C. r. 'Mermaid'
C. r. 'Madame Alfred Carriere'
Solanum crispum 'Glasnevin'
Teucrium fruticans
Schizophragna hydrangeoides
Sophora tetraptera 'Grandiflora'
Trachelospermum asiaticum
T. jasminoides
Vitis amuriensis
V. betulifolia
V. 'Brandt'
V. coignetiae
Vinifera 'purpurea' (purple grape vine)
Wisteria floribunda
W. sinensis

Above right: *Clematis and wisteria combine to clothe house wall with masses of flowers.*

Monthly calendar
JANUARY
Plant new deciduous shrubs or trees. Start pruning roses if you have not done so. Obtain manure for early spring application.
FEBRUARY
In favourable conditions, plant ornamental trees and deciduous shrubs. Prune early summer-flowering clematis, after flowers fade, and late-flowering clematis hybrids. Prune lateral shoots of wisteria and ornamental grape vines. Dig bed for new roses; incorporate humus before planting. Remove twiggy wood from established plants.
MARCH
Lightly hoe shrub borders; begin mulching cycle. Protect *Chaenomeles japonica* from bud-ravaging birds. Complete rose planting and pruning. Prune established roses according to type. Plant evergreens, conifers and silver-leaved shrubs.
APRIL
Mulch trees and shrubs. Plant out clematis from pots. Treat shrubs to prevent aphids and red spider. When rose pruning is completed, apply organic fertilizer. Mulch with animal manure.
MAY
Remove faded rhododendron flower trusses. Transplant evergreen shrubs. Trim to one shoot any multiple shoots on rose bushes. Take action against insect pass. Prune *Buddleia davidii*, *Hydrangea paniculata* and small aromatic shrubs.
JUNE
Support newly-planted climbers. Tie main shoots of non-clinging wall shrubs to horizontal wires until they are strong. Give roses supplementary feeding. Spray against mildew. Watch for insect pests.
JULY
Water shrubs on hot dry days. Prune flowering shrubs that have finished blooming.
AUGUST
Root deutzias, buddleias, philadelphus, berberis and many evergreens. Take root cuttings. Spray roses against black spot. Cut out old wood from established ramblers. Pull off suckers.
SEPTEMBER
Prepare ground for autumn tree planting. Remove all small rosebuds that are unlikely to open before early frosts begin. Shorten extra-long shoots that get damaged in high winds. Check all supports.
OCTOBER
Plant deciduous shrubs, trees and climbers now. Re-new rose stakes. Prepare ground for new roses. Allow soil to settle before planting.
NOVEMBER
Protect tender plants. When planting trees, make sure the hole is big enough to take the roots. Remove newly-arrived roses from packing; sprinkle liberally with water.
DECEMBER
Plan garden now for year-round tree and shrub colour. Rake fallen rose leaves from beds and burn. Start pruning hardy shrub roses.

A down to earth start

What makes up the soil?

Different substances make up a soil suitable for plant growth. For gardening, you ideally need a well-balanced mixture of these substances. Some of the right ingredients will be in the soil you have and other ingredients you will have to add.

The basis of soil is mineral, sandy and clay particles eroded from the earth's parent rocks by incessant rain, wind, sun and water, working over millions of years. These particles are not soluble in water or they would have been dissolved away centuries ago and plants do not make direct use of them because they profit only from materials that do dissolve in water. Nevertheless, they do affect the plant's wellbeing because they affect the way water, air and nutrients circulate in the spaces (called pores) between the particles.

Soil particles vary in size from stones (over 1·5cm [½in] size) through to gravel, coarse sand, fine sand, to silt and then to clay. The spaces between the soil particles vary too.

Sandy soils have large spaces between the soil particles, that is, they are porous. Water runs away freely, sometimes too freely, leaching away plant foods. As the water runs away the sandy soil becomes aerated. So the plant in a sandy soil has air but may lack water and nutrients.

Clay soils on the other hand have small spaces between the particles and so hold water well. Sometimes it is inclined not to drain away at all. Clay will hold as much as 50 percent of its own weight in water, together with many of the nutrients plants need. It helps to stop leaching of plant foods (except perhaps the nitrates). The disadvantage of clay is that although roots need water they also need air which cannot penetrate wet, binding clay.

A good soil will contain a balance of sand, clay and silt (which is sediment deposited by water) to achieve an essential supply of water and air and to give adequate drainage. This is a **loam.** Meadow turf is typical of a loamy soil.

Organic matter is the next most important substance in the soil. This is the decayed remains of plants and animals, for soil has its insects and animals—moles,

Above: *The fragrant double-flowered Philadelphus 'Virginal', like all plants, flourishes in good soil. Often called mock orange. Likes a sunny, bright aspect.*

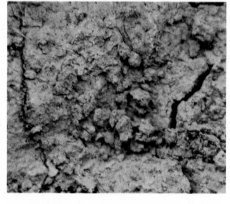

Above: *Topsoil of wet or waterlogged area will lack air (top picture) and subsoil (lower picture) is more grey. Wetness might be from poor drainage, the water table or a spring.*

Above: *Topsoil of heath is sometimes rich in decaying plants but needs nitrogenous manures (top picture). Subsoil (lower picture) could have formed a hard pan that needs breaking up.*

Topsoil over chalk areas might be shallow and lose moisture quickly (top picture) and the sub-soil will be almost all calcium carbonate (lower picture). Add humus-forming mulches.

Below: *Centaurea macrocephala is one perennial that likes light (including chalky) soils.*

The colour of a soil might help you check on its type. Top picture, loamy sand. Lower picture, one of the many types of clay. Clay soils need plenty of cultivation.

Below: *Sanvitalia procumbens, a spreading half-hardy annual, likes a sandy loam best.*

A well-balanced loam gives a supply of water, air and nutrients (top picture). Meadow land is loamy soil. Lower picture, a sandy clay loam. Most loams will make good soils.

Below: *Moluccella laevis, also prefers sandy loam. Flower arrangers like the dried calyces.*

mice, earthworms, slugs, snails, beetles, spiders and microbes. These are all disturbing and aerating the soil, living and dying and adding to the organic matter in it.

The soil contains millions of microscopic organisms called bacteria. The subterranean microbes feed off dead and decaying matter in earth, using some of it themselves and leaving some to dissolve in the water in the soil (called the soil solution) to feed the plants again. The important thing about bacteria is that they get the nitrogen they need for growth from the air and during the death and decay of this bacteria, other bacteria make nitrates from it. So that although nitrates—essential to plant growth too—are continually leached from the soil by rain, they are continually replaced by the soil bacteria.

When you give manure to the soil you are actually feeding your thriving microbes and not so much your plants, but they in turn will feed these for you.

Humus is the final stage of decay for plants and animals. It is a brown-black treacly substance completely decomposed into fine particles like clay but having none of clay's faults. Humus does not compact and although it has not much food value in itself, it holds on to water and plant foods and helps to give a good crumbly texture to the soil. You cannot put humus on the soil, only the organic matter which will become humus.

Acid or alkaline soil and the pH scale

Whether soil is acid or alkaline is an important question that worries many new gardeners.

If the soil is **very** alkaline or acid some plants will have difficulty in growing. There are lime-loving plants and others that prefer or need an acid soil. The majority of plants like a neutral or slightly acid soil, which in most gardens is not too hard to achieve.

However, some soil-testing kits on the market will also indicate deficiencies in nitrogen, phosphates and potash—three essential plant foods not supplied by air and water and possibly lacking in your soil. So a little chemical testing will help you to get to know the soil better.

The acid or alkali reactions of the soil shown by using the testing kit are registered on a scale called pH, the symbol for hydrogen ion concentration (not really a small 'p' but the Greek letter *rho*). Seven on the scale is neutral, below seven means that you have an acid reaction and above it an alkaline one. Each whole number registers a value ten times higher the acid or alkaline reaction than the number before. Many plants like about pH 6·5.

If you do not want to test with a soil kit

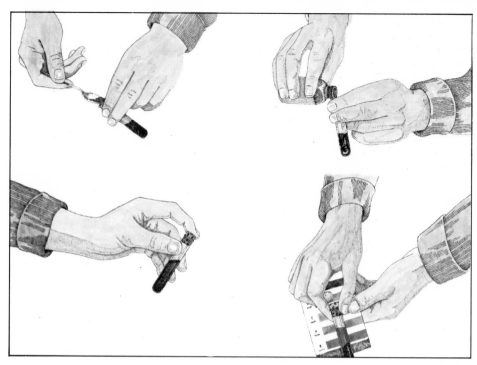

Above: *Testing soil for acidity. Top left, dry soil is put into test tube with a dry spoon. Top right, acidity testing solution is poured carefully on the soil sample. Below left, test tube is corked, then shaken. Below right, the resulting* solution is colour matched to test card. Reading is pH 7. Seven on the pH scale is neutral.

Below: *Nitrogenous fertilizer is applied around each plant and the soil scraped over with cultivator to work in the fertilizer.*

Above: *When lime is needed to reduce the acidity of the soil, it can be spread by hand over the surface in winter.*

Below: *Farmyard manure supplies its nutrients slowly so its benefits can last years.*

then the growth in your area could give some indication of whether soil is acid or alkaline. Rhododendrons, azaleas, heathers, and bilberries like acid soils. Wild clematis, wild cherries, scabious, stone-crops and beeches favour alkaline soils. Check with gardening neighbours if you have just moved in. They will probably know local soil conditions which will help you.

Nurserymen are generally well-informed and know and stock the plants that grow well in the district. Very alkaline soils (around pH 8) can lead to plant starvation because essential foods such as iron or manganese get 'locked up' and can only be released by acidifying the soil. On the other hand, there is a shortage of calcium and available phosphates in very acid soil.

How to treat each soil type

Keep in mind that it is better to under-supply the soil with preparation than over-supply for you cannot retrieve what you have added.

Cure for a **too-sandy soil** is to add bulky, humus-forming material such as well-rotted cow and pig manure. Do not dig it in too deep. You can use other organic matter too, such as granulated peat, and fertilizers applied in small amounts frequently during the growing season. However, sandy soil soon becomes acid so that you may also need frequent but small applications of lime.

You can grow good early vegetable crops in sandy soil—it holds more warmth than clay. If the soil is mulched or irrigated, soft fruits are also successful. For fruit trees and other trees, the soil needs to be more than 37·5cm (15in) deep.

Do not dig over a sandy soil to weather in the winter. Add manure or fertilizer in the spring.

A **too-clay soil** needs plenty of cultivation. Break up large clods with a hoe to encourage plants to grow. Stable manure with straw in it, or granulated peat applied regularly will improve the texture of clay soil. Not all clay soil is acid but when it is, plenty of lime will also help.

Frost is a marvellous clod breaker, so autumn digging in frosty areas is important. Dig over the ground, put in leaf mould and manure or lime, leaving the top of the soil rough and open to the frost. If heavy rains come and lay it down, open it up with a fork again. In addition, gritty sand or well-weathered boiler ash can act as a mechanical aerator.

If clay soil is very badly drained you can lay a simple underground drainage pipe to a soakaway pit, or simply have a soakaway pit. Check drainage by digging a hole about 60cm (2ft) deep, pouring in some water and watching to see if it drains away satisfactorily.

A **land drain** is laid herringbone-fashion along the slope of the land or to a main drain. If there is not a main drain or slope-away and the soil is not solid clay, build the drain to a soakaway pit. This should be 1·2m (4ft) square and deep, filled with broken bricks, pebbles, clinker and other dry debris. Cover the pit with the top soil to hide debris.

If you do not want to build a drain or if it is not possible because of the local water level, build up your garden beds. Drainage is seldom a disastrous problem but if you cannot combat it, plan a bog garden for that area. If one plant does not like the pH of the soil, the damp, the shade or the chalk, then look for another that will.

Should lime be used?

Lime, in gardening terms, is a calcium-containing material used to correct an acid soil. The forms commonly listed in garden catalogues are hydrated lime (slaked lime or calcium hydroxide) and carbonate of lime, sometimes called garden lime. The first is a powder; the second is crushed chalk or limestone.

Lime encourages the busy work of bacteria which break down organic matter liberating plant foods such as phosphates. It also improves the texture of acid-clay soils, aids their drainage and it helps to combat diseases such as club root in cabbage, turnips, etc. All this however, is not a licence to lime indiscriminately or you will over-stimulate the bacteria and bring about a too-rapid breakdown of the soil's humus reserve.

You can test for lime in the soil with soil samples and indicator papers purchased from your garden supply centre, or work

Fallen leaves are a valuable organic material if free of disease. Rake up autumn leaves, put in wire container to rot down into leaf mould. Diagram, right, shows compost heap construction. Most garden waste can be rotted down.

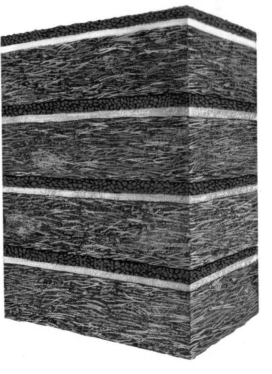

to a rough measure—about 400g of hydrated lime per square metre (approx $\frac{3}{4}$lb per sq yd) a year on an acid-clay, or peaty soil, and about half that on acid-sandy or loamy soil. On the clay type of soil add the lime in autumn. On the sandy soil add in spring and late summer.

Hydrated lime is useful when you want speedy results. Carbonate of lime is slower acting.

If you use carbonate of lime you need about twice as much as the quantity needed for hydrated lime. Add lime to the soil surface, do not dig it in.

Finally, never add lime to any alkaline clay hoping it will be easier to work with, and never lime and manure at the same time; the two are not compatible.

The food plants need to thrive

Plants get food from the mineral salts dissolved in the soil water, or soil solution. They do not feed directly on any vegetable or animal matter so that whether you put in organic or chemical fertilizers, the mineral food the plants take up is the same. They are part of the miraculous biological cycle of the earth whereby plants turn inert minerals into food for animals. Animals and plants die and then microbes turn the dead tissues back into minerals for use by plants.

The first food necessities for a plant are air, water and sunlight. The plant takes carbon dioxide from the air (releasing oxygen for us to breathe) and light energy from the sun, and these together with water are converted into fuel energy contained in sugars. A reserve of sugar is stored in the plant in the form of starch for use during the night and in spring when growth is great and sunlight weak. All these substances are made from carbon, hydrogen and oxygen and are known as carbohydrates. Add the mineral salts taken up in the soil water by the plants, and they can then make their own complicated fats, proteins, pigments and many other things they need for growth.

The main foods in the soil that plants need are nitrogen, vital to all growth, phosphorus, which helps the plant convert and use energy, potassium, used in cell sap and calcium, used in the cell walls. Chlorophyll, the green colouring in plants contains magnesium, and some amino acids in plants need sulphur.

In plants there are also small traces of iron, boron, copper, manganese, molybdenum, zinc and sometimes chlorine and sodium. These are called trace elements and are supplied in some fertilizers.

However, the three vital foods taken up in quite large quantities by plants and sometimes in short supply in the soil, are nitrogen, phosphorus and potassium—the

A site is prepared for a compost heap with a layer of old hedge clippings to ensure drainage and aeration. Wire netting surrounds the heap.

essential ingredients in general fertilizers.

Organic gardening usually means using all the natural decayed matter that you can buy from garden centres or collect from your own garden. Some gardeners discount chemical fertilizers altogether—a plan that is not entirely logical, either. You still need the organic material. The natural decayed matter which allows air to penetrate the soil and roots to grow more rapidly, increases water-holding in light soils, keeps soils at a more even temperature and provides plant nutrients, both the major and minor ones. You can get all this from animal or poultry manure, decayed garden leaves, grass cuttings, vegetable refuse and so on.

However, add to your own materials with bought, spent mushroom compost (if it is a mix with lime do not give to rhododendrons), spent hops, farmyard manure and seaweed (a good source of plant nutrients and trace elements). Weight for weight, organics have less nutrients than chemical fertilizers but their bulk rots down to that vital material humus, and so improves the soil.

If you want to make your own leaf mould, put the leaves into a well-drained pit, or a wire basket, or add them to a compost heap. They should lie from 6 to 12 months.

Manure is a good natural source of plant food and humus, and a useful soil conditioner. Farmyard manure should always be used well-rotted if near plants because the ammonia in fresh manure can damage plants if it touches them. It is also hard to spread evenly. You can use fresh manure on bare autumn and winter earth so that it can break down before spring planting. Do not deeply bury manure; work it in to a depth of 7·5 or 10cm (3 or 4in) and apply plenty of it to receive its full advantages.

Storing manure can be a problem. It loses some of its important ingredients, such as animal urine, if left too long; nutrients are washed out by the rain and microbes are, as usual, busy demolishing the precious pile. So if you have to store the manure because the garden is not ready, keep the heap off absorbent ground;

cover and compact the pile to keep out air and collect any draining fluid in a bucket.

Choose between horse, poultry, cow and pig manure; poultry manure is richer in nitrogen and phosphorus. Keep in mind too that manure heats during the rotting process (a process sometimes used to keep stables warm).

The compost heap

A compost heap is an excellent way to convert garden waste to good humus for the soil. Into a heap or bin should go leaves, clippings, soft but not woody prunings, weeds, spent flowers, fruit and vegetable waste, tea leaves, even dust from the vacuum cleaner.

Make a heap in a shallow pit in the ground or buy wire containers or bins meant for the job. You can make bins yourself from slatted timber spaced a few centimetres apart. If you dig a pit, it needs to be about 30–45cm (1–1½ft) in depth, as long as you like and well-drained.

Put in about 12·5–15cm (5–6in) of vegetable waste, sprinkle a nitrogenous fertilizer or a little manure on top, then a thin layer of soil, another of waste and so on. A little lime added—well away from the fertilizer—will help to counteract the acid set up by the decay. Or you can use a proprietary compost accelerator. An occasional damping with water is also useful. If you are using a pit, cover the top with earth. If bins, use a waterproof lid or polythene sheeting.

A compost heap needs good drainage, a firm but airy composition and dampness. The layer of soil helps to keep the nutrients in, the cover helps to stop the rain washing them out. If the heap is a success, it will warm up to a sufficient heat to kill any weed seeds. Composting takes a couple of months in the summer but longer in the winter. Three bins allow you to have one for spreading, one for rotting and the third for filling.

Fertilizers

Organic fertilizers are the natural humus-forming materials already mentioned such as manure or compost plus others such as bonemeal or bone flour. Inorganic or chemical fertilizers are factory-made or, at the least, factory-refined from natural chemical deposits. Most inorganic fertilizers usually work fairly quickly, dissolving in water, so they are supplied to moist soils. They can also be rather concentrated so do not overdose with them.

Inorganic fertilizers can either supply one special nutrient, say, potash from sulphate of potash, or can be general fertilizers supplying the three main plant foods, nitrogen, phosphorus and potassium; National Growmore is an example.

There are many fertilizers—organic and inorganic—which you can check in the list, together with the main nutrient each supplies and the sort of job each does. If your plants need a nitrogen boost, there is ammonium sulphate, ie, sulphate of ammonia, which is very good on alkaline soils. It can be used on acid soils too as these would have to be limed anyway. You could also use potassium nitrate, dried blood, or hoof and horn. For phosphorus, there is superphosphate or basic slag, the first being superphosphate of lime—a mixture of mono-calcium phosphate and gypsum, ie, calcium sulphate, and the second, basic slag, having a lime content; for potassium, there is potassium sulphate (sulphate of potash) or freshly-made wood ashes.

Right: *The addition of organic material such as spent hops, used here as a mulch, will supply the soil with humus.*

Below: *A straw mulch around dahlias will discourage weeds and prevent the soil surface from panning (hardening) during summer heat.*

Sometimes on the pack of a general fertilizer you will find a series of numbers. This refers to the percentage of nitrogen, 'phosphoric acid', and potash contained in the fertilizer, in that order.

Try to spread a fertilizer evenly and keep it away from leaves and flowers as it might scorch them. Follow the instructions carefully; do not overdose, and keep the fertilizer in a dry place and closed container.

Fertilizers are generally raked into the top 5 or 7.5cm (2 or 3in) of soil. Slow acting ones can be cultivated in a little deeper, about 15cm (6in).

Some of the slower-acting chemical fertilizers are dug into the soil in autumn and winter. The quick-acting ones are supplied during the growing period. Among the slower-acting ones are bonemeal (providing phosphates) and sulphate of potash (providing potash). Mix in with the top 5

or 7.5cm (2 or 3in) soil.

Among the quick-acting fertilizers are superphosphate of lime (supplying phosphates), sulphate of ammonia and nitrate of soda (supplying nitrogen).

A **mulch** helps to conserve water in the soil and protect roots from hot sun. It is a layer of any material over the surface of the soil; even a surface layer of finely-hoed soil or a plastic cover could be considered a type of mulch. However, mulches usually consist of manure or leaf mould, seaweed, lawn or soft hedge clippings, chopped straw, shredded bark or compost. Even pebbles can be used, or pulled-up weeds that are not in flower or seed.

Mulches allow better root aeration by preventing topsoil from compacting, protect the soil from erosion, keep roots cool and moist and prevent water evaporation. That means, of course, that you must lay a mulch over wet soil, not dry.

First, dig and weed the garden bed. Cover it with 7.5–10cm (3–4in) of mulch material. Once it is on, do not dig it in or disturb it. However, do not put down a mulch until the danger of frost is over. Let it decay and then be hoed into the surface by autumn. This is important because the insulating layer of a mulch can increase frost damage to the plant above ground.

Watering—do not merely damp the surface of dry soil, because the water will not penetrate to plant roots where it is wanted. If you water too lightly too often, you encourage plant roots to grow near the surface. Water thoroughly so that the water can penetrate to a reasonable depth. On light sandy soils you will need to water more frequently than on loamy or clay soils.

Weeds These are really plants in the place you do not want them to be, for gardens are planned artificial environments. However, some people allow some weeds to grow because birds, insects, bees or butterflies like them.

If you are waging real war on weeds, cultivate the soil to bring the weeds to the surface to die (they do drink a lot of the water available in a garden bed). Do not cultivate too deeply or you will unearth the seeds of future weeds, cunningly awaiting the chance you give them for air, light and water. Attack them when they are young before they flower and set seed. Hand pull or lightly scratch out weeds around shallow rooting plants. Larger weeds not in seed can go into the compost heap if you are sure your heap will heat up sufficiently to kill them. Otherwise dry them, burn them and use the ash. There are now available a wide range of chemical weed killers, some based on hormones, that will make hoeing and forking incredibly easy.

Fertilizers for general use

Fertilizer and main nutrient supplied	Properties	When and how much to use
Sulphate of ammonia 20.6% N	As soil warms ammonia quickly turns to nitrate by bacteria. Conversion slow when soil temp. below $5°C$ ($42°F$). Called lawn sand when mixed with sand.	Spring and summer at $13-25g$ ($\frac{1}{2}-1oz$) per sq m. Often mixed with superphosphate and sulphate but do not mix with lime.
Nitrate of soda Nitrogen 16% N	Inorganic. Soluble nitrate quickly available to plants.	Spring and summer as top dressing. $13g$ ($\frac{1}{2}oz$) per sq m at intervals of several weeks.
Nitro-chalk Nitrogen 21% N	Ammonium nitrate and chalk, in easy-to-spread granules.	Spring and summer top dressing at $13g$ ($\frac{1}{2}oz$) per sq m at intervals of several weeks.
Urea-form Nitrogen 38% N	Synthetic organic mixture of urea and formaldehyde (sold under trade name). One feed will last several months.	Use any time before sowing or planting. Slow action encourages healthy turf. $25-50g$ ($1-2oz$) per sq m. Can replace hoof and horn meal in soilless composts.
Dried blood Nitrogen $7-14\%$ N	In warm, moist soils a rapid-acting organic fertilizer. Fully soluble form can be dissolved in water for a liquid feed.	Use as top dressing for greenhouse plants throughout season. $50-75g$ ($2-3oz$) per sq m.
Hoof and horn meal Nitrogen $7-13\%$ N	Organic. Acts fairly quickly in warm, moist soils. Long-lasting. Fine grade acts faster than coarser grade.	Open ground and greenhouse. $100-150g$ ($4-6oz$) per sq m. Fine grade for potting compost; coarse grade for perennial borders.
Meat and bonemeal Nitrogen and phosphates $4-6\%$ N $12-14\%$ P_2O_5 (insol)	Good organic type for general use. Phosphates slow-acting; nitrogen fast-acting.	Autumn or winter. Fork into ground. $100g$ ($4oz$) per sq m before sowing or planting. Use in composts.
Superphosphate of lime Phosphate $18-19\%$ P_2O_5	Phosphates are soluble in water, act quickly. Suitable for seed beds and root crops. Does not supply lime.	Use at any time. $25-50g$ ($1-2oz$) per sq m before sowing or planting.
Bonemeal $20-25\%$ P_2O_5 $3-5\%$ N	Organic. The calcium phosphate releases phosphates slowly over long period. Nitrogen works quickly.	Autumn or winter. $100g$ ($4oz$) per sq m before sowing or planting.
Potash nitrate Nitrogen Potash 16% N 10% K_2O	Mixed nitrate of sodium and potassium. Quick acting.	Spring and summer as top dressing. $25-50g$ ($1-2oz$) per sq m. One tspful to about $5l$ ($1gal$) of water during growing period.
Potassium nitrate Nitrogen Potassium $12-14\%$ N $44-46\%$ K_2O	Used mainly in liquid feeds. Suitable for all greenhouse plants when dissolved in water.	1 tspful to $5l$ ($1gal$) of water. Apply regularly.
Sulphate of potash Potash 50% K_2O	Best form of potash for most garden plants. Quick acting.	Use any time. Rake in before sowing or planting. $13-25g$ ($\frac{1}{2}-1oz$). To correct potash deficiency, use $25g$ ($1oz$) in $5l$ ($1gal$) water; wet soil thoroughly.
Wood ashes Potash	Fresh ashes contain potassium carbonate. Heavy dressings could spoil tilth of clay soils or make chalky soil too alkaline.	Autumn or winter. $100-150g$ ($4-6oz$) per sq m well ahead of sowing or planting.
Sulphate of iron Iron	Use to correct iron deficiency in acid soils but not limey ones. Should be powdered finely.	Used in lawn sands.
Magnesium sulphate 10% Mg	Inorganic, crystalline and soluble in water. Used only for magnesium deficiency.	$25-50g$ ($1-2oz$) per sq m or apply as leaf spray using $6g$ ($\frac{1}{4}oz$) to $5l$ ($1gal$) water.

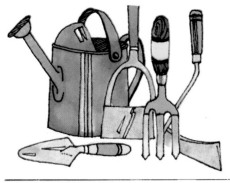

The right tool for the job

You can begin gardening with just a few implements—a spade, a fork, a rake, and a hoe and perhaps a hand fork and trowel. When you have grown a hedge or a lawn, shears and a mower will be needed; for pruning, secateurs and a pruning saw. For watering you need a hose, with sprinkler attachment, and a watering can; for sweeping paths, a broom. For assorted garden jobs, it is useful to have labels, seed boxes, pots, stakes, garden twine, a trug or flat basket, scissors and a sharp knife.

Some of these items can be acquired easily. Pots come from the nursery with plants in them, previous owners of gardens leave about stakes and seed boxes. But make a simple start. Sophisticated purchases can come much later, if needed at all.

Carefully look after the tools you have. Clean them, oil them and keep them sharp. Buy light tools that are comfortable to handle.

A **spade** is used for digging, ie breaking up the soil to improve it for plant growth. The top soil is the top layer to the depth of the spade, which is about 25cm (10in). This is sometimes called the top spit, and this is where the soil nutrients and bacteria are. Spades can be bought in various sizes, 25cm × 15cm (10in × 6½in) is about medium. Handles are usually D-shaped, but some are T-shaped. Handles covered with a PVC sleeve are most comfortable to handle. You can also buy a spade with built-up shoulders to take wear and tear off your shoes. Or you can buy a stainless steel spade; very long-lasting and quick to slip through heavy soil, but expensive. A spade with pointed cutting teeth is also made for heavy soils.

The **fork** is used more for cultivating than for digging. Its thin, strong tines or prongs, penetrate difficult soil more easily. It is very useful for breaking down the heavy clods of earth you dig up into smaller pieces—bang them with the back of the fork. A fork is ideal for lifting plants, causing less root damage. It is useful for raking up, and for forking-over the earth between plants to stop it getting hard and tight and therefore air and water-resistant. Forks can come with a variety of prongs thin or flat—the flat ones being useful for lifting vegetable root crops and potatoes. Purchase a medium-size fork, not too big, with about four prongs.

The hand fork is very useful for planting small plants. You can get one with a long or short handle. The short-handled one is more versatile, but the long-handled fork is good for forking-over the back of borders, etc.

The **hand trowel** is used for all sorts of planting and small garden jobs on rockeries, raised beds, window boxes, pot plants.

Below left: *Keep tools clean and oiled. Store on nails or hooks on the wall.*

Below: *A selection of sprinkler and irrigation fittings and a perforated hose.*

The **hoe** is the main tool for cultivating the soil and attacking weeds. Designs range from almost mattock proportions to neat little cutters. There are two main types of hoe, the draw hoe and the Dutch hoe. The first has a blade set almost at right angles to the handle and the second has a blade running in the same direction as the handle. The first, the draw hoe, is good for clearing weeds and breaking up hard-packed soil and is considered more useful and powerful than the Dutch hoe. Hoeing is hard work on the hands so choose a hoe with a comfortable grip and keep your hoe sharp, so that you can behead weeds as well as draw them to the surface to die in the sun. Hoeing also aerates the soil which is important, and is less likely to damage plant roots than a garden fork.

The **rake** can be used for some very useful work—preparing the soil and breaking it down into fine particles before sowing or planting, making seed drills by using the edge to mark out grooves, for covering seeds, for mounding and shaping earth in garden beds, for taking up anything from grass clippings to autumn leaves. Do not buy a too-heavy or too-long rake. Although more expensive, the best rakes have the teeth cut out of one piece of steel and the head welded to a tapering tube fastened to the handle. These rakes will last. Special, light wire lawn rakes are not meant for the jobs above; a rake with straight fine teeth is needed. Always rake lightly, bringing the rake towards you. To broadcast seeds for sowing in a garden bed, rake the fine earth surface in one direction. Broadcast the seed into these grooves. Then rake in the opposite direction and the seeds will then be covered with soil.

Shears now have moulded handles or rubber or plastic grips for comfort and some have shock absorbers in the handles to reduce jarring. There are wavy-edged blades on some shears that grip as they cut. Start with a good pair of shears with hollow ground blades for a clean cut. Some designs have ball-bearing joints that give a very smooth action and notched blades enable you to cut tough branches. Short-handled shears of the standard shape do the general garden clipping but there are long-handled shears for cutting lawn edges.

You can buy a plastic or rubber **hose**. Generally the first is considered more durable. It is important to get the length right or you will find yourself running out of hose at the farthermost points of the garden. Hose lengths go up to around 50m (approx 120ft) and are 1·5cm–2·5cm (½–1in) in diameter. You need attachments to fix the hose to the tap and a spray head. The spray head should adjust to a fine spray when needed or to a jet. For hose fittings, the

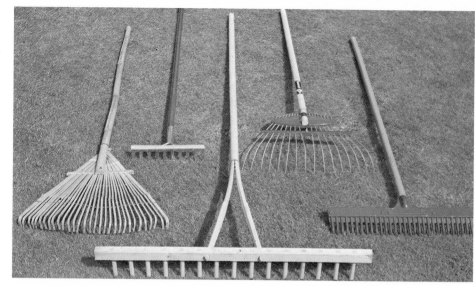

Above: *Garden rakes, left to right, bamboo, iron, wooden, Springbok and rubber. Buy a straight metal rake for shaping and mounding earth or sowing seeds.*

Above: *The Dutch hoe (second from left) and four draw hoes; the two basic types.*

Below: *A selection of shears showing wavy-edge blades (they grip as they cut), centre, curved base of blade cuts small branches.*

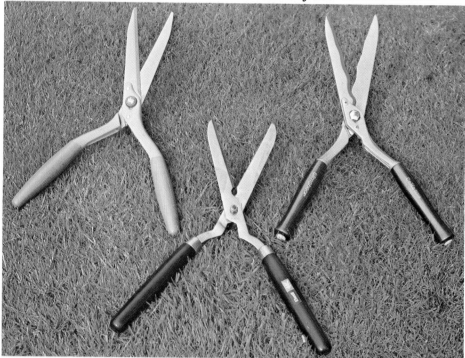

74

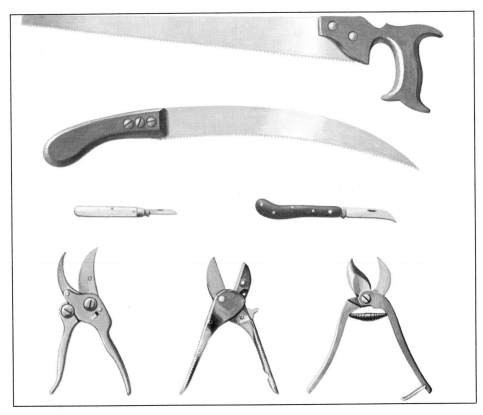

Hoselock fittings cover most needs and allow you to couple hoses together. There are universal tap connectors and sprinklers in the range. You will find a wide range of elaborate and simple sprinkler systems available commercially. Start with an inexpensive one that will give a fine, light spray, and when the garden is more developed, assess better what your particular needs are. Consider having one or two garden taps installed by the plumber in strategic places. It saves a lot of walking.

Secateurs and pruning saw come in varying designs, weights and sizes. For secateurs it is important to get good quality ones and keep them very sharp or you will injure the stems of plants. See pruning chapter for using these two tools. See that secateurs fit your hand well so that you can get a firm grip without discomfort. Start with a simple narrow, light pruning saw.

Left: *Selection of pruning saws, garden knives and secateurs, made for varying size and strength of hand. Secateurs must be kept sharp.*

Below left: *Three types of spades. Spade with teeth is used for heavy soils.*

Below: *Border fork, digging fork, flat-tined fork and in front, small hand fork.*

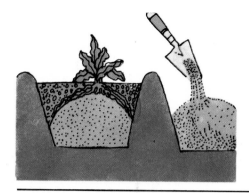

How to plant properly

Before you plant you must prepare the ground by digging, weeding, feeding and weathering. Check your soil type and condition, using the earlier chapter. Preparing it for planting begins with digging. Digging need not be laborious and when you feel like the exercise it can even be quite exhilarating. Here is a simple way to do it.

Digging one-spit deep

This is digging the earth to one spade's depth. Dig a trench approx 30cm (1ft) wide and deep along the back of the garden bed. Remove all the top soil to the opposite diagonal corner to the start of the trench. Now with the trench facing you, dig the spade in 15cm (6in) in front of the trench, lift up the top soil and make sure you throw it into the far side of the trench, breaking up the lumps as you go. Do this line by line right across the garden bed, and when you come to the last part of the trenching use the soil excavated from the first trench to fill in.

Double digging

Double digging is seldom necessary if the subsoil is reasonably well-drained. Double digging aerates the soil, improves drainage and root run of plants. You dig down to about 60cm (2ft). Work in the same way as single digging but when the trench is open the subsoil or second spit of earth is thoroughly broken up with the fork as each bit of it is exposed. Scatter organic matter such as compost or manure over the forked subsoil, then replace the top soil on this layer of broken-up subsoil.

Trenching

Trenching is not often carried out now. The energy needed is never repaid in improved growth. Occasionally, with some soils, inverting the subsoil can be harmful. If you do decide to trench, work the soil down to a depth of almost 1m (3ft). Naturally on stony soils you will not get down that far. Make the trench 1m (3ft) wide as well.

Digging of a heavier type of soil is usually carried out in the autumn and winter and the ground left rough to weather until shortly before being sown or planted. As the weather improves the ground should be worked into the right condition for sowing, for frost will have left the clods quite crumbly. Rake the bed from end to end twice, in opposite directions.

A light sandy soil must be conditioned with a large amount of organic matter during winter digging, or the soil will be eroded by winter weather. Dig in plenty of peat, seaweed, hops, compost, rotted manure. The soil could need liming. Check chapter on soils.

Add a complete fertilizer to the ground about a fortnight before planting, adding it at the rate of about 50g (2oz) to a square metre.

Seed growing

To plant seeds you want a fine crumbly soil which will hold water well.

You can buy special soil mixtures, sometimes called seed composts, for seed sowing. One that suits a wide range of plants is the John Innes standard seed sowing mixture, which was worked out by the John Innes Institute, now of Norwich, England. There is also a John Innes standard mixture for growing cuttings of plants and three other mixtures for various stages of growing plants in pots. The potting mixture can also be used for pricking out seedlings, ie, transplanting seedlings into deeper, richer soil in larger seed boxes.

All seeds need good soil aeration, water, the right temperature (this varies from plant to plant)—and once they germinate plenty of light for short sturdy growth. The earlier a seedling is planted in its permanent place, the sooner it grows well and becomes established. The later in a seedling's life that it is moved the more chance there is that it will be damaged or suffer a check in growth.

Seeds can be grown in a garden seed bed, or in a seed box indoors or out, where the temperature can be controlled—also soil texture and moisture.

Hardy plants can be grown outside in a seed bed and transplanted to their permanent positions later, or they can be sown straight into the place where you want them to grow permanently.

For planting in restricted places, such as between rocks, a two-pronged fork is useful.

For making holes for small plants, the best tool is a small trowel.

Firming after planting is important. Keep new or young plants well watered.

Half-hardy plants usually do better started off in seed boxes indoors or in a frame, under cloches or in a greenhouse. Then they are off to a good start and when planted out in the garden bed they will flower earlier.

Seed beds

Locate your seed bed where it is sheltered and has good soil. You can protect the bed by a frame or cloches if you want to.

Alternatively you can plant the seeds straight into the garden bed where they will grow permanently. If you do this you must thin the seedlings out as soon as you can, to allow the sturdy ones left to develop. Planting straight into the garden bed is usually done during the main sowing time from February to April.

Any seed bed has to be made up of good fertile soil dug or forked-over, fed, and cultivated to a very fine loose texture on the surface. It must be free of weeds, particularly perennial ones. Rake the surface in each direction to remove any little stones or lumps of soil.

If you are planting in a special seed bed or frame you could add some of the John Innes seed sowing mixture or one similar. The ingredients are 2 parts by bulk of loam (John Innes' is partially sterilized), 1 part bulk of peat, 1 part bulk of coarse sand. To each bushel—about four buckets—add 40g (approx 1½oz) of superphosphate and 20g (approx ¾oz) ground limestone or chalk. This mixture, which need not be made if a commercial product is available, will however give you some idea of the ingredients for a good seed bed.

Lime-hating plants however, cannot be sown in a compost with lime in it so prepare the bed with two parts finely-sieved peat to one part of sharp lime-free sand. Strong fertilizers or rich organic materials are not used in seed beds.

Locating your seed bed within a frame is a particular advantage if you are sowing very fine seed because the glass light of the frame stops heavy rain from falling on and dislodging the seed. You can water seeds with a watering can or fine hose spray.

Make the surface of a garden bed where you are planting seeds as close as you can to a seed compost quality. At the very least sprinkle on granulated peat and rake it in until the top soil is light and then add a very light dressing of superphosphate or bonemeal to improve the texture.

Here you will not want parade-ground lines of plants, so make a criss-cross pattern of drills and plant seeds individually or lightly in a random pattern.

Make shallow drills in a seed bed with the hoe turned edge on or with a stick. If you want to get very straight rows peg out a garden line and follow it closely, or use a length of wood. For very small seeds the drills can be very shallow, 0·5cm (¼in) or so, because seeds only need to be covered with their own depth of soil. Straight rows have the advantage of making thinning and hoeing easier.

Water the drills well before sowing and wait until the water has drained away. Then sow evenly along the drills, spacing each seed if it is large enough or mixing seed with fine sand to get a thin spread. It is important to sow thinly. It saves seed and money and gives each seed more space to grow and develop sturdily. Do not consider for a moment cutting off the corner of a seed packet and sowing straight from the pack—the seed will come out in heaps. After sowing, cover with a thin layer of

'Heeling in' is a temporary planting method used until you can position plants permanently. First dig out a narrow trench.

Next, lean plants against one side of trench, away from wind, and replace the soil around the roots of the plants.

The third step is to firm the soil around the roots of the plants. These are lying aslant to keep sap from rising too much.

Once heeling in is completed the plants can remain there for some time but move them before they begin to become rooted.

77

earth drawn back to fill in the drills by using the rake. Firm drills very gently with a flat piece of wood, or your foot.

Seedlings must never be allowed to dry out. Water them with a fine spray.

Seed boxes

Indoors, or in the greenhouse or in sheltered frames, you can grow seed in wood or plastic trays, or clay or plastic pots. Wash whatever you use very thoroughly and any new clay pots must be soaked in water for 24 hours before being used to remove any harmful salts.

Put a drainage layer of crocks (broken pot) or large gravel into pots or boxes covering the drainage holes. Then layer with some coarse earth.

Fill to within 1·5cm ($\frac{1}{2}$in) of the top with a ready-made seed sowing compost.

As with a seed bed, the compost needs to be moist but well-drained. Pots can be stood in water up to their necks before seed-planting, then drained. Water seed boxes and let drain.

Plant the seeds thinly, individually if you can, covering with a very thin layer of soil. Firm with the base of another pot or with a piece of flat wood.

If you have planted too thickly you may have to thin as soon as the seeds show. As soon as they are big enough to handle, prick out into larger seed boxes with richer earth, or transplant to individual pots. You can use the little peat pots which can be planted whole with the plant without disturbing its roots. A plant in an ordinary pot has the advantage usually of being able to be transplanted with minimum root disturbance compared with plants left in large boxes.

Pricking out

Pricking out is an important step in a seedling's life. As soon as the seedlings are big enough to handle easily they are moved into pots or deeper boxes to allow for more root development. If they were left in their original overcrowded condition they would become long and thin and lose their sturdiness. The pots or boxes for the seedlings are prepared in the same way as for the seeds. If the boxes are wood use drainage material over slits, if plastic use coarser sieving material.

Remove the seedlings from the original seed box by levering them up with a flat, thin piece of wood, lifting them out by their seed leaves—never the stem—and putting them in the new place by lowering them into prepared small holes made by a round-ended dibber, or stick. Press the earth around them. Space seedlings about 5cm (2in) apart, and finally, water with a fine spray. Keep the seedlings in a warm, damp atmosphere for a couple of.

Above: *Small seedlings are delicate and easily damaged. Avoid handling them by the stem. They should be lifted carefully by the seed leaf, the first leaves they form.*

Below: *It is easier to firm the soil around seedlings and small plants with knuckles or fingers so that there is no risk of damaging them by treading on them.*

Below: *A good tilth soon forms once the ground is dry enough to rake. Using a line as a guide it is a simple job to draw a drill deep enough for all kinds of seeds.*

Below: *It is a mistake to sow seed too thickly. Pour a little from the packet into your hand and scatter thinly along the drill. Big seeds are best placed singly by hand.*

For seed sowing, any accumulation of rubbish is removed and weeds destroyed.

The second step is to lightly fork the soil to break up clods and create a tilth.

Third step, make seed bed firm by treading gently up and down.

Fourth step, large clods and stones are removed with a wooden rake.

Finally, with a straight metal rake break down top few centimetres of soil into a fine tilth.

Fork over borders and beds in the spring to remove perennial weeds.

days and out of strong light which would make them wilt.

Although sometimes, you will want to collect and grow your own seeds, it is usually easier to grow plants from seeds sold by reliable seed merchants. Some seeds need special treatment before they will germinate. For example, they require a special germination temperature and need to spend some time in winter conditions in a dormant state, or they need a particular amount of light or dark to germinate. Alpine seed, which naturally gets cold winters and melting snow, needs to be sown in boxes and left outside all the winter before it will grow. It has been found that seeds of some of these plants germinate best when piles of snow have been put on the pots or boxes and left to melt naturally. Cotoneaster, holly, primula and others also like a cold dormant period. Alpines also like a gravelly seed compost.

Before seedlings growing in protected frame or greenhouse conditions go outside, they must be hardened off, ie, gradually accustomed to outside temperature and ventilation. This is done gradually by increasing ventilation by raising the frame light or providing more open air conditions so that the plant can acclimatize slowly.

Planting bulbs and corms
The depth at which the bulb is planted is the most important point. If you can invest in a bulb planter that neatly scoops out a flat-bottomed hole the job is made easier. Bulbs of the same type should be planted at the same depth. See the bulb planting chart. A rough rule for bulb depth when planting is that the tips of the bulbs should be about three times as deep as the bulb is wide.

When planting in turf, cut out a slice of turf, plant, and replace turf. If you want a natural group, scatter the bulbs and plant them where they fall.

Two lilies that do not follow the planting depth rule mentioned are the Madonna lily (*Lilium candidum*), which is planted approx 2·5cm (1in) below soil level; and *Cardiocrinum* (Lilium) *giganteum*, planted with the bulb just breaking the surface.

Planting shrubs and trees
Begin of course with fertile, well composted soil. This is most essential.

Deciduous shrubs and trees are planted in the dormant time from autumn to spring. Evergreen shrubs and trees are planted in the spring, when the warm conditions will help the roots to establish.

The plants will arrive from the nursery either balled (with hessian wrapped around earth and roots) or planted in containers. If they were grown in the container there is not the urgency to plant, but if they were simply sold in a container, you must plant quickly, as you must for balled plants or plants posted and packed bare-rooted.

Never let the roots dry out before planting. If you cannot plant immediately, heel the plants into some earth. This means dig a hole, plant the plant at an angle, cover roots with earth and water well. At this angle the sap will rise slowly. Plants cannot be heeled in for too long or they will encourage root growth which will be damaged when they are moved again.

You can wait until growth has started before you put in fertilizer for newly-planted bare-rooted plants, but some gardeners work fertilizer or manure in with the soil *before* planting. Every year feed the plants with a complete fertilizer supplying nitrogen, phosphorus and potash. In spring after rain mulch to keep roots cool. Dig the mulch in before winter.

Tall shrubs and trees must be staked or they will fall easy prey to strong winds. Check newly-planted shrubs to see if they are established and not displaced.

Keep young shrubs well watered, watering leaves as well as roots to help cut down moisture loss.

Step by step guide

1 Dig a hole with slanted sides. Do not guess the depth. You will see a soil mark on the stem of the plant which shows at what level the soil was when the plant was growing. You will see it even more clearly on the plant if you take it out of the container yourself. The hole you dig must be wide and deep enough for all the roots to branch and spread out.

On container-grown plants, slit down the side of the tin with tin snippers. Pot plants can be shaken gently out of the pot, but break the pot if you have difficulty in getting plants out without damaging plant roots.

If moving a plant from one part of the garden to another, again note where the soil level was.

2 In the bottom of the hole make a mound of earth on which the roots of the shrub or tree can be well spread out and supported.

3 Trim off any damaged roots and arrange plant on mound, with roots spread out over the mound. This is where a second person comes in useful for holding the plant. Or you can use a planting board as shown in the photograph.

4 Closely press in earth around the roots. Some gardeners suggest mixing dry potting compost in with the wet earth packed around the roots.

Above: *Planting board holds stem at right planting depth, leaving you free to spread roots.*

Below: *Support stake can go in before shrub is planted. Here, root ball is being spread.*

Below: *Standard rose tied with buckled plastic band. Strips of hessian are an alternative.*

Right: *When planting it is important to take out a hole deep enough and wide enough to enable the root to be spread out.*

Below: *First put stake in, then plant rose standard so that union is just under soil.*

5 Tall shrubs and trees need staking. The stake should be driven in *before* the tree is set in position and the hole filled.

6 Fill hole three-quarters full of earth. Firm.

7 Fill hole with water and allow it to drain away, although if the soil is moist and particularly in winter, this is not necessary.

8 Fill hole to top with soil. When you have finished, earth should be firm but not hard around the plant.

9 Most plants should be cut back to allow for any damage to the roots during planting. This gives the roots less plant to support until they are established, and encourages a good sturdy well-shaped shrub. Deciduous or flowering fruit trees are cut back to very short branches or spurs, although much depends on age of the tree and how it is trained.

Mark the soil or bed level with a stick. Set the shrub to the right depth. You will see a mark on stem at the soil level.

Pack in fine soil firmly around the roots making sure they are in close contact with soil. Level off the soil and firm thoroughly.

Above: *Rose plants sometimes come packed and pruned in polythene bag holding soil ball.*

Below: *A shrub delivered with balled root in sacking. Others are supplied in containers.*

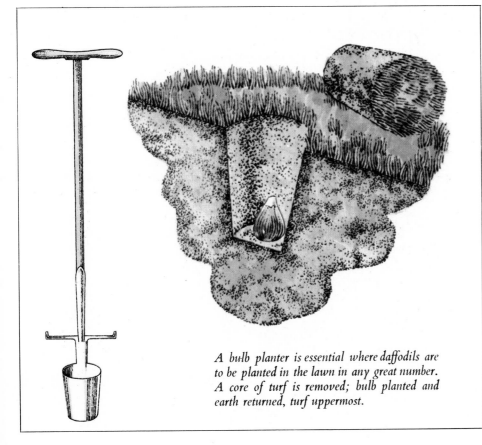

A bulb planter is essential where daffodils are to be planted in the lawn in any great number. A core of turf is removed; bulb planted and earth returned, turf uppermost.

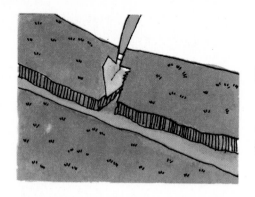

Cultivating a good lawn

Almost everyone would like to have a lawn in preference to an open-paved area. Once a lawn is laid properly, it does not take a lot of work to keep it looking good except for regular mowing. The edges need clipping but if you can edge the lawn with concrete mowing strips it saves extra work.

A lawn makes the perfect background for a beautiful tree planted in it and makes a frame for flower beds. Set a focal point in the middle or a little to one side of the lawn—a sun dial, bird bath or statue, with pavings and plantings around it.

A large unbroken sweep of lawn makes a small garden look larger and more spacious. If you have a square, suburban, fenced garden do not make an absolutely square lawn with narrow beds all round it to the fences. Make the lawn shape prettier, curve it with wide beds on the sunny side of the garden. Make it oval or elliptical in shape.

If you have a larger garden, plan wide grass paths leading from the lawn through wilder areas of the garden.

If you have a small garden with limited lawn area you could grow a chamomile lawn instead of a grass one. It is fragrant

A sweep of lawn with conifers planted as focal points in it, sets off a low shrubbery border.

Preparing the site for a lawn: **Top left:** *Hammer peg in to height of proposed lawn.*

Top right: *Top soil is trodden in lightly to make sure no air-pockets remain.*

Above: *Using a spirit level, hammer other pegs in to the same height.*

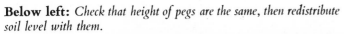

Below left: *Check that height of pegs are the same, then redistribute soil level with them.*

Above: *The soil is raked to a good tilth before sowing the grass seed.*

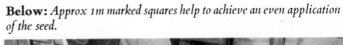

Below: *Approx 1m marked squares help to achieve an even application of the seed.*

and almost maintenance free. The chamomile used is *Anthemis nobilis*, the common chamomile, which will spread itself. It withstands dry weather better than grass and needs no mowing but will not stand the hard wear of frequent foot traffic. In California and Australia, many ground covering, low-growing plants are used for small lawns where grass won't flourish.

There are various grasses that you can grow for a lawn, some giving a very fine textured lawn that won't take hard family wear, others giving a coarser, more hard-wearing lawn.

About six types of grass are used for lawns, each with various useful characteristics. Chewings' fescue, for example, cuts well and makes a good quality lawn but its winter colour is poor. Bent grass, usually combined with Chewings' fescue, also cuts well. These do not have the wear-and-tear and drought resistance of smooth-stalked meadow grass. Many lawn grasses are seed mixtures sold by seed merchants and if you buy from a reliable, experienced source you should get the type of lawn seed at the price you want. Manufacturers of most mixtures list what is in them and these points might help you check up on the advantages and disadvantages.

Perennial ryegrass (*Lolium perenne*), the late flowering, leafy, persistent strains are best for lawns, including the Aberystwyth

Right: *Sowing seed thinly by hand. When sowing from bucket or bag it is harder to distribute the seed evenly.*

Below: *It is difficult on some shapes of lawn to mow in different directions but diagonal mowing can give a glamorous finish.*

strain 'S.23'. There are continental varieties—'Heraf', 'Pelo', 'Sceempter' and 'Melle'. Perennial ryegrass does not form a very dense sward on its own and will not flourish if cut very close. It needs reasonable fertile ground and frequent mowing in growing season, and to be cut to 2·5cm (1in). It is a very hardwearing lawn.

Timothy (*Phleum pratense*). There are new

leafy cultivars of this agricultural grass and it has good winter colour and recovers well after wear. However, it is slow to establish itself from seed and does not compete well when mixed with perennial ryegrass or other grasses. The cultivars are quite expensive but the resulting lawn is 'playing-field' quality only.

Rough-stalked meadow grass (*Poa trivi-*

alis) is a fairly vigorous grass sometimes used in the cheaper mixtures.

Smooth-stalked meadow grass (*Poa pratensis*) has some good cultivars including the Dutch variety 'Prato'. Slow to establish but eventually a dense, durable, drought-resistant sward, it does not like close mowing; 2–2·5cm (¾–1in) is about the right cutting height.

Annual meadow grass (*Poa annua*)—a short lived perennial is seldom sown but often found because it is an excellent invader of existing lawns. It is not very resistant to drought or winter weather.

Red fescue (*Festuca rubra var. rubra*)—is found in good lawn mixtures but does not stand close mowing and so will not make the aristocratic heights of lawn growing. 'S. 59' however is a fine-leaved winter green type which forms a good lawn alone or with other mixtures. 'Oasis' and 'Brabantia' are continental varieties.

Chewings' fescue (*Festuca rubra sub spp. commutata*) is usually mixed with Browntop bent to make the best fine lawn and sometimes added to the other lawn mixtures. Very good quality seed is available mostly from America and Holland ('Highlight' and 'Brabantia' are Dutch). However, this variety does not have a good winter colour.

Browntop bent (*Agrostis tenuis*) comes mostly from America and is mixed with Chewings' fescue for high quality lawns. It is a dense turf and does not mind close mowing. It is used with other mixtures of lawn seed too, because it is a valuable bot-

Above: *A well-mown lawn does more for a garden than any other single feature.*

Below: *Water lawns so that moisture penetrates deeply to roots. Use a sprinkler.*

Below: *Providing there is enough sun even a small town garden can have a lawn.*

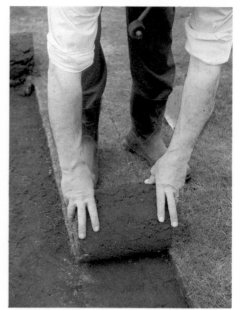

This is the way that lawn turf is cut. You may want to cut and re-lay your own sometime.

The turf is lifted or cut free with turfing iron or sharp spade.

Once cut or lifted free, the turf is rolled up like a carpet.

Place a line of turf around the perimeter of the lawn area.

Cut each piece of turf in half to start the second row of laying, so joints are staggered.

Butt the second row of turf against the first. Lay turf with staggered joints.

tom grass. Creeping bent (*Agrostis stolonifera*) is more popular than Browntop bent in America in the same climate belt as Britain and there is at least one satisfactory variety in Britain called 'Penncross'.

Crested dogstail (*Cynosurus cristatus*). A tough, rather coarse, tufted grass which is good for lawns that get hard wear. It is partially shade tolerant. A common constituent of the cheaper lawn mixtures and invariably used for sports grounds.

Preparing the site

The lawn needs to get as much sun as possible because most lawn grasses will not tolerate mowing and shade without dying away. The ground needs to be graded gently into slopes and curves, with no

steep slopes or awkward corners. This is to make lawn mowing possible and safe.

Fifteen centimetres (approx 6in) of topsoil is needed on the site, no debris and no weeds, if possible. The lawn does not have to be level, it can slope in any direction but the surface needs to be smooth. You can usually smooth out small bumps and dips with a load of topsoil. Gentle slopes will help the lawn drain after rain.

If you already have a lawn, think in terms of trimming it to a better, curved shape and smoothing out the gradients to make a pleasing nearly-flat or undulating surface.

If you want to change levels more drastically you must remove the topsoil. Alter the levels by moving the subsoil about and

then put back and smooth out the topsoil again.

In all levelling and shaping, do not work with the soil when it is very wet.

If you have to dig up a section of land to prepare it for lawn, it is a good idea to do it in the winter so that frost can break down the clods. Then you can rake it down and prepare a fine surface in the spring. If you are digging soil—or adding topsoil to an area for lawn—then you can add in some sand and peat to a heavy soil, or very well-rotted manure to a light, sandy soil to improve the texture.

A summer's fallowing is valuable. Growing a potato crop on the ground will help condition the soil and reward you with new potatoes.

When laying turf, the ends are butted firmly together to make a neat join.

If a lawn area is bumpy, lift turf, level soil surface below, then re-lay turf.

Next, make a fine, firm soil bed by firming and treading down the soil after raking it free of any rough material, smoothing down any small bump and filling out any tiny depression. Then rake it all once more and tread it down this time working in the opposite direction.

You can now choose your lawn laying method. You can seed the lawn using a lawn seed mixture. Or you can lay turf, ie, small oblongs of already-growing grass. Sowing from seed is much cheaper than laying turf but you have to wait for results. The lawn you get from either method will depend on the quality of the seed or the quality of the turf. For a beginner it might be a little harder to judge the turf quality—but check it for weeds,

disease, good looks (it will not look any better laid) and close texture.

If you are using seed apply the following fertilizer a few days before sowing: 1·3kg (3lb) sulphate of ammonia, 1·3kg (3lb) fine hoof and horn meal, 1·3kg (3lb) dried blood, 2·5kg (6lb) powdered superphosphate, 2·5kg (6lb) fine bonemeal, 1·3kg (3lb) sulphate of potash, per 100 square metres.

If you are laying turf apply the same fertilizer mixture, leaving out the dried blood, and the sulphate of ammonia and increasing the fine hoof and horn meal to 2·5kg (6lb), raking it in a few days before turfing.

Lawn from turf

Turf can be laid in the autumn, when it would be too late for seeding, and if all goes well be ready the next summer to be used as an established lawn. Turf laid in the spring and summer runs the risk of drying out and then doing badly.

When you buy the turf it should be healthy, mown, stone-free, dense and a good colour.

Delivered turf is usually in 30×90cm (1×3ft) oblongs, each 3cm (1¼in) deep. You can have 60×30cm (2×1ft) oblongs. Do not order delivery until the weather is right for laying turf.

Begin by laying a single line of turf around the perimeter of the lawn site. Then lay turf across the site, working forwards so that you face the unturfed part and are not stepping on it and spoiling its condition. Where you have to walk across the new turf, lay planks down. Lay each line of turf with staggered joints, as if you were brick-laying and push each turf flat and tight against its neighbour.

If a turf stands up a little or sags down, adjust the level of soil below it. When all the turf is laid, roll with a light roller and then scatter a sandy compost over the top, using 2·5 to 2·7kg (4 to 5lb) a square metre, and gently brush it in.

Turf lawns sometimes need top dressing with bulky material such as sandy compost or a mixture of soil, sand and peat, to smooth out the surface and fill in cracks and dips. Work it in carefully by dragging a brush or rake over it.

During the first year the grass will need mowing regularly but do not mow the grass very closely.

Lawn from seed

The best time to sow lawn seed is about the end of August when weeds are a little on the wane. You can sow a lawn in spring but in this season there is greater risk of drought from a dry May and weeds are more vigorous.

Choose your lawn seed, keeping in mind

whether you want a fine, ornamental lawn or a coarse, hard-wearing one. (See above for seed types and mixtures.)

Sow on a dry, raked surface, dividing the seed into half and scatter one half over the site in one direction and the other half over the site in the other direction. Rake the seed in very lightly—grass seed should not be deeply covered.

When the grass is showing through, roll it to firm the soil around grass roots so that the grass can be mowed later.

If you find birds are eating the seed, or enjoying a dust bath, tie cotton strings attached to sticks over the area.

Newly-sown lawns should not be mown until the grass is about 5cm (2in) high. Then carefully top it. It is useful before mowing to roll the lawn area and then wait until the grass is upright again before mowing. Hand-weed the grass whenever you see weeds emerging.

Never let the grass grow too long. Gradually lower the height of the cut in successive mowings until you achieve the height you want.

The surface of a seeded lawn will not be as level to begin with as a turfed lawn. A monthly top dressing during the first year's growth will help to make the surface much smoother. A few weeks after the original sowing, some bare patches may show up where the seed missed the earth. Over-sow these as quickly as possible—you will find that the growth of the new seed will soon catch up with the old.

A disease known as 'damping off' can attack a newly-sown lawn. It is more inclined to do so if the seed is sown or washed by rain into little heaps. The seed can recover by itself but if the attack is serious, treat the grass with a fungicide such as Cheshunt compound or with a dry dust mercury fungicide.

Mowing

A light mower is recommended as the use of a heavy model over a period of time compresses the topsoil. Do not cut a new lawn very close; cut it high and gradually lower the cut to about 2·5cm (1in). Even the finest lawns should not be cut much below 1·3cm (½in). Close cutting weakens the grass; ryegrass should never be below 2·5cm (1in). Very fine lawns need mowing about two or three times a week in summer and ordinary lawns about once a week. Mow the lawn in different directions each time it is cut, and do not mow the lawn when it is wet.

A lawn should not get much above the height you have planned before cutting, because infrequent mowing damages it.

If you let the grass cuttings lie on the ground, you return some of the soil nutrients to the soil although if left in heaps it can encourage earth worms, coarse grasses, weeds and a soft surface, so a grass catcher attached to the mower for collecting the grass cuttings is advisable.

Looking after the lawn

Top dressing is a good way to keep a lawn in good health and with a smooth surface. For most lawns a sand, soil and peat mixture with a texture rather like a good loamy soil, should be spread over the lawn and then worked into the surface by dragging over it with a twig broom or the back of a rake. Apply the top dressing lightly.

Lawn on a rich soil might need fertilizer only occasionally. On the average lawn, apply once a year. A good mixture is 1·3kg (3lb) sulphate of ammonia, 450g (1lb) fine hoof and horn meal, 450g (1lb) dried blood, 2kg (4lb) powdered superphosphate, 450g (1lb) fine bonemeal, 450g (1lb) sulphate of potash, applied on 100 square metres. Mix with about 1kg (2·2lb) of sandy soil to make the application easier and more even. Water-in the fertilizer if it does not rain, otherwise you will damage the grass. Avoid liming a lawn.

Regularly brush or lightly rake the lawn to improve its appearance and raise runners of clover, etc, which you can then remove by mowing.

In the late summer, on old very fibrous lawns, scarify with a wire rake to thin out some of the fibre while there is still some growth.

On most lawns a good forking every three or four years, to make holes for water and air to enter, will help the lawn flourish. Remember also to water the lawn well in dry weather before it turns brown.

For weeds you can use a selective weedkiller, for example, a hormone weed killer is one type widely used by gardeners today. If you do use a weed killer, the grass clippings should not be used in the compost heap. Weeding by hand is laborious but effective if the lawn is small and you have the time.

When choosing a **lawn mower** to buy, consider these points: price, the cost of maintenance, after sales service, reliable running, long-lasting finish, energy or fuel used, and what sort of handling it needs. The simplest and cheapest mowers are the ordinary manual types driven only by man —or woman—power! These are probably the cheapest but are obviously better for a small lawn area. As with cars, within the type you choose, you tend to get what you pay for. A self-propelled model, for example, saves a lot of effort but costs more. If you decide on a powered mower, the first decision should be which type to buy— whether to have an electric-powered mower or petrol-driven type, and here you must

consider safety first, manoeuvrability and noise. If you want a petrol-driven mower, the next choice is between the cylinder type and the rotary cutting type and here the first is a better choice for the very fine lawn but the second is sturdy, and in wide use. For all mowers, safety must be checked carefully—a rotary mower should have a safety shield, for example, and an electric mower, a transformer. Another consideration is the type and size lawn you have.

Rotary mowing machines cut by a horizontally-set rotating blade under the mower. Cylinder mowers have blades which turn in the same way as the old hand push-pull mowers. Another possibility is the hovercraft mower which is of the rotary type but rides on a cushion of air.

Look for these refinements in a mower —silencing, easy adjustment of the cutting height of the blades, safety precautions (to stop a flying blade, electrical accidents, rubbish being kicked up), firm handlebars, easy storage. Consider too, how much effort has to go into pushing it along (larger diameter wheel sizes ride more comfortably on rough land), its grass collection, mobility and the weight of its collecting boxes, and how easily it starts.

Weigh up these pros and cons of the various features available:

The rotary grass cutter does not give such a fine finish to a lawn, but it can serve the dual purpose of cutting lawn and

rougher grass. Cheaper versions vibrate and are noisy, more expensive models can be more silent and also self-propelled. Rotary mowers do not cut around trees or over edges very well.

The hovercraft type of mower can cut low without scalping the grass, and is safe and easy to push.

Fabric grass bags are cumbersome but light. A grassbox when removed should not leave an unprotected, potentially dangerous opening.

A wide machine cuts quickly but can scalp the grass on an uneven lawn more easily.

Most of the cylinder mowers are self-propelled and their cut is fine. Grass boxes on some models are cumbersome and their handlebars are not often the folding type needed for easy storage.

Electric mowers are very silent and require little maintenance but the cable can be a nuisance and potentially dangerous. However, a low voltage model operated through a transformer is available.

Battery mowers need more maintenance than mains operated mowers but are manoeuvrable. Some designs are not so well balanced for handling; and their batteries need replacing every few years.

If you can afford it, there is a mower that you can ride on. If you have large lawns and reluctant mowers in the family it might be worth sacrificing the money to buy this particular model.

Above left: *Young perennial weeds appearing in the lawn can be weeded by hand.*

Above: *The grass on a newly-sown lawn should be only lightly clipped over.*

Left: *Isolated lawn weeds can be given this 'spot treatment' with weedkiller.*

Above: *Putting top dressing on the lawn ready for working it in.*

Below: *Working in the top dressing using the back of a rake.*

Above: *The lute is another tool which can be used to work in soil.*

Below: *Brush off surplus top dressing with a twig broom.*

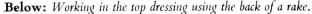

Monthly calendar

JANUARY
Mow lightly when soil is dry enough. Trim edges. Order any new seed.

FEBRUARY
If the lawn is soggy, pierce surface with fork at 15cm (6in) intervals; sprinkle a peat and coarse sand mixture over it.

MARCH
Sweep, lightly roll and rake lawn before mowing. Prepare ground for new lawn, either seed-sown or turfed.

APRIL
Sow seed (but better sown in August); lay turf. Give established lawns first feed of the year.

MAY
Regularly mow new lawns. Use weed-killer on weeds in established lawns.

JUNE
Mow twice weekly. Rake lawn once or twice before cutting (for weed control). Apply fertilizer.

JULY
Weed new lawns, if necessary.

AUGUST
Sow seed if not done in spring. Frequently mow established lawn. Leave the cuttings of final cut to help retain moisture.

SEPTEMBER
Raise mower blades. Rake lawn to remove dead lawn and weed runners. Top dress with slow-acting organic fertilizer. Late summer is a good time to lay turf.

OCTOBER
Re-seed bare patches. Fill-in hollows and top dress. Turf can be laid until December.

NOVEMBER
Remove fallen leaves regularly with a twig broom or lawn sweeper.

DECEMBER
Give special attention to uneven lawn edges; turn turf at worn edges.

The garden framework ~ paths to pergolas

On the right path

Paths are vital for easy, practical movement around the garden. You can push a wheelbarrow more smoothly and tread less dirt into the house when paths and pavings are wisely placed. The best paths give more than practical convenience. They are landscaped for pleasure too, out of materials that please the eye of the passer-by and plants that intrigue or enchant him.

Make paths as wide as possible. In sunny, dry or well-drained areas of the garden, lawn paths are ideal and in shady damper places you could use cobblestones, pebbles or gravel. If gravel paths are near the house be careful to choose a medium grade—fine gravel sticks to shoes and large pebbles are not very comfortable to walk on. Lawn paths on the other hand are a pleasure to walk on but are not ideal for paths where there is much traffic in wet weather.

Concrete is a versatile material for path-laying. It does not have to be straight. It can be laid in asymmetrical curves, like giant tear drops, or in a wide and gently curved arc. The advantage of tear drop or stepping circles of concrete is that plants can be grown between the sections to

Ready-made paving slabs are edged with river stones and pebbles. Pebbles and flower beds are separated by rounded edging strips.

Above: *A path of bricks laid herringbone fashion is set between wide flower borders.*

Below: *Stone steps cloaked with aubrietias, trailing perennials that like the sun.*

soften the outline of the concrete by overlapping its edges.

There are interesting finishes that can be given to concrete. Various aggregates can give it a texture which ranges from a polished surface like terrazzo, which has to be professionally done, to rougher or more pebbly finishes that you could probably do yourself with a bag of ready-mix concrete and some water-worn stones, pebbles or gravel. The beach and river provide beautiful pebbles which you can make into your own personal mosaics, laid in sections in the concrete path.

A path near the house can be laid with alternate squares of concrete or quarry tiles and pebble mosaics.

Concrete can be coloured but do not forget that the colour needs to be muted and natural looking as it could dominate the garden with a garish intensity when the sun shines on it.

Concrete set in curves and softened by plants can be quite as charming as stone flags or bricks. Circular stepping stones of concrete with pebble beds and creeping plants between them make an unusual path across a front garden to the door.

Bricks, flagging and paving stones are easier for the amateur to lay and have the advantage of being able to be lifted and set in another place if the layout of the garden is later changed.

Before you lay a path make sure the foundation is a secure one. Bricks can be laid on a bed of sand or fine cinders, followed by a 2·5cm (1in) layer of liquid cement. Lay the bricks—or you can use flagstones—far enough apart to allow more liquid cement to be poured between them.

Patterns of bricks can be varied in the laying, from herringbone to basket-weave. If you have a large old tree, lay the bricks in circles at the base of the tree trunk—it makes a perfect place for a seat.

Ready-made paving slabs are again easy for the amateur to lay providing he has a strong back. Concrete paving slabs can be laid as stepping stones on gravel. Otherwise lay them on a bed of sand. Because the squares are factory even, they lend themselves to interesting symmetrically-shaped paths, with plantings between them.

Paving slabs of natural stone are more expensive and are better for large-paved areas, being softer-coloured and more natural looking.

You can use concrete or stone for path edgings or as stepping stones through the lawn to a seat.

Sawn timber discs treated with a wood preservative also make good stepping stones across gravel or pebbles.

Left: *Wide, well-proportioned steps give a spacious look and provide easier walking.*

If you lay loose pebbles or gravel as a path, it is really essential to have properly built-up edges to the path to hold the gravel in place, or it will continually wash away leaving you with dirt paths and gravel garden beds. When the coping or built-up edges are finished, fill the path with any hard dry fill for about 7·5–10cm (3–4in) and then put the gravel on top. Roll it to compress in place.

Pink or white marble chips also make a good-looking pathway but like gravel needs laying on dry fill and needs to be at least 5cm (2in) in depth to discourage weeds from growing. For immaculate gravel you need some weedkiller or the old-fashioned remedy of strong salt and water. Or you can lay the gravel or chips over a layer of a thick outdoor-grade of polythene.

A little more permanent than gravel is tarmac or asphalt which will last for years if well-laid. For those who are not fond of its blackish colour, there are different colours available or pale chips can be embedded in it.

Path plantings

Many of the rockery plants that climb, spill, trail or creep will also suit path planting. So will prostrate shrubs that hang over stark corners of masonry shrouding them in green, gold or silver. Many of the herbs such as chamomile and thyme do not mind being occasionally walked on.

Edging plants include alyssum, lobelia, candytuft, dwarf nasturtiums and French marigolds. Creeping Jenny (*Lysimachia nummularia*) has buttercup yellow flowers and will grow in full sun or part shade. You can grow alpine strawberries along the path.

Grow some of the lovely fragrant plants beside paths, mock orange blossom, daphne, violets, belladonna lilies, and the fragrant annuals—mignonette, wallflower, dianthus and carnations.

Steps

Steps take you where you are going but they can do it in a straight no-nonsense sort of way or they can do it gracefully. Many ground-covering plants do very well against the warmth of stone or concrete.

Try to give steps an interesting point of arrival—such as a small garden of herbs, massed tubs of plants, a special weeping shrub or tree beside the door.

Plants that should not be planted near steps and paths are ones with long arching canes that reach out to slap the passer-by or arch above in the rain quivering with more raindrops than you care to collect. Plants that prickle or sting, give some people allergies, are poisonous and inviting to children, or drop messy, slippery fruit

and blossoms are all ones that should be banished from the by-ways of the garden.

Fences

Screens and fences protect from the wind, mark the boundary, shelter plants, support climbers, turn open space into a sun trap, and give the garden privacy and orderly divisions.

Place windscreens where they will filter the wind but not stop the gentle summer breezes. The solid fence makes the best privacy screen but the slatted or partly open fence or wall makes the best wind-break. The speed of wind should be slowed down and broken up but not completely blocked, for this makes the wind rise and swoop down further on in the garden.

It is essential that a fence should be in good repair. Even the simplest board fence looks sturdy and attractive if standing up-right, and looking firm. A fence does not have the masonry strength of a wall, any plants still clinging to it on its way down will hasten its end and theirs. So if you are having a fence built, see that posts are strong, 10–15cm (4–6in) square, and set at close enough intervals. They can be con-crete or timber but all timber should be treated with wood preservative. A solidly-built frame around a timber fence often improves its attractive look and its struc-tural strength. This particularly applies to a fence of trellis or laths.

Screens and fences can be constructed in many ways.

Light trellis work makes a romantic screen but it must be well-constructed and properly stained or painted. Trellis makes a good wind and sun filter and provides support for climbers or creepers.

Slatted timber screens or fences also filter the sun and wind and let in light; 10 × 2·5cm (4 × 1in) laths of redwood set in framework are very handsome. Fences do not have to be one long line along the boundary. They can be shorter screens, stepped in such a way that the far one is a boundary marker, the next one hides the

Above: *A world of blues—bugle, helichrysum, stachys and houseleeks flank the path.*

Above: *Small-scale steps for a small sunken garden planted with alpines, herbs and shrubs.*

Left: *A pathway curving out of sight gives interest to a garden.*

Above: *Interwoven wooden fencing erected in units makes a good privacy screen.*

Above: *A paling fence backed by a well-kept hedge is a good boundary barrier.*

Above: *Wattle fencing is rustic-looking. It would make a good screen for a utility area.*

Left: *Concrete grille blocks can be built into an attractive screen wall and windbreak.*

Below: *Pre-cast walling blocks are particularly suitable for low walling like this.*

utility or dustbin area, the next supports perhaps a beautiful climber.

Basket weave fencing makes a handsome privacy screen, particularly if stained an attractive colour. There is also a woven wattle fence that gives a rustic look, or a cleft chestnut fence that looks practical and attractive and can be bought in rolls. Look on the market for other ready-made fence units that you can put up yourself.

Horizontal boarding can be laid in overlapping or slatted patterns or like a ranch fence. It looks strong, gives a long and pleasant perspective to a garden and supports climbing plants well. It is not so suitable for a formal or small town garden.

Most fences have a mood conveyed by their design and the materials used. Half the success of a good fence is to choose one that suits your garden atmosphere.

Walls
Walls give privacy, close off one area of the garden from another, and give shelter for a court or terrace.

Walls weather in time but not all are made of handsome materials or laid imaginatively and few look better bare than with plants against them.

Plants show off their shapes against walls and soften the hard look of masonry with branches of cool green. Many grow better for the shelter of the wall.

There are lovely creepers that turn red and gold in the autumn, like the Virginia creeper, and put out their furled red tips in spring, only to change to brilliant green. Against sheltering walls you can grow tubs of plants, climbers, creepers, espalier shrubs or trees. A surprising number of shrubs and trees will take shaping including camellias and cotoneasters (see chapter on fruit for shaping fruit trees).

Cotoneaster lactea and pyracanthas are both evergreen, with brilliant autumn berries. *Chaenomeles japonica* (also called Cydonia or flowering quince) is a deciduous shrub which needs to be persuaded to the right shape. To do this, leave the plant unpruned until autumn and then shorten the lateral shoots well back. Also cut or pinch back forward-pointing growth. In a small garden bed by a sun-lit wall yellow *Euphorbia epithymoides*, scarlet chaenomeles and purple-blue grape hyacinths make a brilliant April trio.

Plant climbers and espalier-shaped shrubs about 22·5cm (9in) from the wall base so that roots are not cramped against the wall foundations. See that the earth is well-prepared before you plant, and well-fed.

Plants and trees against walls are among the first to dry out in warm or windy weather, so water thoroughly about once a week in dry weather and mulch over moist soil during the summer months.

Pergolas

Some of the most beautiful plants are climbing ones. There is wisteria, with its lavender or white spikes which hang like garlands, or honeysuckle, with its very fragrant creamy, red-flushed flowers, or clematis and the climbing rose.

Pergolas will support plants like these and provide a useful link between the house and garden. A pergola displays a climbing plant to perfection, allowing it to form an archway of greenery or to hang out a canopy of flowers.

A pergola must be well-constructed with strong posts and joists. It is a professional building job, unless you are an experienced handyman with posts being firmly founded in concrete.

The timber can be dressed or finished—giving a clean-cut, rather modern look, or undressed, whereupon it looks more rustic, more peasant-style for the true cottage garden. For this, you could use pillars of round, natural trunks.

Height of the pergola needs to be about 2·5–3m (8–10ft) depending on what will climb it, and whether a lot of room is needed for hanging flowers. If the pergola is built against the side of the house, the height might be more determined by the architectural look of the addition. The posts should be sunk 60cm (2ft) into the ground. Keep in mind that a pergola has to carry a lot of weight when the climber

Above: *Pergola posts spanned by trellis supports and climbing roses make effective screen.*

Above: *Overlapping chestnut fencing supported by concrete posts.*

Below: *Polygonum baldschuanicum is a quick-growing climber for pergolas.*

Above: *Thunbergia alata, black-eyed Susan, an evergreen and warm-climate twiner.*

Above: *Passiflora caerulea, passion flower, is a beautiful climber that needs a warm wall.*

Left: *Clematis viticella 'Ville de Lyon' rambling over a pergola. Clematis likes cool roots, heads in the sun and fertile soil. Prune back in late winter.*

matures and if heavily covered will create considerable wind resistance.

Space the upright posts about 2–2·5m (6–8ft) apart and the joists, or crosspieces, over the top at the same distance but, if you like, extending by 30cm (1ft) or so beyond the post line. The top plates which sit on the posts, or piers, and support the joists, must be firmly attached with bolts or something similarly strong to the top of the posts.

Once the main structure is built, then you can add stays or bracing pieces of wood to give extra rigidity and provide more climbing places for plants or hanging baskets.

One of the pleasures of a pergola is the way it casts shadows in the sunlight and filters bright light. If you want to increase this filtering you can fill in some of the roofing area with slatted timber.

Do not add too many extra pieces of wood to the main structure or the effect will be confusing; a pergola should look simple, strong and permanent.

See chapter on 'Learn the language of gardening' for planting lists and cultivation method for climbing plants to cover walls, fences and pergolas.

Hedges

Perhaps the softest and most harmonious screen for a garden is the living one of a hedge. A hedge can shut out the wind, screen you from neighbours, divide off one part of the garden from the next—and as a bonus produce brilliant colourings or sweet blossoms. If you need a hedge for privacy then it has to be compact enough not to be seen through. A good idea is to double plant, putting more shrubs in front of the hedge line or staggering two rows of the same hedge plant.

Give serious thought to an unclipped hedge if you prefer it. It does not give quite the same orderly look but if the plant is well-chosen it adds its own natural beauty to the garden.

A hedge planted with a mixture of evergreen and deciduous shrubs giving various shapes and colours can be like your own hedgerow, a haven for animals and birds, and planted at the base with all the hedgerow flowers. Hawthorn, holly, hornbeam, elm and hazel are one possible hedgerow planting. Common hawthorn can be raised from seed, but it needs to winter outside between layers of coarse sand (this is called stratifying) for a year.

A hedge, being hopefully a permanent structure, needs a good start in life.

Prepare the site before the plants arrive from the nursery and this can be done at any time during the winter unless the

Below: *The common box, Buxus sempervirons, is a good evergreen hedging plant.*

Below: *Berberis thunbergii atropurpurea grows to 2m, makes a fine deciduous hedge.*

ground is too wet or deeply frosted. Mark the line of the hedge with a garden line— that is, a stake driven into the right position at either end and a straight string stretched between them. Now dig a trench along the line one-spit deep and from 30–120cm (1–4ft) wide. Remove this good topsoil to the side and break up the subsoil, adding to it plenty of humus-making material such as peat, compost and farmyard manure. Replace the topsoil, breaking it up well and incorporating two handfuls of bonemeal to every metre of length. Leave the soil to settle for a couple of weeks or so.

When the plants arrive from the nursery, heel them in at one end of the trench you have dug, ie temporarily plant them at a slant so that the sap does not rise quickly.

Beginning at the other end, dig the trench again about 30cm (1ft) deep and the width for the plant to go in comfortably— and plant each hedge plant at intervals of about 45cm (18in). Each plant will touch its neighbour in about two years.

If you want a very compact hedge you can reduce the 45cm (1½ft) intervals to 30cm (1ft).

Water the plants well. Never let the plants become dry. Their first springtime is critical.

Good hedge backgrounds are made by yew, holly, cypress and the conifers— *Chamaecyparis lawsoniana*, American arbor-vitae or *Thuja occidentalis*, *Thuja plicata*

Below: *A mixed hedge of copper beach, yew, box and hornbeam gives a tapestry effect.*

Above: *No plant makes a more charming, low, flowering hedge than lavender.*

Above: *Rose-covered pergola is an eye-catching feature beside garden steps.*

Left: *A hedge of Fuchsia magellanica flowers in summer, giving good screening. It is rich in colour and gives a good hedge shape.*

(syn. *T. lobbii*), Monterey pine or *Cupressus macrocarpa*, Chinese honeysuckle—*Lonicera nitida*, the evergreen barberries *Berberis darwinii*, orange-yellow flowers followed by plum-coloured berries, height 2–2·5m (6–8ft) and *B. x stenophylla*, golden-yellow flowers and about the same height. The last two are trimmed when flowers fade.

Rose hedges are satisfactory when you do not need garden privacy in the winter as they become more or less seen-through. Shrub roses will make a hedge. So will tall-growing floribundas planted about 60cm (2ft) apart. 'Iceberg' and 'Queen Elizabeth' are two varieties. Hybrid musks are another possibility for a hedge which is fragrant and beautiful. Other deciduous hedges for summer privacy and display are flowering currant (ribes), forsythia, hawthorn or beech. Beech hedges can be either green, copper or purple-leaved.

In an old garden you might have overgrown hedges of blackthorn, hornbeam, myrobalan plum and hawthorn (quickthorn). You can rejuvenate them by hard pruning during the winter months.

A fragrant low hedge can be made of lavender if you want to divide one area of the garden from another. Rosemary makes a good hedge for the herb garden.

Where you need a windbreak

A dense screen against the wind is not as effective as a lighter more open one. If the wind can be filtered through open-work fence or loose hedge or trees, its strength is broken down and it moves gently through past your garden plants. A solid fence, wall or hedge forces the wind upwards over the structure and it then swoops down to the garden with increased force.

So hedges and plants make good wind-filtering screens provided they do not mind the wind themselves. They also allow more light to plants on the sheltered side.

Bamboo makes a good shelter belt against wind, so try *Arundinaria nitida*, *Phyllostachys nigra* and *P. viridi-glaucescens*. Give them a mulch of compost in spring plus 25g (1oz) of sulphate of ammonia per square metre. Plant 90–120cm (3–4ft) apart in May, and trim at the same time of the year.

The daisy bushes are good wind-hardy shrubs. *Olearia x haastii* has small grey foliage and white daisy flowers. *Olearia macrodonta* has glossy grey-green leaves with silvery backs and white flowers. The first grows from 150–240cm (5–8ft) and the second up to 3m (15ft). Both flourish in chalky or sandy loam.

Monthly calendar

JANUARY
Clear algae and moss from paving. Prepare site and let settle before planting new hedge.

FEBRUARY
Examine climbers' supports. Complete repairs. Kill weeds before they grow on paths and driveways. Apply light dressing on soil in preparation for new hedge.

MARCH
Put plants and seeds in wall crevices. Plant evergreen or deciduous hedges. Protect young hedge on exposed sites with wattle hurdling. Lightly clip rose hedges.

APRIL
Lay new paths. Prune back flowering shoots of hedges that have flowered. Hoe around newly-planted shrubs.

MAY
Check fence support posts. Make sure supports for climbing plants are strong enough. Clip fast-growing formal hedges. Spray overhead and mulch evergreens and conifers.

JUNE
Flower borders can be improved by addition of perimeter path or edging not more than 15cm (6in) wide. Spray rose hedges against black spot, mildew and greenfly.

JULY
Plants spreading over walls need close attention, especially climbing roses. Feed well. Mulch newly-planted hedges. Leave spring-planted hedges untrimmed the first year. Trim other hedges that have flowered to a general wedge shape; widen at base, taper at top.

AUGUST
Lay paths. Treat soil base with weedkiller first. Take care with lavender hedge pruning. Lightly trim new growth only.

SEPTEMBER
Consider constructing raised beds. Complete annual trimming of mature hedges. Plant evergreen hedging shrubs at the end of the month. Prepare site in advance.

OCTOBER
New spring-planted beech, hornbeam and quickthorn should be drastically cut back to encourage hedge with well-clothed base.

NOVEMBER
Planting sites for deciduous hedging should be deeply dug and well-supplied with manure or compost. From now until March, deciduous hedges can be planted.

DECEMBER
If considering new hedges, consider berry-bearing ones. They look at their best now.

The pleasure of a rock garden

If you want to give a flat garden more interest or improve the slope of a small hillside garden build a rockery.

The creeping, climbing, trailing, cushion-like, and spillover plants are often called alpines, although not all of them come from mountain places. Some are crevice plants, liking very dry conditions with little soil and are happy to grow in the cracks of walls or rocks. Others like shade and a well-drained stony soil. Others still like to be in the sun but with their roots kept in cool places under stones.

The attraction of rockery plants is their miniature beauty and their year-round colouring for many are perennials. Together they can form an intricate and rich pattern of colour and shape, changing from month to month.

Rockeries should look weathered, natural and not like just a heap of stone.

The natural position of a rock is to have the worn weathered sides uppermost and the side where it was cut or lifted from the earth, still face downwards. On a natural rock face you can see how the rock is stratified in the same way across several rocks. The rocks in a rock garden should also be laid on their natural bed with the rock seams or grain running the same way, and with the faces of the rock sloping in the same direction.

Before you start to plan your rock garden, study other people's efforts. In many parks you can find expertly-built rockeries.

You must have a well-drained area. If you have a natural bank or ridge then it is probably well-drained unless the soil is very heavy. If it is really boggy land, then you might be wise to consider a rock pool and bog plants rather than a rockery. However, you can drain the site by building a soakaway pit under it or a drain about 60cm (2ft) down and 60cm (2ft) in from the front of the rockery. On normal or sandy soil you should not have drainage problems even for a flat-site rockery.

It is harder to construct a rockery with a natural look on a flat site. You could start by excavating to 30cm (1ft) deep and filling the base with about 12·5cm (5in) of coarse ash or rubble. Build over this a gentle mound of earth, using sandy loam.

If you buy the soil make sure it is free of weeds. Eradicating weeds from among rocks is a very hard task.

Building a rockery on a slope is much easier because your bank of earth is already there and does not have to be made by you. If the bank is rather steep, then rockery stones should be angled well back into the slope to retain the earth and direct water back into the slope. On a gentle ridge of land you can use just a series of well-anchored flat stones, dividing one part of the garden from the next.

Or you can make a slightly different kind of rockery, by outlining small terraced beds with stone, as shown in the step-by-step pictures. Decide whether you prefer this or the large weathered rocks placed more at random with planting pockets between them. To some extent it depends on the local stone available and the plants you want to use. Terraced beds suit massed azaleas, for example, whereas the natural boulder look is ideal for spillovers, trailers and creepers. For these, some planting pockets must be deep and some shallow, some filled with gravel and earth and some with earth.

Remember whatever your design, that you are building a rock garden so the rocks need to be seen too. Do not get them completely covered with mounding growth. Keep some beautiful faces of rock entirely free of plants and leave some rock outlines clear.

Rocks for the rockery are best found on your own land or taken from a local quarry because they need to be naturally worn and weathered and to be in keeping with the local terrain. It is also far cheaper to use the nearest possible source of stone. Man-made materials such as concrete or brick cannot be used for a rock garden because they cannot pass for a natural outcrop of rock. They are good materials suitable for drives, paths and raised beds but not for rockeries.

All rocks must be embedded well into the soil. If they are unstable they can be quite dangerous. Do not place rocks on end.

If you are stepping natural boulders or rocks up a slope, about three-quarters of

A rock garden of regional sandstone. Approx 10 tonnes (10 tons) of stone was used.

Above and below: *The stone is taken to the site and levered into the right position.*

The stone is bedded firmly into place so that the natural stratification lines on the rocks run in the same horizontal direction.

Last step of the actual building of the rockery is to brush the stones clean of soil. The stones should show clearly in any rockery.

The steps through the rockery are completed first so that access to the rest of the rockery, while working on it, is made easier.

The rockery is now complete before the planting begins. This is a more formal rockery layout, with terraced beds.

The topsoil taken from the rockery site is used for beds when the building of the rockery is completed.

Shrubs are planted first to form a background or framework for the alpines and other rockery plants.

the rock should be embedded in the bank with only a quarter to an eighth of it showing clear. Lie it on its broadest part. No higher rock should overhang a lower rock. The rocks should be following the line of the slope and sloping back into it—so that rain runs back into the slope and soil is not washed down and away. The rocks must support and retain the earth in the planting pockets. If you are using an expensive and rather beautiful rock you can expose a bit more of it, providing you are certain it is absolutely safely anchored with earth rammed well around it.

Pebbles can often be successfully combined with this sort of rockery, arranged to help hold the earth, or dropped in a heap at the base of some plant or at the feet of a small stone statue. Use water-worn pebbles with beauty of their own from a loch, river or beach.

If you are building terraced beds, then each level of retaining rock should be solidly based, with a third of each stone buried in the soil in front of it. This means the planting bed in front of the stone will cover one-third of the stone and the planting bed above and behind it will cover about seven-eighths of the stone.

Soil and planting

A good mixture of soil for a rock garden is 4 parts loam to 2 parts organic matter to 1½ parts grit, the grit being fine stone chippings, gravel or sharp sand. Some plants that like a well-drained soil, such as the gentians, can have more grit added to their planting pocket. Dust the rockery soil with bonemeal and mix it well in with the other ingredients.

As you fill in the beds or planting pockets and place the rockery stones, see that there are comfortable platforms of stone or stepping stones for you to use when you plant and care for the rockery plants. A rockery garden does not take very much looking after once it is established but it is very annoying to find that to get to one plant you have to tread on another. The area of the stepping stones can be covered with pebbles, chips or gravel where some plants will gradually encroach and others will seed.

Do not choose plants that multiply very fast by means of rhizomes—stems running horizontally beneath the earth surface. These will take over and be very hard to remove. Rampant-growing plants will also take too much work to keep in check. Plants to avoid are snow-in-summer (*Cerastium tomentosum*), the creeping *Veronica filiformis*, *Helxine solierolii* and *Ajuga reptans*.

When choosing alyssum, aubrieta and arabis, keep in mind that they give a gay display for a short time early in the year

Above: *Terraced rock garden now awaits plants to transform it.* **Below:** *Saxifrages grown in pots are being planted out now that they are in flower.*

Alpines for special purposes

Full sun and a well-drained soil

Achillea	Cytisus	Hypericum	Phlox
Aethionema	Dianthus	Helichrysum	Potentilla
Alyssum	Draba	Helianthemum	*Saponaria ocymoides*
Antennaria	*Dryas octopetala*	Iberis	Sedum
Armeria	Erysimum	Linum	Sempervivum
Aubrieta	*Gyposphila repens*	Oenothera	Thymus
Campanula garganica	Hebe	Penstemon	Zauschneria

Shade or half-shade

In Scotland and northern England these plants may be grown in almost full sun as long as there is sufficient moisture.

Anemone nemorosa	Epimedium	*Omphalodes*	Shortia
Astilbe	Gaultheria	*cappadocica*	Thalictrum
Cassiope	Hepatica	Primula	Trillium
Cyclamen	Meconopsis	Saxifraga	Trollius
Dodecatheon	Mimulus	(Kabschia section)	

For a lime-free soil

Andromeda	Calluna	*Gentiana sino-ornata*	Rhodohypoxis
Androsace carnea	Epigaea	Lewisia	Shortia
Arcterica	Erica (most)	*Lithospermum diffusum*	*Trifolium alpinum*
Cassiope	Gaultheria	Rhododendron	*Viola pedata*

Lime-loving or lime-tolerating

Achillea	Cyclamen	*Gentiana dinarica*	*Primula auricula*
Acanthus	*Cypripedium calceolus*	Gyposphila	*Primula marginata*
Aethionema	Dianthus	Hepatica	Saxifraga, (with a few
Aubrieta	*Dryas octopetala*	Helleborus	exceptions)
Carlina	*Gentiana clusii*	Leontopodium	

Above: *The double daisy, Bellis perennis flore pleno, is a neat carpeting plant.*

Above: *A rock garden in early spring. Choice of plants should give continual colour.*

Below: *Very steep rockery is planted with crevice clumps of saxifrage, phlox, dianthus.*

Above: *Sempervivums or houseleeks flourish in sunny crevices without much earth.*

but look indifferent for the rest of it—so do not allow them too much space.

Some of the crevice-growing plants are more easily planted while you are placing the stones.

Shrubs to be planted first

Most rockeries have some dwarf shrubs planted with alpines to form evergreen backgrounds, provide seasonal change and give height. There are many to choose from and they are planted first so that you can judge their overall effect. Consider some of these plants—dwarf rhododendrons, Kurume azaleas, daphne, *Lavender spica*, rosemary 'Miss Jessops', miniature roses, New Zealand flax, *Cotoneaster microphyllus thymifolius*, and among the evergreens, *Juniperus communis* 'compressa' which is silvery, and *J. horizontalis* or *Chamaecyparis obtusa* 'Juniperoides' or *C. obtusa* 'Pygmaea'. Fuchsias, dwarf broom, hebe and many of the ericas are other choices. Once you begin to plant the small shrubs and dwarf trees, the outline of the rockery then takes shape. You need to grade the heights and contrast upright growth against spreading growth.

Dwarf shrubs for the rock garden, small beds, ground covers, banks:

Berberis stenophylla 'Corallina Compacta'
Ceanothus pumilus
Cotoneaster microphyllus thymifolius
Cytisus X beanii or X kewensis
C. procumbens
Daphne blagayana
D. cneorum
D. collina
D. retusa
Fuchsia 'Tom Thumb'
X Halimiocistus sahucii
Helichrysum selago 'Major'
H. pimeleoides 'Glaucocaerulea'
H. albicans
Hypericum moserianum 'Tricolor'
Potentilla fruticosa mandshurica
P. f. 'Munstead Dwarf'
Prunus prostrata
Dwarf Rhododendrons, particularly:
   impeditum, calostrotum, campylogynum, racemosum
   'Forrest's Dwarf', 'Carmen', 'Chink', 'Jenny'
   ('Creeping Jenny'), 'Blue Tit'

Dwarf conifers

Abies balsamea 'Hudsonia'
Cedrus libani 'Comte de Dijon'
Chamaecyparis lawsoniana 'Pygmaea Argentea',
   C. l. 'Rogersii', 'Minima Glauca'
C. obtusa 'Nana'
C. pisifera 'Boulevard'
Cryptomeria japonica 'Nana' ('Bandi-sugi')
C. j. 'Vilmoriniana'
Juniperus communis 'Compressa'
J. chinensis 'Procumbens'
J. horizontalis 'Bar Harbor'
Picea mariana 'Nana'
P. pungens 'Procumbens'
Pinus pumila
P. mugo 'Pumilio'
Podocarpus nivalis
Thuya plicata 'Rogersii'

Left: *Primula vulgaris spills over rocks. Many primulas are native mountain flowers.*

Above: *Iris histrioides 'Lady Strawley's Form' flowers early, grows about 30cm high.*

Above: *Flowerheads of Pterocephalus parnassi, a low-growing perennial for the rockery.* **Below:** *Raymonda myconii has a rosette of crinkled leaves and purplish flowers.*

Above: *The perennial, Adonis vernalis, is an excellent rockery plant.*

Above: *Thuya orientalis minima glauca, a dwarf conifer with good colouring.*

Left: *Pinguicula alpina, butterwort, is insectivorous. Grows in a rather dry place.*

Above: *Rockery plant-mates, left, Alyssum saxatile and right, iberis, white candytuft.*

Right: *In this dry crevice dianthus and sedum create good contrast. Both like sun and a sandy loam, each have many good varieties.*

Above: *Aubrieta deltoidea loves lime and sun. Cut back hard after flowering.*

Below: *Ranunculus lyallii, a rock plant from New Zealand, with flowers spanning 10cm.*

Above: *The bright purple flowers of Gentiana septemfida. Flowers mid to late summer.*

Below: *Edraianthus serpyllifolius major, a prostrate grower liking gritty soil, and sun.*

Plants to keep in mind

For a cool corner, the hardy cyclamen tubers can be planted in gritty soil rich in organic matter. Cover the tubers with about 3·5cm (1½in) of soil. For a warm spring, plant *C. repandum*, with its pink flowers; for summer *C. europaeum* with fragrant soft pink to rose-red flowers; for autumn there are the pure white or deep pink flowers of *C. neopolitanum*. When the leaves die down uncover the top 3·5cm (1½in) of soil and replace with rich, manured soil.

The dianthus family will come out with summer flowers. This is a huge family including perennials. Try *D. arvernensis*, ash-grey pads and deep pink or pure white flowers, *D. deltoides* 'Flashing lights', crimson, long flowering and 15cm (6in) tall, and *D.* 'Little Jock' a lovely hybrid with pink flowers on short stems. *D. neglectus* does not like lime and has large pink flowers on short stems. *D. alpinus* has rose to crimson flowers and grows from 7·5–10cm (3–4in).

Iberis sempervirens is a perennial candytuft that likes a sunny place. *I.* 'Snowflake' has superb white flowers. It grows 30cm (1ft) in height. In the small rockery you could plant instead 'Little Gem', which is only half its height.

In shady planting pockets plant some bulbs, including *Erythronium* 'White Beauty' with cream-white lily-like flowers on 22·5cm (9in) stems. The related dog's tooth violet *E. dens-canis* has lovely mottled leaves and rose-purple flowers. There are various iris you could choose but you particularly want the winter-flowering *Iris unguicularis* (syn. *I. stylosa*), the Algerian iris.

For lime-free soil there are autumn-flowering Asian gentians such as *G. sino-ornata*, *G. farreri* and their hybrid *G. x macaulayi*. They flower from late August onwards into the depth of winter, but they will not tolerate a chalky soil.

The sun roses or helianthemums give you plenty of choice and summer-long flowers. They range from 15–45cm (6–15in) high, are evergreen and like a sunny bank or planting pocket. It sometimes helps to trim them lightly with shears in late summer to keep them compact. There are yellow,

Above: *A firm, cushion-forming plant, Saxifraga x jenkinsae, growing on scree and rock.*

Left: *Campanula fragilis, a tufted perennial for a gritty soil, sunny position. Grows to about 15cm. There are many more varieties.*

Below: *Dwarf genista, broom, is easily grown and excellent for dry banks or stony ground.*

white or pink flowers. Other plants helped by a light trim after flowering are the dwarf hypericums. They demand full sun.

Try these sort of combinations for an attractive look—*Festuca glauca*, a bristly 15cm (6in) blue-grey grass, with velvety green *Raoulia* to carpet the earth and creep into ledges, clumps of ericas, creeping thymes, bronze New Zealand flax and dwarf, golden juniper. Or a yellowish-green carpet of *Sagina* with its tiny white flowers contrasting with *Hypericum reptans* which has bright yellow flowers and the pink flowers of Lady's pincushion, the thrift or sea-pink, *Armeria maritima*.

The crevice plants

Saxifraga lingulata, now known as *S. callosa* is one of the huge saxifrage or rockfoil genus and comes from the Maritime Alps. It forms silver-grey rosettes and then little offset rosettes, geometric in their neatness. A sun-loving plant, in summer it produces white flowers on 30cm (1ft) long stems. *Ramonda*, from the Pyrenees and Alps produces lavender, white or pink flowers in early summer. *Haberlea* likes to grow in vertical fissures in the shade and to be well-watered in summer; *Primula marginata* also likes a cool place or shady bank. *Gypsophila*, a Mediterranean native,

Above: *Eriophorum angustifolium, cotton grass, likes shallow pool edge or boggy ground.*

Right: *Variegated ivy, a form of Hedera helix, climbs or trails over rocks or walls but needs keeping in check.*

Below: *Sea pinks, Armeria maritima, look lovely massed in the rock garden.*

microphylla, bronze-green foliage and crimson, spiny seed heads and *A. novae zealandiae*, a bronze or green ground cover studded in summer with red-brown, short stemmed burrs.

The achilleas flower in early summer. *A. tomentosa aurea* 'Grandiflora' has ferny, grey-green leaves and short-stemmed golden blossoms. *A.* x 'King Edward' (or *A. lewisii*) is even more dainty with lemon yellow flowers. *A. prichardii* has silver leaves and white flowers.

There are many campanulas (bell flowers) to choose from, flowering from mid to late summer. Plant *C. cochlearifolia* (syn. *C. pusilla*) bearing blue or white bells on 7·5cm (3in) stems. It threads its way about but not destructively. *C. carpatica* has large, showy flowers and can spread 30cm (1ft) high and wide. There is also *C. portenschlagiana* (*C. muralis*) to provide a purple carpet and *C. garganica* to trail along crevices.

Liking a cool position is *Chrysogonum virginianum* with golden flowers appearing continuously over a slow carpet of leaves, from mid-summer into the autumn. Also look for some of the genus *Dianthus* family to give you delicious drifts of flowers.

Dryas octopetala drapes its woody stems over a warm rock and carries dark green leaves and large flowers like those of a white dog rose.

Once established, *Geranium cinereum subcaulescens* will cover a metre of ground with a brilliant mass of clear carmine-red, dark-centred flowers from May until the end of summer. *G. renardii* is a good contrast, with lobed leaves forming a green velvet mat and ash-grey flowers lined with a darker colour. *G. dalmaticum* is deep pink although there is a white form. These are the cranesbills, the true geraniums. They like a sunny, well-drained position.

Sheltered from full sunlight *Houstonia caerulea* is a charming blue-flowered creeper, carrying flowers on 7·5cm (3in) stems in May and June.

Potentilla x *tonguei* spreads outwards and carries from May until October a succession of crimson-blotched, apricot-coloured flowers. It grows 7·5cm (3in) high and likes plenty of moisture, whereas *P. megalantha*, forms mounds and has large yellow flowers.

Carpets made of various forms of thyme, *Thymus serpyllum* (*T. drucei* or *praecox*), in sunny places will form a fragrant cloak for small bulbs.

Among the thrifts is *Armeria caespitosa* which forms dark green compact hummocks studded with pink flowers. Alpine phlox are indispensible forming mats of countless flowers but these are spring flowerers so do not give them too much space. Try *P. subulata*.

is available in lovely dwarf varieties which take to a sunny scree. Dwarf dianthus or pinks are fragrant. *Sedum* or stonecrops is another large genus with a choice of colours, habit and flowering season, and one or two black sheep, disastrously rampant. Try however, *Sedum* 'Ruby Glow' and consider *S. spathulifolium* (with fleshy leaves and golden flowers) and *S. cauticolum* (with crimson flowers) for other places in the rockery. *Lewisia* loves moist sunny crevices, comes from North America and is a pretty pink or white-flowered plant. Another succulent (with fleshy leaves) that does not mind half shade is

Chiastophyllum, and the mountain houseleek (sempervivum) likes sunny chinks in the rocks. *Erinus alpinus* is a crevice plant for sun or light shade. It has pure white, red or pink flowers and seeds itself, often very freely.

Carpeters, trailers and cushion plants
Acaena is a genus of carpeting plants from New Zealand and South America which should not be planted near small plants because it will over-run them. They cover the ground growing and flourishing in chinks. Try *A. buchananii* with pea-green leaves and yellow-brown seed heads, *A.*

The following plants are suitable for late-flowering colour, shady places, hot, dry positions; or gravelly places in the rock garden:

Late-flowering—*Polygonum vaccinifolium, Solidago brachystachys, Sternbergia lutea, Saxifraga fortunei, Gentiana sino-ornata, Sedum* 'Ruby Glow' and *Potentilla x tonguei.*

Shade—cassiopes, ramondas, haberlea, 'mossy' saxifrages, *Maianthemum bi-folium,* astilbes, cyclamen, *Linnaea borealis, Omphalodes verna,* trilliums, *Tiarella cordifolia* and *Mentha requienii.*

Hot, dry positions—*Zauschneria californica,* sedums, sempervivums, *Acantholimon glumaceum,* helianthemums, hypericums, cytisuses, genistas, *Lithospermum* 'Grace Ward' (no lime) and alpine penstemons.

Moraine or scree—This is very gritty soil. Any cushion-forming saxifrages, *Edraianthus pumilio,* cushion dianthus, *Silene acaulis, Minuartia* (syn. *Alsine*) *verna, Anacyclus depressus, Crassula sedifolia, Erodium chamaedrioides* 'Roseum', *Gentiana verna, Helichrysum milfordae* (syn. *marginatum*) and *Ranunculus montanus.*

A beginner's choice of 50 plants suitable for the rock garden

Achillea 'King Edward'
Aethionema pulchellum
Androsace primuloides
Antennaria dioica rosea
Armeria maritima 'Vindictive'
Aster alpinus
Campanula cochlearifolia
C. garganica
C. portenschlagiana
Chiastophyllum oppositifolium
Cyclamen neapolitanum
Dianthus arvernensis
D. deltoides
Dryas octopetala
Epilobium glabellum
Erinus alpinus
Genista pilosa
Gentiana septemfida
Geranium subcaulescens
Gypsophila dubia
Helianthemum 'Jubilee'
H. 'Mrs Earle'
H. 'The Bride'
Hypericum polyphyllum
Iberis 'Snowflake'
Leontopodium alpinum
Linaria alpina
Linum alpinum
Lithospermum 'Grace Ward'
Oenothera missouriensis
Omphalodes verna
Penstemon pinifolius
Phlox douglasii 'Snow Queen'
P. subulata 'Temiscaming'
P. subulata 'Model'
Polygonum vaccinifolium
Potentilla tonguei
Primula frondosa
Pulsatilla vulgaris
Ranunculus montanus
Saxifraga aizoon rosea
S. aizoon lutea
S. X sanguinea superba
S. irvingii
Sedum spathulifolium purpureum
S. cauticolum
Sisyrinchium brachypus
Thymus serpyllum 'Coccineus'
Veronica 'Carl Teschner'
Zauschneria californica

Above: *Small pool surrounded by rocks and stones, planted with primulas, pinks, cistus.*

Below: *Astilbe hybrid 'White Queen', for moist soil, bog or stream-side.*

Making a pool from a fibreglass shape. Mark out the area to be excavated.

Allow more space than the actual outline of the fibreglass shape.

Put in marking pegs around the outline before beginning to dig.

Dig out the rectangular area. This should be able to accommodate the pool shape.

Now try the pool shape for size and depth. Remove any sharp stones from the hole.

The rim of the pool shape should rest level with the lawn surface.

The edging tiles or stones and turf are fitted around the pool to hide the edge.

Smaller pools are added here so that a waterfall effect can be made.

The finished pool. Plants will soften the new look.

Rock pools

Even a small pool gives you the scope to grow some of the prettiest bog or water plants or to keep a few fish.

The very simplest, smallest pool will not of course support fish because it would freeze completely in winter and be too hot in the summer. The tiny waterlily, *Nymphaea pygmaea helvola*, will grow in 15cm (6in) of water. It has pale yellow flowers. A large, shallow stone bowl, or plastic pool, old bathtub or pot, would all make simple water gardens, using the more shallow water plants, polished pebbles and attractive rocks. Make your own mosaics around or in them, using the small Italian glass mosaic tiles, or broken pot and china, pebbles or broken glass.

A pool for fish and water lilies is probably best dug out of the earth and lined with reinforced concrete. The pool is stepped in layers to take the deep and shallow water plants. This sort of pool needs to be at least 38cm (15in) deep and, like all pools and water gardens, should have a place in the full sun. Oxygenating plants also like fairly deep water, and these provide vital oxygen in the pool to help it maintain clear water and good balance. They should be planted at the rate of ten to every square metre of water surface.

If you are excavating for a pool, use the earth dug up for making a rock garden beside the pool. Making a pool can be quite a large-scale affair so do not undertake it too lightly, but well-sited and planted, it can be one of the most appealing parts of the garden. It does need some almost-professional knowledge to get the engineering right; no leaks, sloping walls to ease ice pressure in winter, proper reinforcing for the concrete (water exerts considerable pressure), overflow and drainage. Paving too, around the pool is an asset, keeping earth from being washed down and drying out faster around a seating area.

A formal shaped pool (a square, omega, rectangular or oval), placed near the terrace or house needs proper edging and paved surrounds, with planting pockets left in the paving for poolside plants, such as variegated rushes (*Scirpus albescens*), flax, or pampas grass (*Cortaderia argentea*).

Plants that oxygenate the water and are planted deep in the pool are American pound weed (*Anacharis canadensis*), *Lagarosiphon major* (syn. *Elodea crispa*), *Hottonia palustris*, callitriches, *Ranunculus aquatilis* and various members of the water milfoil family (*Myriophyllum*). Grow the plants in shallow containers, baskets, boxes or pans, with loam and a little charcoal.

Decide when you are building a pool whether you will use containers for your plants or plant them in earth at the pool base or on the ledges. Fibreglass pools do not retain the soil in place on the ledges. If you plant straight into pool base, you can leave plants to grow undisturbed for several years but when you do want to adjust or reorganize, it is a bigger job than just lifting out containers. On the other hand, containers usually mean that plants need repotting from time to time.

Water lilies grow with their roots in the mud at the bottom of the pool and their lovely fragrant flowers and leaves on the surface. Choose hardy ones because they are easier to look after. For a pool 17·5–38cm (7–15in) deep, choose the shallow rooting varieties such as 'Conqueror', rosy-crimson, 'Aurora', buff yellow or 'Laydekeri rosea', rose pink. These will not succeed in deeper water but the ones for deep water do not mind being planted in shallower water than their ideal 60–90cm (2–3ft). Plant from May to July, using special water lily pots or baskets filled with rich loam, and well-rotted manure. Water lilies need sunny water and can take up a lot of space as they grow, so do not overplant as they will crowd each other.

Above: *The marsh marigold or kingcup is a spring-flowering bog garden plant.*

Above: *Sagittaria sagittifolia, the arrowhead, has leaves floating on and below the water.*

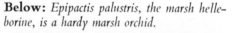

Below: *Epipactis palustris, the marsh helleborine, is a hardy marsh orchid.*

Below: *Scirpus tabernaemontani zebrinus, variegated rush grows to 130cm in bog or water.*

Reeds and rushes can either be grown in wet or bog soil, near or in the pool in water 5–10cm (2–4in) deep. Cut them back after planting to about 22.5cm (9in) until their roots have taken hold. Also plant them where you can control their rapid expansion. Sweet flag (*Acorus calamus*) is another plant for pool-sides or the bog garden with sword-like leaves, scented foliage and again, rampant habit.

Calla is a useful marsh, bog garden or pool-side plant with a small white arum-like flower, 15–22.5cm (6–9in) tall. It has red berries in autumn, will tolerate semi-shade, and is fertilized by water snails. It likes thoroughly damp leaf mould. In wet soil that must not dry out, grows the native kingcup or marsh marigold, a 30cm (1ft) tall, hardy perennial with butter-yellow flowers that blossom in spring.

One of the most beautiful irises of all, the Japanese water iris, is a bog plant, although it will grow elsewhere. It is *Iris kaempferi* and there are purple, rosy lilac, blue and white cultivars. Although it likes damp rich soil in the growing season it likes drier conditions for the rest of the year. *Iris laevigata* has large brilliant violet-blue flowers borne on 60cm (2ft) stems in the summer and will grow in bog soil or water up to 10cm (4in) deep. There are also the water flag iris, *I. pseudacorus* and *I. sibirica* and its hybrids that thrive in boggy, sunny conditions.

Lysichitum belong to the same family as the native arum and are striking flowers for the bog garden or water-side. They are sometimes known as skunk cabbages although, accurately, this name belongs to one of their relatives.

Above: *Dodecatheon meadia, the shooting star, likes a half-shady, moist and leafy soil.*

Above: *Alchemilla mollis, lady's mantle, grows among rocks or as ground cover in shade.*

Above: *For walls, hedge-banks, rocks, try the fern Asplenium adiantum-nigrum.*

Left: *Ranunculus fluitans floats its threadlike leaves and white flowers on the water.*

The reeds or rushes are water-fringe plants, inclined to be rampant.   *Irises and ranunculus planted in moist soil pockets by a rock pool.*

Monthly calendar
JANUARY
Clear around emerging bulb flowers. If surface of rock pool is frozen, ensure there is hole open in ice.
FEBRUARY
Clear debris. Loosen surface of rock garden; apply top dressing with appropriate chippings over it.
MARCH
Plant out newly-acquired plants. To complement watercourse, plant trailers (aubrieta, alyssum, helianthemum). In pool, plant *Hottonia palustris*, the water violet.
APRIL
Divide bog and rock plants. Catalogue and label plants (if not already done). Complete new pools. Spring-clean established pools. Feed fish to breeding condition. Order new aquatic plants.
MAY
Spray against pests. Take cuttings. Construct peat bed for dwarf rhododendrons. Fish in the pool are ready to spawn.
JUNE
Pot-on seeds sown in April. Sow seeds of rare rock plants as they ripen. Plant aquatics. Watch new lily leaves for midge attack; remove if affected.
JULY
Lift and divide iris which grow from rhizomes. Fish-spawning time so make sure pool is not starved of oxygen.
AUGUST
Take cuttings of dwarf rhododendrons. Plant spring-flowering bulbs and corms. Divide and replant established bulbs. Watch out for aphids. Blast them from foliage with hose jet; fish will eat them from water's surface.
SEPTEMBER
Transplant evergreen rock garden shrubs. Continue planting spring bulbs. Clear pool of decaying vegetation. Take measures to prevent leaves falling into water.
OCTOBER
Construct any new scree or rock beds. Clear peat gardens of dead foliage. Plant water-side perennials. Time for extending the water garden or constructing a waterfall.
NOVEMBER
Top dress rock garden. Spray against pests during dry spells.
DECEMBER
Cover cushion plants with chicken wire to prevent bird damage. Remove dead plants.

Home-grown vegetables

The vegetable garden needs to be in a sunny, open part of the garden, for most vegetables object to shade from trees, shrubs, walls or fences. You can have shelter of a wall or fence on the north side, for the coldest winds blow from there. The compost could go near the vegetable garden and you need paths around and through it for easy cultivation and picking.

Vegetables of one species, such as cabbages, use up different quantities of plant food from vegetables of another species, for example, potatoes. So you can make better use of your soil by regularly changing or 'rotating' your vegetable crops. This also prevents a build-up of pests ready to attack any one kind of vegetable. For

example, if you grew nothing but cabbages or their close plant relatives in the same ground over and over again you would impoverish the soil and might build up a thriving colony of club root parasites. Adequate manuring and liming of the soil would prevent this.

A crop rotation plan usually covers a time span of three years. For example, you could follow the cropping plan charted here, which also gives an accompanying manuring and liming plan. This is important, for some plants do not like manure and some do not like lime—and yet it is vital to keep up the best soil fertility and structure.

Generally speaking, in a vegetable plant-

ing plan, legumes (plants producing pods) and leaf vegetables follow potatoes, the potatoes follow the root crops, and the root crops follow the leaf vegetables—or alternatively, the legumes and fruit crops like sweet corn or tomatoes follow the root crops and potatoes, and the root crops and potatoes follow the leaf vegetables like cabbages and Brussels sprouts (the brassicas).

Leaf crops need beds rich in nitrogen and they are heavy feeders. When vegetable crops are produced intensively the soil can begin to lack lime, an essential ingredient

The vegetable garden can yield an abundance of healthy, fresh, delicately-flavoured food.

for many vegetables but particularly the cabbage family. As you will manure the ground heavily for them to give them the nitrogen, you also increase the acidity of the soil, and therefore need to add lime—at a different time from the manure.

The root vegetables on the other hand, such as carrots, beetroots and parsnips grow badly-shaped if given a recent dressing of well-rotted manure. So they are planted after a year's crop of leaf vegetables—the ground is then sufficiently rich for them. Add wood ashes or a complete fertilizer like Growmore to the soil a week or 10 days before sowing.

Fruit crops like sweet corn, tomatoes, capsicum and marrow like soil that has been well-manured in the winter and also fertilized.

The legumes—peas and beans—are great users of phosphorous so that superphosphate fertilizer should be used to enrich their soil.

Cropping plan

First season:

Plot A   cabbages, Brussels sprouts, cauliflower, broccoli, turnips.
Limed in late autumn if necessary. Manured or composted during winter digging.

Plot B   beans, peas, miscellaneous small crops.
Manure or compost can be forked into trenches for peas and beans. Wood ashes or a complete fertlizer like Growmore can be applied just before sowings are made.

Plot C   potatoes, carrots, beetroot, lettuce, onions.
No liming for potatoes, manure or add compost during winter digging. Carrots and beetroot can have wood ashes forked in if available and a complete fertilizer like Growmore applied just before sowings are made. Lettuce and onions should go into ground dug, manured and composted during previous winter digging.

Second season:
The crops shown in Plot C above will grow on Plot A, crops in Plot A on Plot B and those in Plot B on Plot C.

Plot A   potatoes etc
Plot B   cabbages etc
Plot C   beans etc

Third season:
The position of the crops will be as follows:

Plot A   beans etc
Plot B   potatoes etc
Plot C   cabbages etc

Fourth season:
In the fourth season, the rotation starts off as in the first year.

Above: *The young shoots of purple sprouting broccoli are ready in spring. It is the most hardy broccoli and can overwinter safely.*

Below: *Garden peas, First Early variety, were sown in autumn, have come through the winter and will provide an early crop.*

Above: *A well-grown head of cabbage.*

Right: *Swiss chard, or seakale beet.*

Below: *Lettuces grown as a catch crop on the ridges of celery trenches.*

While following your rotational cropping plan, keep in mind that you want to carry out a kind of orderly delivery of vegetables to the family kitchen. Start by sowing a small to medium amount of any one vegetable and plant at intervals to keep a reasonable supply going. This is called successional sowing. For example, you can sow a short double row of radishes outside in early April, followed by a sowing between the pea rows in mid-April. Then sow a few more in May, June and July. Then you will have fresh young radishes for salads from May to October. Lettuce seeds can be sown in small batches between March and August. For peas, choose early, mid-season and late varieties. Sown at around the same time—they bear one after the other. There are potatoes which grow for lifting in June and July and some other varieties that mature more slowly for late summer use. A main crop of potatoes is not dug up and stored until autumn.

When planning a steady supply of vegetables you can often use space where one vegetable has finished and it is not yet time to plant another. For example, radishes can be sown on the ground that will be used for outdoor tomatoes. The radishes are harvested before the tomatoes go in. Or you can use soil banked up on either side of leek and celery trenches for radishes and lettuces. This use of ground between crops harvested and new crops being sown is called 'catch-cropping'.

Inter-cropping

This allows two plants to grow in the place of one to give more produce from the small vegetable garden. For good results the soil must be very fertile so that neither the first nor second crop is starved of food. It is also essential that the vegetable rows should run from north to south so that shade from the taller plants does not fall on the shorter plants. Any shade would encourage spindly growth and poor crops.

Here is an example of inter-cropping. Rows of peas which grow 90cm (3ft) high are sown 90cm (3ft) apart and in this space radishes, spinach or lettuce are grown.

In the simple outline of vegetable planting that follows, many vegetables have not been included, some because they need blanching. This does mean extra thought and work for a gardener if it is done on a larger scale. But these less well-known vegetables have been included—Lamb's lettuce (Italian corn salad) and land cress for their usefulness. The first two, *Valerianella locusta*, an English native, and its slightly better Italian equivalent flourish when green produce is getting short. Land cress or American cress (*Barbarea praecox*) is a substitute watercress and very good in both summer and winter salads.

Vegetable growing can be fascinating. When you have tried your hand at some of the old favourites, check the catalogues for many more, and they will also give broad directions for planting.

Vegetables among the flowers

There are many places in the garden where vegetables could be grown among the flowers to save space in the vegetable plot. Rhubarb can grow in the same place for years and is quite handsome, and so are many other fruit and vegetables such as capsicum, tomatoes, carrot tops, many of the herbs, including parsley, mint and thyme.

Beetroot looks attractive planted among the annuals. Runner beans, especially the purple-podded kind with their bright scarlet blossoms, can be grown on tripods at the back of the border. Alternatively they, and marrows, could grow over a child's teepee frame of lashed poles. Cut-and-come again vegetables such as handsome Swiss chard and its coloured variety 'Ruby Chard', and the oak-leaved, salad bowl lettuce can be grown in groups among flowers—and stay there until the end of the summer.

Cloches

Cloches are very simple climate controllers that can allow you to plant on unprotected open ground when you otherwise could not because of the cold or wet. They also stop birds attacking young plants, for example, taking the fruit from strawberries or pecking at lettuces.

A cloche is a simple framework of wire or metal which supports a plastic or glass 'tunnel' that goes over the plants. You can buy several designs in both materials: glass lasts longer and provides better winter protection but plastic is light and cheaper. You can make your own cloche with strong wire and sheets of polythene. The wire hoops are spaced at about 60cm (2ft). The plastic goes over them with the edges trapped under the soil.

You must be careful to keep cloche-protected ground watered because rain cannot reach it and the extra heat under the plastic or glass causes rapid drying out. Plenty of humus in the soil will also help conserve moisture.

Compared with cold frames and greenhouses, however, cloches need little attention and allow you to make sowing of radish, lettuce, onions, broad beans and peas from late February to early April. Wind, frost and bird damage is banished. When the weather warms up or the plants grow too large, the cloches are moved to cover other crops.

In the south and the Midlands the cantaloupe melon is a good summer cloche

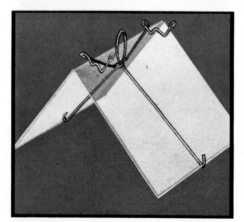

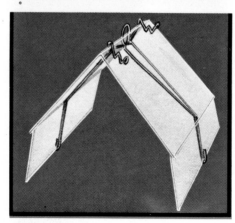

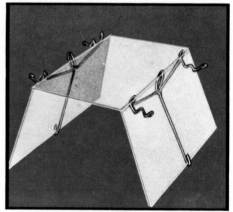

Top picture: *A well-shaped truss of tomatoes ripening in early summer, The plants were given cloche protection after planting out. Bush varieties are particularly suitable for cloche protection.*

Three types of glass cloches. **Above left:** *tent cloche;* **above:** *a flat-top barn cloche;* **left:** *a barn cloche. The barn-type cloches are best because they allow more headroom and can therefore accommodate more vegetables. The flat-top barn shape allows this too but crops might not develop so quickly because winter sunlight is reflected off the flat top and roots might get less moisture draining to them than from the angled barnshape.*

Above: *Sweet peas benefiting from cloche protection, with a catch crop of lettuce.*

Below: *Cloches stood on end are a useful way to protect any plant from cold winds.*

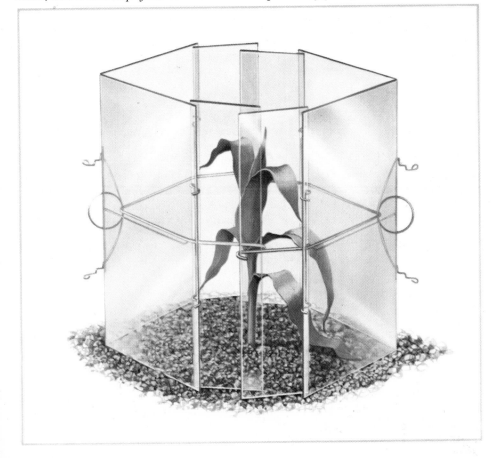

crop—in colder areas, try growing the ridge cucumber.

In autumn use cloches to help dry off the onion crop, ripen the last of the outdoor tomatoes and protect the last lettuces.

In winter, cloches protect lettuce, endive, spring onions and cabbage plants.

Using a garden frame

These can be used for other plants besides vegetables but it is particularly useful for vegetables because it can extend the growing season and the variety of food you produce.

A frame has four sides of wood, metal or glass and a removable glass top called a light. Because the glass traps the sun's heat, you can grow plants earlier or later in the season, or plants that like a lot of heat in the summer. Some frames have brick, concrete or wooden sides and just a glass light. You can probably make a simple one yourself, and it costs much less than a greenhouse.

The frame needs to be large so that the temperature is more even and there is space for crops. A small frame is affected very quickly by outside temperatures, and needs to be ventilated on all sunny days, particularly from March to October.

During the summer, melons and cucumbers can be grown in the frame, and in the winter, lettuce, cabbage, cauliflower and onions.

You can prepare a seed bed in early March and sow lettuce, summer cabbage, Brussels sprouts, leeks and onions as soon as the weather seems good enough for quick germination.

Sow seeds for tomatoes in peat pots and sink them in the frame bed in early April. Later in the month the same could be done with dwarf and runner beans, ridge cucumbers, melons, pumpkin and marrow.

Good summer frame crops are self-blanching celery, tomatoes, melons and cucumbers. Tomatoes and celery plants set out in mid-May can be grown without the light (glass top) by June but with melon and cucumber, set out in early June, the light is not removed except for ventilation.

A greenhouse

You may choose to have a greenhouse, though you will have more than enough scope if you have cloches or a frame. Greenhouse culture can be rather complicated and because of the bigger area required it needs constant attention. A certain balance of light, humidity, ventilation and heat is needed. However, in a cool greenhouse you can grow things earlier and later, as you can with a frame, and in a slightly warmed greenhouse you could get out-of-season crops like tomatoes in June and cucumbers in July.

Monthly calendar

JANUARY

Planning the vegetable garden starts now. Study seed catalogues. Place orders for seeds and seed potatoes. You might look for lettuces that do not 'bolt', ie, run to seed quickly, or long-standing cabbage which keeps a good heart longer. Sow peas, early broad beans and shallots—providing ground and conditions are right. If you sow dwarf broad beans, plant 90cm (3ft) apart for single rows and 120cm (4ft) apart for double. Then later you can sow quick-maturing lettuce and radish or corn salad between rows.

FEBRUARY

Sow broad beans, shallots, garlic. Look at standing crops such as perpetual spinach and parsnips which will run to seed soon. Keep cutting spinach hard. Lift parsnips; store them.

If you have cloches or frames, sow Brussels sprouts, cabbage, cauliflower, lettuce and leeks, short horn carrots, globe beetroot, white Lisbon onions and radishes. If you can spare frame space then spinach, cauliflower, turnips or potatoes could be left to mature after sowing, giving a welcome early crop, but use varieties suitable for forcing.

If you have greenhouse sow seed of celery, celeriac, lettuce.

Celery is a bog plant in its wild state, receiving plenty of food and moisture, so water plants frequently; feed with liquid fertilizer.

Leeks are planted out when big enough to drop into 23cm (9in) deep holes made with dibber. Plants grow up from holes. They like really rich soil.

MARCH

As soon as soil can be easily raked and drills drawn, and provided there is no strong wind, sow early-maturing varieties of stump-rooted carrots, cabbage, lettuce, spinach, onions, broad beans, early peas, parsnips and turnips. Lettuce can be sown in permanent positions at about three-weekly intervals. Also plant carrots, chervil and turnips at intervals. The brassicas—cabbage, cauliflower, kale etc, are often best planted first in nursery bed which is raised and mounded for warmth and good drainage. Soil should be fine so that shallow drills can be made. Sow seeds thinly so they are not checked by a transplant—for vegetables need to grow quickly and without any check to be at their best. Transplant when two real leaves have developed. Potatoes can be planted in warmest part of vegetable garden.

If you have frame or greenhouse—peas and beans grown in them earlier can be hardened and planted out at end of month.

Annual herb seeds can be sown—basil, borage, chervil, coriander, Florence fennel, sweet marjoram, summer savory.

APRIL

Plant seeds of vegetables including sowings missed earlier—sow turnips between rows of peas and beans, globe beetroot, quicker to mature than long-rooted types, spinach beet, main crop carrots can go in and still some early maturing varieties. Later in month, sow second earlies and main crop peas, mangetout peas. Sow brassicas, sprouting broccoli, summer and winter cauliflower, Brussels sprouts, cabbage for summer, autumn and some for winter, savoy cabbage—use club root and cabbage fly preventive. Grow catch-crop of radishes near parsnip or lettuce. Sow onions. Support peas that were planted earlier with mesh or canes. Earth up potatoes that are showing.

Two-year-old asparagus roots bought from specialists can be planted this month to crop next year. Existing beds should be top dressed. If you wish to plant own seed, soak for 24 hours then sow now.

Plant out broad beans or peas sown earlier, transplant brassicas that are ready. Feed spring cabbage. In warm, sheltered place sow French beans.

In cloche or frame sow dwarf varieties of runner beans, capsicum, celery, cucumbers, sweet corn, tomatoes for outdoors, marrows.

Sow annual and perennial herbs.

MAY

Still sow chicory, cauliflower, garlic, cucumber, perennial broccoli, which will yield for several years (plant 90–120cm [3–4ft] apart)—in cold districts swedes and kale are more likely to survive than winter cabbage or savoy. Sow also New Zealand spinach, French, haricot and runner beans (guard against slugs). Stake climbing beans as early as possible, delay planting in northern areas. Thin out vegetables sown last month. In cloche, frame or greenhouse—sow marrow seeds, sweet corn in single pots, outdoor tomatoes.

Sow herb seeds and plant out canister-grown herbs.

JUNE

By now you should be enjoying first vegetable crops.

Save space by growing quick maturing salad plants among slow maturing crops like marrows and courgettes (zucchinis), or using temporarily empty space for nursery rows of brassicas which are soon planted out. Sow quick maturing carrots ('Shorthorn'), beetroot, kohl-rabi, radish, lettuce, peas, chicory, Chinese cabbage, French, runner and broad beans if not sown earlier. Earlier-sown broad beans can now be picked and young 7·5cm (3in) long pods cooked with beans in them. Nip out tips of

bean plants now—these can be eaten but taken out to prevent black fly infesting them. All pests are very active now. Inspect peas for thrips and other plants for aphids, caterpillars. Spray potatoes against blight at end of month. Transplant all seedlings in good time to stop them being checked, and harden off; transplant plants from frame and greenhouse, such as celery and leeks.

JULY

Weeds are having their hey-day, so do quick light hoeing between vegetables every other day to kill weed seedlings before they flourish and germinate. Mulch to save work too, with nettles, turnip and radish tops mixed with another mulch or unsprayed lawn mowings. When the crops finish, fork mulch into soil. Early potatoes and peas finish this month, lift out with fork; use ground for carrots, pulled in autumn or early winter. Where potatoes are soon to be lifted, plant brassicas in furrows made by earthing up around potatoes. When potatoes are lifted, level earth. Sow turnips, and later in month, turnip 'Golden Ball' for winter use. Sow small onion 'Silverskin'; for pickling, sow seed thicker to keep onions small. Sow broad and runner beans in south, also sow spring cabbage, parsley, winter radish. Plant out brassicas. Feed and water marrows. Cut courgettes regularly to make them produce fruit more profusely.

AUGUST

Sow Brussels sprouts for use next summer and autumn. They remain in seed bed all winter and are transplanted in spring. Later still transplant to permanent positions. Sow last batch of lettuce outdoors but be prepared to protect with cloches should cold nights come early. Sutton's 'Spring Beauty' is good crop to sow now, being extremely mildew resistant, or 'Continuity'. Land cress or Lamb's lettuce can be sown for late winter and spring salads. Sow winter spinach from now until the middle of September in sheltered place.

Lift shallots and autumn-sown onions if foliage has faded completely. Do it when weather is dry; clean and remove soil and loose skin. Onions can be sown in autumn as well as spring, for example, 'Autumn Triumph' and 'Reliance'. Leave unthinned, even unweeded, until spring when they can be used as spring onions or transplanted. Autumn sown 'Lisbon' and 'White Portugal' are two very good spring onions that must be pulled before Christmas because they are not hardy.

Lift and store beetroots but some globe beets can be left until needed or until frost threatens.

SEPTEMBER

Busy planting and harvesting month. All late winter and spring cabbages, late kales and savoys are sown so that they can become established by winter. Winter radish, onions, land cress and prickly or winter spinach can still be sown in open. Also sow seed of Brussels sprouts and lettuce, but must be removed to frame later. Produce should be harvested before frosts come. Marrow, pumpkin, squash gathered now will keep to following spring if handled gently, picked with part of stem and hung in airy place in string bag, or stood on cushion of paper on shelf. Place must be frost-free and dry and marrow wood-hard when picked.

Bring haricot beans indoors. Pull entire plant and let dry. Leave in shell until pods are crisp to touch. Potatoes must be gathered quickly, much sunlight turns them green and inedible. Store at temperature of about 4°C in frostproof larder. Dig out main crop carrots about middle of month. Gather tomatoes and ripen green ones in dark place. If some crops are not quite ready—salads, globe beetroot, carrots, radishes, cover with cloches until ready. Compost discarded vegetable tops, except potatoes—burn to guard against blight in future years.

Check empty ground for next year's crops, plan rotation, dig deeply, dress with manure or lime and leave rough for winter frost to condition.

OCTOBER

Spring cabbage can still be planted but this is month for lifting and storing all roots; dig any vacant ground to leave fallow for winter. Cover any salad crops with cloches if you have them, Lamb's lettuce and land cress are hardy but are better for being covered, so is spinach beet. Protect any cauliflower heads from frost by snapping a leaf or two near curd to hang over and protect it.

If you have frame, sow winter lettuce and forcing varieties; transplant to another frame or greenhouse later.

NOVEMBER

With winter upon the vegetable garden, cloches come into their own. Broad beans and early peas can be grown in warm areas or under cloches. Broad beans to sow now include dwarf 'Aquadulce Claudia' which will winter and crop under cloches. 'Seville' is also hardy with shorter pods that mature early. Round-seeded peas such as sugar pea, 'Feltham First' and 'Meteor' can be sown.

DECEMBER

Finish all digging now, leaving clods to be broken down by weather and turned to fine crumbs by spring. Carry on with salad crops under cloches. Write away for seed catalogues so you can order what you want early. Check tools and clean trays, check stored marrows and other food. Bring in potted herbs of chive, mint, etc to over-winter in house.

Above: *Runner beans are easy to grow but will not resist frost.*

Right: *This late variety of Brussels sprout is a tall one, with large sprouts.*

Below: *Radish 'Scarlet Globe'.*

Below right: *Carrots thrive in cultivated sandy loam previously manured for earlier crop.*

Fruit in the garden

Summer can be fruitful and lush with nature's bounty. Even a small garden can accommodate quite a lot of fruit trees, and other fruits—strawberries, raspberries, gooseberries, currants.

Let us start with **strawberries** because they can be grown simply in a vegetable or flower bed or barrel. They grow happily in 30cm (1ft) deep soil, well supplied with humus. Soil that has been well-manured earlier for a crop of vegetables will do nicely. The strawberry bed needs full sun and shelter from spring winds. Perhaps the easiest type to grow for the beginner is the perpetual-fruiting alpine strawberry. From a spring sowing, they will provide you with a delicious crop within four months, and will crop during the summer and autumn for that year and future years. The seed is best sown in February, March and April, transplanted to boxes when large enough to handle and planted out 15cm (6in) apart from April onwards.

When planting out, the base of the crown should be just at soil level, and the roots should sit spread out on a little mound of earth within the planting hole. Fill in, firm the soil well. If you are not increasing your supply of plants from runners then cut them off with the scissors as they appear. To keep strawberries free of mud, you can lay straw on the ground, but do not do it until the warmer weather as mulches reduce temperature around the part of the plant above ground. Strawberries like plenty of moisture.

If you are growing strawberries in a barrel, you need 5cm (2in) diameter holes for each plant. As well, make holes in the bottom and put in a drainage layer of crocks. Adequate sun and rich soil (John Innes potting compost No 3 is a suitable potting mix that is available) is also needed.

Some people think that **raspberries** vie with strawberries as the most exotic fruit of summer. One garden row can give you many delicious desserts. As with strawberries, you must begin with very reliable, preferably certified stock because the plants are subject to many diseases. Raspberries like full sun but can stand a little shade. Raspberries will grow in most soils even chalky soils, but they prefer an acid one

A barrel of strawberries, good-looking and good eating. All sides of the barrel need sun.

and they must have good drainage, plenty of moisture, and good soil.

The raspberry is a hardy perennial and is planted ideally in early autumn (in a row running north to south) but can be planted between autumn and spring in good conditions. Do not plant too deep—the roots should be covered with no more than 7·5cm (3in) of soil.

Prepare the raspberry bed in summer by weeding and digging in a generous amount of well-rotted compost or farmyard manure, about 5kg (10lb) per square metre, and more on sandy soils. Dig in a dressing of 25g (1oz) per square metre of superphosphate, for raspberries need phosphates. Add more decayed manure annually in November, forking it only into the top 7·5cm

(3in) of soil. Mulch to keep soil moist in April. Some gardeners think that a dressing of sulphate of potash should be given in autumn. When plants are well-established, do not dig near their roots.

The **loganberry** is treated similarly to the raspberry and arose as a seedling cross between an American blackberry and a raspberry. As flowering is late, it is a good fruit for areas where there are spring frosts that damage early-flowering plants. They fruit from August to September and can go on for 15 years or more. They love rich soil, an annual mulch of farmyard manure in late autumn, or a feed of fish manure.

To reduce disease infection from old to young canes, the young canes are trained fan-wise on the opposite side from the old canes. The two ages of canes occupy alternate sides annually. Ten to 12 fruiting canes are kept per plant and fruiting canes are cut down to ground level after they have fruited. Two good varieties are 'LY 59', a virus-free clone available since the 1950's, and 'American Thornless' which is a pleasure to prune and ideal for a small garden. Both give good crops.

The black, red and white fruiting currants and the gooseberry are all related and are hardy, deciduous fruit-bearing shrubs.

Currants take up quite a small space, fruit prolifically and like rich, moist soil. Red and white currants withstand drought better than blackcurrants, but flower early so are not so good for districts with spring frosts. Blackcurrants tolerate some shade but it delays ripening. Blackcurrants fruit from July to early September, red and white from late June to late July. You can plant cuttings of the bushes, or put in one to two-year-old bushes between October and mid-March; the earlier the better. Plant bushes with about 5cm (2in) of soil above the roots. Mulch bushes in April with manure and feed in the spring with a 50g (2oz) per square metre of sulphate of ammonia or Nitro-chalk and in the autumn, with 25g (1oz) per square metre of sulphate of potash. Pruning is done in the winter for red and white currants, and on black currants after fruiting.

The **gooseberry** is native to Britain and has been cultivated since the 13th century. It is a good choice for a small garden but flowers early so will not suit spring frost areas. It likes full sun if you want an early crop, and north or east walls if you want a late crop. You can plant gooseberries between plum trees which like good manuring too. Plant gooseberries from November to April on ground well-manured earlier. Cover roots with 7·5–10cm (3–4in) of soil. After planting, shorten back the leading shoot by half and side shoots to two buds. Mulch in spring, water well, and give a spring dressing of sulphate of potash, 50g (2oz) to the square metre. Bonfire ash will supply potash too.

Anyone can grow an **apple tree**. You can shape an apple tree as a cordon, fan, espalier, bush, pyramid, standard, which is just as well because you need more than one apple tree to achieve cross-pollination and get a good crop. Several are sufficiently self-fertile to produce a reasonable crop, such as the old, very late sort 'Crawley Beauty'. However, it is best to have several trees flowering at the same time.

You can have a family tree with several cultivars grafted on to the same trunk. To choose several cultivars of apple trees successfully, it is useful to know that there are diploid and triploid apple trees. These are trees with different chromosome arrangements, the important thing being from your point of view that the triploid apple cultivars are not very fertile. Therefore you need at least two diploid trees in your collection. Choose from the lists given; some cultivars in the same group for cross-pollination.

Apple trees like deep loam. Plant from November to March, firm the soil well and tie the tree to a substantial stake. Give trees a spring mulch of rotted manure and dig it in during the following autumn. You can also use an inorganic fertilizer of a sulphate of ammonia, superphosphate and sulphate of potash mix, if you feel the trees need it in spring. Hoe it in lightly to beyond the tree spread. Apples are one kind of tree that likes to grow in meadow (loam is in any case a meadow type of soil) with grass and clover cut short beneath it. This discourages tree growth but encourages fruitfulness. Dessert apples take on better colour and can be stored longer.

Apple trees bear fruit in two ways. Most do it on short lateral branches called spurs. A few however, also bear a large percentage of fruit at the end of one-year-old shoots. These are called tip-bearers.

Among varieties that train particularly well as cordons are 'American Mother', which has good flavour but an irregular crop, 'Cox's Orange Pippin', excellent flavour and fair crop, 'Egremont Russet' with very good regular crops, 'Lord Lambourne' good flavour and crops and most of the

'Merton' types listed. These are dessert apples and there are many more to choose from so check with a reputable supplier and discuss with him what is best for the soil and space you have.

Training apple trees to a shape. There are certain shapes such as cordon, espalier, bush or fan in which plants can be trained either for decoration or for more practical purposes—to take up less space, cast less shadow, be easier to harvest from and protect fruit on. Apples and pears are good trees for shape training and it means you can grow more of your own fruit in a small garden. They should be bought already grafted on to a dwarfing stock.

To train an apple tree to a **cordon**, you begin by buying a one-year-old grafted apple tree which comes with a single stem and possibly a few sideshoots, sometimes called feathers. Then you train this 'maiden' as it is called, to become a single cordon, with one main stem, or a double or triple cordon, that is, with two or three main stems. The single stem cordon can be vertical, oblique or horizontal but it is worth remembering when deciding on a shape that near-horizontal shoots bear more fruit than vertical ones. The oblique cordon can also give greater stem length.

In the **fan** shape the branches spring from a short leg and spread out like the ribs of a fan, all growing in a flat single dimension.

The fan tree can be trained against supporting wires.

Pyramid-shaped trees are small bushes on dwarfing or semi-dwarfing stock that are compact enough for the small garden. The branches radiate from a main stem. The lowest branch is little more than 30cm (1ft) from ground level and is the longest and oldest branch. The branches progress to the shorter and newer ones as you go up the tree. Space the branches at about 20cm (8in) intervals up the main stem and let them grow out in different directions, so that fruit and leaves get maximum sunlight and the fruit harvested is well-coloured and good quality. A dwarf pyramid will carry a heavier crop than a cordon.

Allow for wider planting distances—1m (3½ft) apart in rows 2.2m (7ft) apart—as against 90cm (3ft) apart and rows 2m (6ft) apart for cordons.

The pyramid apple does spread more than the pyramid pear. You can buy a 3-year-old pyramid tree already on its way

to the right shape or buy a maiden. Avoid buying tip-bearing varieties of trees; tip-bearing pears are less common than apples.

The **espalier** fruit tree is trained along horizontal wires in a flat shape. Espalier actually means a 'fruit wall' and is the framework on which fruit trees are supported. You need an upright post every 3m (10ft) securely fixed in the ground and about 2m (6ft) tall, with horizontal wires fixed at 38cm (15in) intervals along the posts connecting them. Support the end posts well, for wires must be pulled tight so that they in turn can support the fruit. Fruit trees are then planted along the fence and trained against the wires. The result is very effective and space-saving and you can get good crops with a little concentrated work. You can either train the horizontal-growing branches to go straight along the wires, or you can turn them up at the ends to form a U-shape across the tree.

Dwarf bushes are varieties grafted or

Left: *Immediately after planting raspberries the canes are cut back to a bud at 60cm.*

Above: *Raspberry 'Malling Landmark'. Raspberries need plenty of moisture.*

Above: *Fasten each raspberry cane individually with raffia or garden twine.*

Above: *Alternatively, you can let canes grow full height then loop them over and tie.*

Left: *'Ellison's Orange', a dessert apple. Apples are picked when they part easily from spur.*

Below: *Apple blossom. Apple trees live long and healthily, and provide fruit for decades.*

budded on to dwarfing rootstocks and the trees need not exceed 2·2m (7ft) in height, making them easy to look after and harvest from. Even more important they can be planted fairly close together to save space in the smaller garden. The trees only need winter pruning of the weaker side shoots or laterals. Branches come almost from the base of the tree and grow cup-shaped if the leading main stem of the maiden is cut back to encourage side shoots to grow from below the pruning cut.

Pears have been growing in Britain since Roman times and were extremely popular in Tudor times. They live longer than apples, are less subject to pests or disease but need more warmth and protection. They flower early and are vulnerable to spring frosts. Not all varieties are suitable for growing in the open in most parts of the country. Varieties have to flower at the same time and pollinate each other.

All dessert pears can be cooked if they are picked slightly unripe but there are special varieties for cooking or for making perry, the pear equivalent to cider.

Pears like a slightly acid soil but will grow in an alkaline one. They are not so fussy about drainage but demand plenty of moisture. Give them if you can, a rich deep loam. The trees tend to get very large for a small garden so bush-type trees, cordons, pyramids, fans or espalier trees, grown on suitable dwarfing root stocks are the best choice. See apple section for various tree-training shapes.

Planting should be done between leaf fall and March, the sooner the better if the soil is satisfactory. It is very important that the union between the scion (the variety you have chosen) and the rootstock which it is grafted onto, should be well above soil level—at least 10cm (4in). The dwarfing effect of the rootstock will be lost if roots are formed by the scion. The tree will take years to bear. If there are two unions on the tree (this double grafting is sometimes done by nurserymen) the lowest union must be 10cm (4in) above the soil.

After the planting, staking and making firm, put down a 5cm (2in) deep mulch of garden compost, well-rotted farmyard manure, peat or leafmould, to keep the soil moist if there should be a dry spring. Keep well-watered.

Plant cordons approx 1 × 2m (3 × 6ft) apart, fans and espaliered trees 3·5 × 4·7m (12 × 15ft) apart, dwarf pyramids 3·5 × 4·7m (4 × 7ft) apart, bush trees about 4m (12ft) apart.

Give a spring mulch of manure and fork it in during the autumn or you can use inorganic fertilizer—50g (2oz) of superphosphate of lime, 25g (1oz) of sulphate of ammonia and 12·5g (½oz) sulphate of potash, sprinkled as far as the tree roots extend,

Flowering times for apples

Very early
Aromatic Russet (B)
Gravenstein (T)
Keswick Codlin (B)

Early
Adam's Pearmain (B)
Beauty of Bath
Ben's Red (B)
Bismark (B)
Cheddar Cross
Christmas Pearmain (B)
Discovery
Egremont Russet
George Cave
George Neal
Golden Spire
Irish Peach
Laxton's Early Crimson
Lord Lambourne
Lord Suffield
McIntosh Red
Melba (B)
Michaelmas Red
Norfolk Beauty
Patricia (B)
Rev W. Wilkes (B)
Ribston Pippin (T)
St Edmund's Pippin
Scarlet Pimpernel
Striped Beefing
Warner's King (T)
Washington (T)
White Transparent

Early mid season
Arthur Turner
Belle de Boskoop (T)
Blenheim Orange (TB)
Bowden's Seedling
Bramley's Seedling (T)
Brownlee's Russet
Charles Ross
Claygate Pearmain
Cox's Orange Pippin
D'Arcy Spice
Devonshire Quarrenden (B)
Early Victoria (Emneth Early) (B)
Emperor Alexander
Epicure
Exeter Cross
Fortune (B)
Granny Smith
Grenadier
Howgate Wonder
James Grieve
John Standish
Jonathan
King's Acre Pippin
Kidd's Orange Red
Lord Grosvenor
Merton Pippin
Merton Prolific
Merton Russet
Merton Worcester
Miller's Seedling (B)
Ontario
Peasgood's Nonsuch
Red Victoria (B)
Reinette du Canada (T)
Rival (B)
Rosemary Russet
Sturmer Pippin
Sunset
Tydeman's Early Worcester
Tydeman's Late Orange
Wagener (B)
Wealthy
Winter Quarrenden (B)
Worcester Pearmain

Mid season
Allington Pippin (B)
Annie Elizabeth
Chelmsford Wonder (B)
Cox's Pomona
Delicious
Duke of Devonshire
Ellison's Orange
Golden Delicious
Golden Noble
Herring's Pippin
Lady Henniker
Lady Sudeley
Lane's Prince Albert
Laxton's Superb (B)
Monarch (B)
Orleans Reinette
Sir John Thornycroft

Late mid season
American Mother
Coronation (B)
Gascoyne's Scarlet
King of the Pippins (B)
Lord Derby
Merton Beauty
Newton Wonder
Northern Spy (B)
Royal Jubilee
William Crump
Winston
Woolbrook Pippin (B)

Late
Court Pendu Plat
Edward VII
Heusgen's Golden Reinette

Very late
Crawley Beauty

B=biennial or irregular flowering varieties. T=triploid varieties with poor pollen. Those not marked T are diploid varieties. Coloured sports eg Red Millar's Seedling usually flower at the same time as the parent.

and raked carefully into the surface.

Cherries There are many flowering as well as fruiting kinds, the first are bred mainly for display.

A sweet cherry, *Prunus avium* which you might be able to fit into your garden (it grows between 10–20m (30–60ft) is available in black or white varieties and is hardy, although the blossom could be damaged by spring frosts. These cherries are not able to be grafted on to dwarf root-stock and they resent hard pruning, although you can try a fan shape or bush. There are early, mid-season and late cultivars of the sweet cherry and fruits that are yellow, red, dark red, black, crimson or purple.

The sweet cherries are not self-fertile and can only be fertile with certain other varieties although there are some universal donors compatible with all groups. The trouble is that your garden has to accommodate not one large cherry tree, but at least two, and those two must have blossom times overlapping. It is a good idea to check with a reliable nurseryman on what to choose, deciding on whether you want early or late fruiting, what colour cherries, etc.

One way out of the pollinating problem, is to plant a sour cherry tree such as the bush morello which grows only to about 4·7m (15ft) and is self-fertile and able to pollinate any sweet cherry flowering at the same time. You could use the sour cherries for cooking, bottling, jam-making or making cherry ale.

Sweet cherries fruit on spurs formed on older wood. Sour cherries fruit on shoots formed the previous season. You can train a sour cherry as a fan shaped tree—see pruning chapter.

Sweet cherries like deep, loamy soil and a spring mulch of farmyard manure (approx 55kg [1 cwt] to 10 sq m [10 sq yds]) or Nitro-chalk 50–75g (2–3oz) per square metre; and an autumn application of 25–50g (1–2oz) per square metre of sulphate of potash.

Protect cherries from birds by using netting or rayon spider's web material.

Above: *Space-saving 'family fruit tree' where a selection of varieties of one fruit are grafted onto a common root stock.*

Plums They flower early and so are susceptible to spring frosts, so try and give them the protection of a wall. They like a 62·5–75cm (25–30in) rainfall and good sunshine, and a well-drained soil with plenty of humus. Plums do not favour soils overlying chalk, but will grow in them. They give better and more regular crops if they are pollinated by compatible varieties.

Plums can be grown as semi-dwarf pyramids pruned to about 3m (9ft) and then you might be able to ward off birds with netting, etc.

For training as a pyramid, a maiden (one-year-old) is planted. See 'pruning pyramid plum'.

Plant plums between November and March when soil is suitable.

Once the tree is bearing good crops it needs plenty of nitrogen so supplement a yearly mulch of compost or manure with a nitrogenous fertilizer.

Plum tree wood is brittle so watch that summer gales do not damage branches laden with fruit.

Damsons are a type of plum, ripening a little later than most plums. They are not very sweet but good for jam. Bullaces, another type of plum-like fruit ripen even later, and can be eaten but are good for cooking. Gages are a special sort of plum which have their own characteristic, full, juicy flavour.

Below: *Training apple trees: 1 One-year-old maiden 2 Fan-trained tree 3 Dwarf pyramid 4 Espalier shape 5 Cordon 6 Bush.*

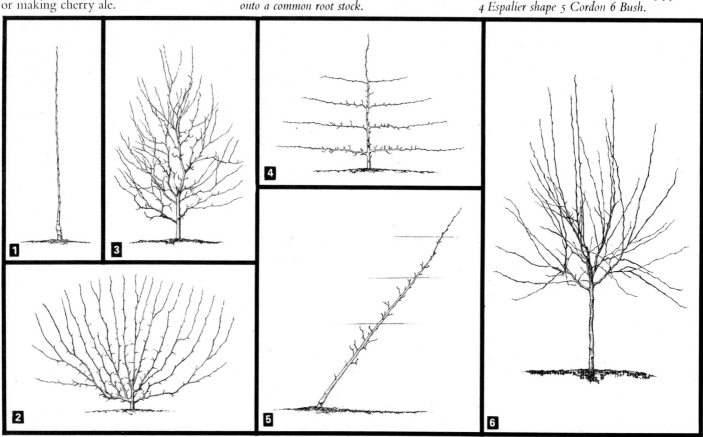

Above: *Fan-trained apple tree. The branches are in a flat plane, growing from a short leg.*

Below: *Pears ready for picking. Do not leave on tree too long or they won't store well.*

Above: *Damson 'Merryweather' has purple skin and yellow flesh, ripens in autumn.*

Monthly calendar

JANUARY
Weather allowing, plant newly-arrived fruit trees. Trim leaders of apples, pears and cherries if needed.

FEBRUARY
Before growth starts, prune young plums that are to be fan-trained. Prepare to protect blossom from frost. Apply artificial fertilizers.

MARCH
A final chance to plant fruit. Refirm soil around earlier plantings; secure ties, apply mulch.

APRIL
Spray fruits before they blossom. Cut back leaders of maiden plums. Pinch out blossoms on new trees.

MAY
Protect strawberries in flower from frosts.

JUNE
Spray apples early against red spider mite. Watch gooseberry bushes for hatching sawfly caterpillars.

JULY
Prune cordon pears early in the south of England; two weeks later in the north. Spray loganberries. Start to shorten side shoots of trained fruit trees.

AUGUST
Pick early apples and pears. Plant summer-fruiting strawberries.

SEPTEMBER
Complete strawberry summer-planting. Prepare ground for November fruit planting.

OCTOBER
Cut down fruited canes (to soil level) of blackberries (when all fruit is gone).

NOVEMBER
Fruit tree planting season—never plant in wet, sticky soil.

DECEMBER
Prune secondary growth on cordon apples and pears. Do not prune stone fruits. To prevent brown rot, pick off and burn old fruit.

The herb garden

Herbs have a history going back to the ancient Egyptians and the earliest Chinese dynasties, when they were used for incense, embalming, toiletries, medicines and cooking. Today, we like many of them for cooking and some of them for health and beauty, and many more for pot pourris, herb pillows and sweet-smelling sachets.

Two classic uses for herbs are the *bouquet garni* and *fines herbes*. The first is a little bunch of thyme, bay leaf, parsley and perhaps marjoram and rosemary. The second is a mixture of chervil, chives, parsley and tarragon finely chopped together.

Start your herb garden in a small way, with the herbs you use for cooking planted near the kitchen door. Spare some good soil among the perennials for the annuals to be planted each year, or have a small, separate annual bed. You can plant herbs in the rest of the garden too—thyme creeping among paving stones, lavender hedges, marigolds and nasturtium and rosemary among the shrubs. Nettles you will probably have anyway and they are also good activators for the compost heap.

Herbs like good drainage and shelter from the wind and some compost applied in the spring or autumn, but they are not fussy and do not need rich soil.

Allium sativum (Garlic). Technically a vegetable rather than a herb (although always used as a flavouring not as a vegetable), garlic is a member of the Lily family and related to onions and chives. The separate cloves from each bulb are planted in light well-composted soil in a sunny position about 2·5cm (1in) deep and 15cm (6in) apart in the early spring.

The bulbs can be lifted when the leaves have died down in the late summer then hung up in a dry place.

Allium schoenoprasum (Chives). This perennial plant produces clumps of mildly onion-flavoured green spears. Chives, which grow to 15–40cm (6–16in), make good edging plants in summer and have pretty mauve-blue flowers for cutting. Sow in early summer.

Anethum graveolens (Dill). This is a beautiful feathery herb, growing to 45–90cm (1½–3ft), and is sharply aromatic. It is a hardy annual and has leaves similar to

Above left: *Majorana hortensis (syn. Origanum majorana), is the annual sweet marjoram.*

Above: *Lovage, Ligusticum officinale, is a useful herb for stocks, stews or fish sauce.*

Left: *There are many different mints with flavours from spearmint to pineapple.*

Below left: *The ovate bulbils of garlic, Allium sativum, usually called cloves.*

Below: *Broad-leaved garlic, a British native, likes a light, damp soil and sun.*

Above: *Dill, Anethum graveolens, looks rather like fennel, but among its differences, has a hollow stalk. The leaves will flavour fish or vegetables. Dill is an annual so you can let some of the plant flower and seed itself.*

Below: *The British native borage, Borago officinalis, is also an annual grown from seed each year. Leaves have a stinging, hairy surface. Use fresh leaves in salads, vegetables, fruit and alcoholic drinks. Grow it in the sun.*

fennel but blueish-green in colour and more delicate. In late summer it has yellow flowers that look lovely in flower arrangements, and whose seeds are used for pickling cucumbers. Sow the seeds in late spring in well-drained soil in a sunny place and give the plant quite a lot of water. As it is quick-growing from seed it will do well in pots or boxes on a window-sill.

Angelica archangelica (Angelica). This giant biennial, which grows 1·5–2m (5–6ft) tall, has huge green umbels. The seeds should be sown in autumn—they are only viable directly after the parent plant has shed them. If possible plant them in rich damp soil in a fairly shaded position. Germination is slow, but once the plants are established they will seed themselves. Angelica needs a fairly large garden, but it is also good for cutting for the house.

Anthemis nobilis (Chamomile). Chamomile makes an unusual and fragrant lawn; the stems go along the ground and white daisy-like flowers rise up 30–35cm (12–14in). Flowers are dried to make a most refreshing tea. The seeds are sown in the late spring. It seeds itself as well as spreads and will grow in any soil if it gets some sun. You have it forever once it is established.

Anthriscus cerefolium (Chervil). This is slightly similar in appearance to parsley but is more delicate and fern-like. It is an annual and grows to about 30cm (1ft). Chervil appreciates a shady place, grows best when sown in late summer in well-drained soil and is one of the earliest herbs to be used after the winter. Usually sown at intervals throughout the year and used very young. It has a slight aniseed flavour.

Artemisia dracunculus (Tarragon). This is the true French tarragon and considered the best; *Artemisia dracunculides*, is the Russian tarragon, which has slightly less flavour. Tarragon can almost never be grown from seed but it can be grown from root divisions or cuttings planted in spring. The French variety will probably not set seed in a temperate climate. The Russian variety is a very strong grower and tends to spread rather like mint if not controlled. The French variety grows to 60cm–1m (2–3ft), the Russian to 1–1·5m (3–5ft). Both like a light soil and a dry sunny position but will grow in a wide range of soil types, even clay.

Petroselinum crispum syn. *Carum petroselinum* (Parsley). Parsley is a biennial and another member of the *Umbelliferae* family. It is full of vitamins, particularly vitamin C. Sow the seeds from spring to midsummer in drills 30cm (1ft) apart, in fairly damp soil in a shady place. Parsley is slow to germinate, but it transplants easily and makes an excellent edging plant.

Coriandrum sativum (Coriander). This

attractive feathery annual grows to about 45cm (1½ft) and provides both leaves—with a flavour somewhat like dried orange peel—and seeds for the kitchen. Sow the seeds in rich light soil.

Foeniculum vulgare (Fennel). With its fine feathery foliage and yellow umbels of flowers, fennel, grows to 1·2–3m (4–6ft). It is a perennial, but should be transplanted before the tap root has grown too long. A well-established plant does not take kindly to being moved.

Laurus nobilis (Bay). This is the sweet bay tree. A mature tree may grow to 5–7m (15–20ft) tall or more over 20 years. It has small yellow flowers in spring followed by purplish berries in a warm dry summer. You can grow it from seed sown in the spring, but this is sometimes difficult to do and it is easier to buy it as a small pot plant. Grow it in well-drained soil in a sheltered position or keep it in a pot on a shaded balcony or verandah.

Lavandula officinalis (Lavender). Most people know lavender, with its grey-green needle-like foliage, spears of fragrant flowers and a scent which is perhaps, the most refreshing in the world. Increase by green cuttings about mid-summer. Grow in a sunny position in poor soil. Although flower-stems may be removed before winter it is not advisable to trim the bush until any spring frosts are over.

Ligusticum officinale syn. *Levisticum officinale* (Lovage). Lovage is a giant-sized perennial, growing 1·5–2·2m (5–7ft) high with yellowish flower umbels in late summer. It prefers rich moist soil. Either sow the seeds in spring, or divide roots in spring or autumn. Both the leaves and seeds are used and are very pungent, being noticeably stronger than other herbs.

Lippia citriodora (Lemon Verbena). This shrubby plant can grow to over 3m (10ft), and has long, pointed lemon-scented leaves, and small mauve flowers in late summer. Lemon verbena was introduced from Chile in 1781 and is not hardy. Grow it from a cutting planted in late spring in light, well-drained soil in a warm, sheltered position. In sheltered places it will probably survive the winter outside. Alternatively, you can grow it in a pot and take it indoors or into the greenhouse if a frosty winter threatens.

Melissa officinalis (Lemon Balm). This hardy herbaceous perennial grows high with light green, deeply-veined, heart-shaped leaves, strongly scented of lemon, and small whitish flowers. It is easily grown in most soils from seed sown in spring, or by root division in spring and autumn. It also seeds itself.

Mentha (Mints). There are over 40 varieties of mint and many hybrids of which a few, all perennial, are well-known. They must be grown from root division

Above: *Lemon-scented thyme, Thymus citriodorus, is perennial.*

Below: *Parsley needs picking well in the summer or the plants will grow coarse.*

which is not a problem. It grows well in moist rich soil and spreads very fast so, ideally, it should be grown on its own with the roots restricted either by planting it in a box plunged in the earth or by driving down slates around it. The most common varieties of mint, all edible, are: *Mentha piperita* (Peppermint). This grows 30–60cm (1–2ft) tall with longish pointed leaves and has purple flowers in autumn. It is the oil from this plant that is used for peppermint flavour. *Mentha rotundifolia* (Apple Mint, Round-leafed Mint). This grows 60–90cm (2–3ft) tall or more, with round furry leaves and has purplish-white flowers in summer. It is often used as a substitute for spearmint and, once tasted, is usually preferred to it. *Mentha spicata* syn. *Mentha viridis* (Spearmint, Lamb Mint, Common Green Mint). This is the one generally used for mint sauce. It grows 30–60cm (1–2ft) tall with pointed leaves and has purplish flowers in autumn. Keep the plant pinched down to about 15cm (6in).

Monarda didyma (Bergamot, Bee Balm, Oswego Tea). This perennial has aromatic foliage and honeysuckle-shaped scarlet flowers. It grows readily from seed, and should be sown in the summer for flowering the following year. It will grow to 75cm–1·5m (2½–5ft) depending upon the soil, and position. In light rich soil you can grow it in full sun; in hot dry soil it prefers some shade and should be well-watered.

Ocimum basilicum (Basil). Common or sweet basil is a half-hardy annual and grows in good warm conditions to about 30cm (1ft) high. It has roughly triangular leaves and cream-coloured flowers. A delicate plant, basil does best of all under glass as it needs heat to bring out its clove-like flavour. Sow the seeds in late spring. Give it the sunniest position in the garden. When a young plant is established, keep pinching out the top to make it bush out.

Origanum (Marjoram). These perennials are among the most useful culinary herbs, and one of those that make up a traditional *bouquet garni*. *Origanum majorana* syn. *Majorana hortensis*. (Knotted Marjoram). Although a perennial, in temperate climates treat it as a half-hardy annual. Sow it outside when the soil has warmed up, sometimes as late as the end of May. It can be sown earlier in heat and set out in a warm sheltered bed. (If frost threatens protect the plants with cloches.) *Origanum onites* (Pot Marjoram). This is green-stemmed and generally white-flowered. It can be grown in a pot indoors for use during the winter. *Origanum vulgare* (Wild Marjoram). This has reddish stems and generally purple flowers. It is indigenous to the limestone hills of Britain, where the temperate climate gives it a similar, but somewhat milder, flavour to that of pot

Above: *Sweet basil, Ocimum basilicum, gives a delicate aromatic flavour to food.*

Below: *Chives, Allium schoenoprasum, are a grass-like hardy perennial. Grow it near a tap or water. Cut back leaves only to 5cm.*

Above: *For a steady supply of herbs throughout the year, dry your own in an airy, dark place or gentle heat. Herbs have dozens of uses.*

marjoram. When grown in hot climates such as southern Italy, however, it is known as oregano and has a pungent taste.

Rosmarinus officinalis (Rosemary). This evergreen shrub makes a large sprawling bush 2m (approx 6ft) or more in height with blue-mauve flowers in spring. It should have a reasonably sheltered place in sandy well-drained soil and, although it is hardy, it cannot withstand severe frost. A dry, warm, sunny border suits it best—and if it is happy it can live for 20 years. Seed can be sown in early summer, but rosemary is normally grown from rooted cuttings or bought plants.

Salvia officinalis (Sage). This is a little shrub about 60cm (2ft) high with narrow greyish-green leaves and spikes of purple flowers. Sage will grow almost anywhere but, like most herbs, is happiest on well-drained soil and needs a warm, sunny position to develop fully its aromatic oils. If growing from seed, sow in early summer in a seed box. Transfer to a nursery bed before transferring to final position. Sage can be grown in a pot. It is increased by root division or cuttings. Renew the plants every three or four years as they get thin and woody.

Satureja (Savory). Savory is a very useful aromatic kitchen herb and looks like a long-leafed thyme. Two varieties are grown: *Satureja hortensis* (Summer Savory). This is a little bushy annual which grows to 45cm (1½ft) and has pink flowers in late summer. Grow it from seed sown in early summer. You can also grow it in pots indoors throughout the winter. *Satureja montana* (Winter Savory). This hardy dwarf evergreen grows 30–45cm (1–1½ft) tall and is extremely useful for a flavouring in the winter when everything else is dead. As it is a perennial it is perhaps preferable to summer savory. Seeds can be sown in a fairly light soil in late spring.

Thymus (Thymes). Thyme, a perennial evergreen, is another of the very popular herbs used in bouquet garni and stuffings. Insert the cuttings in early summer in a sunny, sheltered position in well-drained soil which is not too rich. *Thymus vulgaris* (Common Thyme). This grows in the shape of a low bush about 30cm (1ft) high, and has strongly-scented tiny leaves. *Thymus citriodorus* (Lemon Thyme). This is of creeping growth, only 15cm (6in) high and grows well amongst paving stones.

Tropaeolum majus (Nasturtium). Nasturtiums are such a part of the flower garden that it is perhaps a surprise to find them in the herb garden. But the spicy, peppery leaves are very rich in vitamin C and the fresh flowers are delicious in salads. Nasturtiums are annuals and are extraordinarily easy to grow, although subject to black fly. Sow the seeds in late spring.

Above: *Lemon balm, Melissa officinalis.*

Left: *Winter savory, Satureia montana.*

Below left: *Bay, Laurus nobilis.*

Below: *Variegated form of sage.*

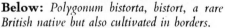
Below: *Polygonum bistorta, bistort, a rare British native but also cultivated in borders.*

Below: *Caraway and yellow woad, whose purple seed pods were used for making a dye.*

Verbena officinalis (Vervain). Vervain is grown in herb gardens mainly because of its ancient use to ward off evil powers, although in France a tea is still made with it. It is a pretty perennial plant which grows to 45–60cm (1½–2ft) high with pointed leaves and spikes of mauve flowers. Sow seeds in spring where the plant is to grow, thereafter it will seed itself.

Harvesting and drying herbs Harvest herbs when their aromatic oils are most powerful, and their flowers when they are most perfect.

Pick herbs just before they flower, in the early morning when the dew has dried and before the sun is hot. Pick flowers when they are just open and absolutely unblemished.

Harvest seeds when they are ready to fall; and roots at the end of the season. Pick only just enough to lightly cover whatever drying shelves you have arranged and leave the leaves on the stem. Handle the leaf and flower as gently as you can to prevent bruising. As you pick herbs or flowers lay them gently one deep in flat boxes.

The drying place This can be an airing cupboard, platewarming compartment of the oven, clothes drying cupboard or warm, well-ventilated and darkened room. Leave cupboard or oven door open because the movement of air is essential to carry away the humidity of the drying plant.

The shelves themselves are best made from wooden frames with open-weave cloth like cheesecloth, hessian or muslin stretched over them, or with the flat bottoms of cardboard boxes laid across. Do not use wire framework.

If you can alter and regulate the heat, one method is to begin drying with a temperature of about 32°C (90°F) for a day and then to reduce the heat to 21°C (70°F) until drying is finished. The drying space should only faintly smell of herbs, a strong smell means too much heat and escaping aromas. Do not add a fresh batch of herbs until the first batch is dry or you will add more humidity to the air. Turn the herbs as they are drying.

Experiment with your drying arrangements until you can get maximum colour and smell in the herbs.

Flowers are sometimes dried more slowly and at a lower temperature than herbs, eg rosemary flowers.

Air drying involves tying a bunch of herbs or flowers together and hanging them upside down in a dry and airy place and is an older method of drying herbs and flowers. It is more satisfactory in a warm climate than a humid one and is an easy method but you will not retain so much colour and scent in the herbs.

Herbs used regularly can be grown outside your kitchen, in a garden layout as shown.

129

Pruning practice made easy

Pruning basically means using secateurs or a saw to shape and train plant growth, cut out old or diseased wood and encourage strong growth, flowers and fruit.

A form of 'soft pruning' called pinching out, deshooting or disbudding is also used to manipulate plant growth. This can be done with your fingers. To pinch out, nip off the top growth of the main stem thus encouraging the plant to grow outwards with more side stems (called laterals) rather than up. To disbud, rub off the buds or shoots on the stem of the plant to discourage side growth or side stems growing in the wrong direction and so the main stem grows vigorously upwards. In most plants the main stem dominates the lateral or side growth and so, pinching out the top encourages bushy lower growth.

Before you pinch-out on young plants, let a good number of leaves develop on the main stem as new side growth comes from the angle between leaf and stem (the axil).

If you are disbudding to produce a tall main stem (also sometimes used to get a good fruit or flower harvest), remember that no bud is likely to re-form there.

Even well-nourished plants have limited energy to direct into production. If you remove dead flowers and young fruits, then the plant produces more flowers. If you leave them, the plant turns from flowers to fruit and seed production.

Pruning equipment
Choose your **secateurs** to fit comfortably into your hand. It is less tiring for a woman to use a light pair for light pruning and a heavier pair for the harder work. The secateurs must be sharp or you will bruise stems and make harder work of your pruning.

You must make a sloping cut which sheds rain better—about 1cm (½in) above the bud and parallel to the direction of its growth. If you make the cut too far above the bud the short bit of stem between your cut and the bud may die back and possibly will harbour infec-

tion. If you make your cut at too steep an angle so that it extends behind the bud, the bud will dry out and die. You can make a cut on a shrub or tree level with a joint on a larger branch.

Be careful not to twist the secateurs as you cut for you can mangle the end of the stem, which makes a good site for disease to enter. For the same reason, it is better to treat larger pruning cuts with a proprietary wound-sealing compound.

Secateurs have to be kept very clean. If you cut a virus-diseased cane and then cut a healthy one you can spread the virus; clean the secateurs in-between the two jobs. Oil the joints and the blades.

Above: *A thin-bladed small pad saw is useful for thinning out basal growth.*

Above: *Use sharp secateurs and cut just above the bud to avoid damage or dying back.*

Treat large pruning cuts with a lead-based paint or with a proprietary sealing compound.

Right: *A hand saw with a long narrow blade cuts awkward branches where they cluster at the base of a shrub.*

The woody base of some shrubs and certainly trees are beyond the capacity of secateurs to cut and you will make your hands sore trying to use them. For this work you need a **pruning saw** which can also get a good bite at canes growing very close together at the base of a shrub. Be careful not to bruise neighbouring canes. There are several types and sizes of pruning saws available; a small pruning saw is quite successful for roses and general work.

Pruning knives are not advised for the beginner. There are expert nurserymen who wield them with skill but secateurs are all you will ever need.

Pruning shrubs

Pruning should never interfere with the natural plant shape. If it has elegant, long-arching canes, to cut them midway is to interfere with its shape without a good reason. If you do want to take out some very old wood and encourage growth of new wood, cut an old cane at the base letting other arching canes take its place. The aim of pruning a shrub is at most to help it along a little but the shrub should stay as natural-looking as it can.

When autumn comes it is tempting to get out your secateurs and tidy up the straggling growth and dead flower spikes but confine your enthusiasm to cutting off the dead flowers only. It is best to prune nearer the spring. Beginner gardeners should leave pruning young shrubs for more than a year or two until the growth pattern is clear and there really becomes a need to cut out old wood.

Among the early-flowering shrubs that need pruning after flowering are forsythia, *Kerria japonica*, *Spiraea arguta* and *S. thunbergii*, philadelphus or mock orange, weigela and diervilla. They will make unproductive thickets if the older growths are not cut away.

Prune forsythia before the leaves fully develop and the flowered wood can easily be seen. Do not prune it too heavily or it will grow leafy, non-flowering growth.

Certain deciduous shrubs produce bigger and better flowers if pruned hard back each year; among those are *Buddleia davidii*, *Spiraea japonica*, *S. X bumalda* and *Caryopteris X clandonesis*. The first is pruned back hard in March before growth begins; the next two are also pruned to the ground in March and will flower in the summer on young wood; the last should have the previous season's shoots cut back to two buds, and will flower in autumn.

Deciduous varieties of ceanothus, the dogwoods, *Hydrangea paniculata*, hypericums, fuchsias, *Tamarix pentandra*, hybrid tea and floribunda roses will give better displays if cut back in the spring just before growth begins.

Evergreen hedges that can be cut back in spring are box, laurel, lonicera and privet.

For pruning purposes plants are divided into two main groups by the way they grow. The first group of plants flowers and fruits on the current year's growth, called the new wood. The second group of plants flowers and fruits on last year's growth, called the old wood.

If a plant flowers and fruits on the new wood, it probably does so late in the season, around autumn. If it is flowering and fruiting on old wood then it probably flowers early in the year, around spring. There are exceptions to this however, some plants flowering on both types of wood.

The plants flowering late on new wood are pruned usually in the dormant period just before growth starts again. When plants flower on old wood early in the season, they are pruned after flowering so that they have the rest of the year to grow more canes for production of flowers the following year.

Perovskia atriplicifolia, a shrub with striking greyish-white shoots, benefits from cutting away all dead growth in early spring.

Perovskia 'Blue Spire', pruned back earlier, will now produce good flowering shoots in the summer.

When you see a variegated shrub with a pure green branch, cut it off right back at its junction with the main stem. Do the same on all shrubs where strong shoots grow into neighbouring shrubs.

Rose pruning

Before you prune you should have some idea why you are pruning a rose.

You prune to keep a rose healthy by cutting out dead wood or damaged wood which is subject to disease, and wood already diseased which could infect the whole plant. You cut too, for shape, if, for example, you have a rose hedge, or to stop the bush growing in the wrong direction. You also prune to maintain young, healthy growth and to cut out weak, old growth which cannot support good flowers.

Most experts advocate gradual pruning of roses from about the turn of the year through to March or April, except for the ramblers which are pruned when their flowers are finished. For pruning others, wait until the leaves have fallen so that you can see what you are doing. Some experts leave pruning roses until the new growth has started in the spring, when canes damaged by winter frosts can be cut out too. By early spring you can see which eyes are putting out strong new shoots and which are heralding weak growth. In early spring, you can also rub out unwanted shoots with your fingers and give the rose bush more of the shape you want.

However, you can start to prune your roses on any day in January when the weather is favourable.

Like all plants, the growth of a rose has a distinctive pattern. A cane on a rose bush starts its life low down near the crown of the bush—where the bush is grafted to stock. The cane grows, bears leaves and tapers towards the top in the first year. In the second year, it bears lateral shoots coming off the main cane and ending in a prolific display of flowers. In the third year, sub-laterals grow off the laterals and produce fewer flowers than the year before.

The growth of perpetual or hybrid tea roses is a little different but the principle is the same. Every shoot, even in the first year's growth tends to have a flower bud and, because this stops further growth of the shoot, the plant produces laterals in the first year and then more flowers. However, every stem growing from another stem is thinner than the stem it grows from, until it is too thin for supporting flowers—then the whole cane is removed to make way for younger canes.

Pruning rambler and climbing roses is again slightly different. Ramblers are pruned by cutting back the flowering canes either to the base of the plant or to the

Above: *Forsythia, spring-flowering shrub that is pruned once flowering is over.*

Above: *In tree or shrub this type of branch is removed to stop chafing and overcrowding.*

Above: *The head of a standard rose before pruning has some twiggy and dead wood.*

Above right: *After pruning, all twiggy growth and dead wood have been removed.*

Right: *Pruning a newly-planted climbing rose by shortening the long growths. As growth begins, encourage it by watering and mulching.*

Below: *Fuchsia magellanica can look dead in late winter but prune off shoots close to the base and you will get great summer display.*

132

Above: *Once-flowering rambling roses have flowered canes cut out. Tie new canes in.*

Below: *Dormant buds can be encouraged to grow by cutting back the laterals.*

Above: *Removing dead flowers allows further followers to be produced.*

Below: *Pruning a newly-planted bush rose by cutting back growth quite close to ground.*

place where a new cane grows from an old one. The flowering canes cut out flowered in their second year of life and their disappearance gives space for new canes to grow, and in turn, flower. If the rambler has not enough new canes coming on, this does happen with a few varieties, then cut back laterals to the main cane.

For climbers encourage the plant to have more than one base stem, or it may become a thick bare trunk as the years go on. Prune off its flowers in the first year of planting to give it more strength to establish itself if it seems reluctant to climb, and shape it to its support. Cut out old twiggy and crowded growth and any that is damaged or diseased. To encourage new base canes from time to time, cut out one of the old ones.

Fruit shrub pruning

Raspberries In the first year, cut off canes to within 25cm (10in) of the ground, in the spring, cutting just above a swelling bud. This encourages good basal growth. In succeeding years, cut off old canes close to the ground after fruiting and these will be replaced by new canes shooting up which will bear fruit the following year. Keep the number of young strong canes to about five or six, and pinch out their sappy tips in early spring. Burn all prunings. Varieties fruiting in summer are cut back after fruiting. Varieties fruiting in autumn have fruiting canes cut back in the dormant season.

Blackcurrants Prune after harvesting the fruit. Remove about a third of the older branches to maintain vigour and induce sucker shoots to form below ground. Retain a good supply of last year's shoots, spaced evenly over the bush. Blackcurrants fruit on previous season's shoots.

Redcurrants Prune in late winter, by shortening the leading shoots by a third and the side shoots to two or three buds. Summer pruning in July promotes fruit bud formation. Shorten the side shoots to five leaves and leave the leading shoots unpruned. Red and white currants fruit on spurs formed on the old wood.

Gooseberries Prune in summer, cutting side shoots to six leaves in July to promote bud formation and to remove mildew-infected tips. Tear out suckers; cutting them only encourages them. Winter prune the bushes in November or leave until the spring if birds attack buds. Shorten leading shoots by one-third and reduce side shoots very short to about 3·5cm (1½in) for heavy crops, and to two buds for large dessert berries. Prune upright bushes to outward pointing buds and weeping bushes to upward pointing buds.

Fruit tree pruning

You must first of all know whether your

apple or pear tree is a tree that bears fruit on spurs, ie short lateral branches, or one that is tip-bearing, ie bears its fruit on the end of one-year-old shoots, from a terminal (end) fruit bud. Fruit buds are larger and more prominent than growth buds and often stand out from the branch, or form clusters. The bud at the tip, that is, the end of a shoot, is called a terminal bud. The majority of apple and pear trees are spur-bearing. One spur tends to develop out of another spur and on old trees the spur system becomes too confused and the fruit too crowded thus resulting in inferior fruit. The cure is to shorten the spur system during the autumn or winter pruning, or to remove some spur systems entirely.

You must have sufficient unpruned laterals in tip-bearing trees to get a good crop. There are tip-bearing pears too.

You prune fruit trees to cut out diseased, overcrowded or damaged growth, to let light into the centre of the tree, to shape (if you are training an espalier tree, or cordon, etc), and to encourage regular, earlier yields.

Again, know something about how the trees grow. They are perennial and by natural means alone they would take several years to crop; by using dwarfing rootstocks, this time is shortened. Vigorous rootstocks delay cropping but yields are greater. The majority of the best fruit is found on the younger branches—on fruiting spurs—with smaller, inferior fruits on the older wood. This younger wood is generally found towards the outside of the plant and has larger and more plentiful green leaves which feed the fruit buds. On the older branches, leaves tend to be small, fewer and perhaps faded. So if you replace old or ageing branches with younger ones, you encourage the production of high quality fruit.

Below: *Ribes sanguineum, the flowering currant, also has stems that have been pruned back.*

Apple trees Any winter pruning is done as soon as possible after leaf fall. Any summer pruning is done around July or August and involves cutting back the current year's side shoots to 10–15cm (4–6in).

This is only done for trees trained into shapes—the leading shoot is left unpruned. Secure the suitably-placed shoots to your training espalier or to a support.

Standard apple trees, large trees over 5m (18ft) or so, are not suitable for average gardens but if you have one do not summer-prune it. Bush trees which grow to about 5m (18ft) are not summer-pruned either. In winter, thin out branches of standards; remove damaged, diseased and crowded wood. On bush trees, in winter, weak growth can be shortened right back.

Pyramid shaping begins when the maiden, one-year-old apple tree, is shortened back to within 45cm (18in) of the ground after planting. In the following winter each new leader is pruned to 25cm (10in),

On the flowering currant, the old wood that has flowered is cut right back and the shrub is left, as above, with only new shoots remaining to flower next year, below.

if vigorous enough, above the cut made the previous winter. The direction of the top bud at each cut is chosen on the opposite side of the cut before, so that an upright main stem is made. When the tree is 2m (7ft) high (it might take years), the top can be removed in mid-summer to restrict growth.

In winter, the side shoots, which you pruned back a little in the summer on your trained apple tree, are now shortened back further—to within 2·5–5cm (1–2in) of their base, while the tree is dormant. Leave the extension shoots on espalier trees unpruned.

Pears Pear trees are just as suitable as apple trees for growing in cordons, pyramid or on espalier. They are pruned and shaped in the same way as apples.

Cherries Prune sweet cherries to keep the tree open, to cut away dead wood or crossed branches, and to shorten straggly growth after flowering. Do this in spring or mid-summer to prevent the gumming sap coagulating and to lessen the chances of disease entering the wounds.

Pruning a sour cherry to fan-shape
After planting, shorten the previous season's growth on the leading branches by half and cut back side shoots to 7·5cm (3in). Sour cherries fruit on shoots formed the previous season. Shorten the leaders each year. Annually replaced side shoots are tied in parallel to the branches building up the fan shape. Replacement shoots are chosen in May and August; one near the base of a fruiting shoot and another at its tip, to draw sap to the fruit. All other shoots are pinched out when small. The tip of the terminal shoot itself is pinched out when 7·5–10cm (3–4in) of growth has been made. After the cherries have been harvested, the fruited shoots are pruned back at their junction with the selected replacement shoots. These are then tied into the fan shape as the earlier shoots were.

Pruning a pyramid plum
Plant a maiden and cut it back to 1·75m (5ft) the following March. If less than 1·75m (5ft), allow it to grow on for another year. Any side shoots above 45cm (18in) from the ground should be shortened by half and any below 45cm (18in) should be cut off. Towards the end of July or August, when new growth has finished, cut back branch leaders to 20cm (8in), making the cut to a bud pointing downwards or outwards. Cut side shoots back to 15cm (6in). Do this each year. Leave central leader of the maiden in the summer of the first year but in April of the second year, cut it back to a third of its length. Do this each year until the tree grows to 3m (9ft). Thereafter, shorten new growth on central leader each year to about 2·5cm (1in).

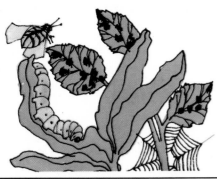

Pests
and diseases

In the garden some insects and animals seem to be about more than others and a few of those are described here. As the insect world is endlessly varied and inventive in its breeding and eating habits, it cannot be covered here in great detail.

When it comes to bacterial, fungal and viral diseases the enemy is often unseen and can be harder to deal with. You can buy Ministry of Agriculture booklets on chemicals for the gardener to use—all garden societies and the Ministry are only too anxious to suggest safe and sensible remedies for garden pests and diseases. Good nurserymen will help with advice too.

Where possible use the simplest means for a cure—picking off or pruning affected parts and burning them, destroying a plant, rotating crops, keeping the garden free from weeds and rubbish cover for breeding insects, or encouraging the predators of the garden who are your friends—birds, frogs, toads, ladybirds, some beetles and centipedes. Never spray open blossoms as this will kill the visiting bees. Do not let pest control get out of proportion. It is not always worth using thoroughly toxic and persistent sprays in cases where it only means losing a flower or two, or an unsightly plant that could easily be burnt.

If you spray, begin by using the sprays based on natural substances such as derris, pyrethrum and nicotine. These will help control a large range of the ordinary pests such as aphids, red spider mite and sawflies. Washing soda (approx 1kg (2lb) to approx

Top: *Caterpillars of the Lackey moth attack fruit trees. They congregate together.*

Above: *Aphids or greenfly are sap-sucking, and like a variety of plants.*

Left: *The codling moth lays its eggs in fruit trees; the caterpillars tunnel into fruit.*

Right: *The caterpillar, at the fruit core, is pinkish and 1cm long. Once fed, it departs.*

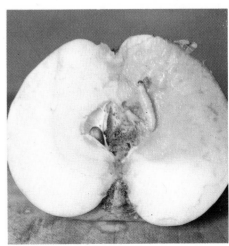

5·75l (10 pints) of rain water) is a cheap although not terribly effective remedy for powdery mildew—you can add 200g (8oz) of soft soap to the mixture if you like.

It is important when using sprays or poison pellets to consider the neighbouring gardens, animals and children, as well as your own. Always follow the directions given by the manufacturers very carefully. Never increase their recommended dose on the theory that if one dose is good, more will do better. More could be extremely dangerous and at best kill the plant.

Always allow the time recommended (or more time for added safety) to elapse before eating any treated fruit or vegetables.

Lock chemicals away and see that each is labelled very clearly with its name clearly marked POISON. Never decant any garden chemical into harmless-looking bottles or jars. Do not use DDT in any way or form as it is considered a highly dangerous chemical.

The **greenfly or aphis** These are sap-sucking insects. During the summer the females, without mating, produce living young who in turn give birth to their young— and so in a very short time a few greenfly have become hordes. They can be brushed off the bush, squashed, watered off or sprayed off with an insecticide. Remember not to use DDT which kills off all their natural enemies, eg ladybird larvae. Bees and ants on the other hand like the sticky 'honeydew' secretion produced by green-fly (also sometimes black or red), but this substance leads on to a black sooty mould. If the problem is severe, use malathion. A large bird population will also be on your side, helping to eradicate the pests.

Caterpillars can be found in all sizes and shapes with all kinds of moth and butterfly parents. They love leaves but sometimes will eat flowers. Sometimes they will be found rolled up in a leaf, safe from sprays and powders. Picking them off the plant is the best idea. Once egg laying begins derris will kill off those laid by the white cabbage butterfly from mid-summer onwards. Eggs are also laid on the underside of leaves of nasturtiums and stocks. Caterpillars are larvae and make their homes in many places —in the soil (cutworms), inside fruit (cod-lin moth), in leaf mines (the lilac leaf miner) or in wood (the leopard moth), or in webs. Prune webbed or bored shoots as soon as possible. If you are truly beset with the pests, resort to derris or pyrethrum.

Thrips like all pests will carry disease from plant to plant. They damage and malform buds, flowers, fruit and leave silvery blotches on leaves. They are minute and lay eggs in the bud and young leaves. There are lily, gladiolus, onion, pea and bean thrips, and if you have to protect

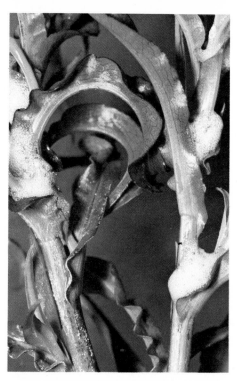

Above: *Rose leaf hoppers cause mottling, they leap off leaf when disturbed.*

Left: *Cuckoo spit is the froth which hides the larvae of frog hoppers.*

Below: *The rose leafrolling sawfly causes this type of damage and distortion.*

Below: *The eggs of the cabbage white butterfly. Check for these.*

Below: *The large white butterfly, a brassica pest. Watch for this pest on cabbage.*

Above: *The eggs of the adult sawfly are hatched on many plants including food crops.*

Above: *The larva (caterpillar) of the birch sawfly. Sawflies attack many trees and plants.*

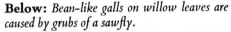

Below: *Bean-like galls on willow leaves are caused by grubs of a sawfly.*

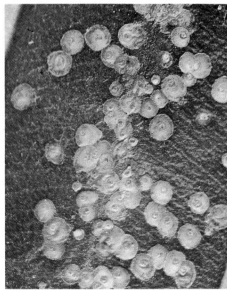

Above: *Oleander scale also attacks many other plants from aucuba to cyclamen.*

Above: *Willow scale on ceanothus. There are many different scale insects.*

Left: *Eelworm attack in narcissus bulbs.*

vegetables you can use malathion, but leave for a few days before harvesting. There are all sorts of **chafers** whose grubs live in the ground, sometimes for years, where they do quite a lot of damage to roots and underground stems. They are more likely to be found in a light, sandy soil. The chafers can sometimes swarm and wreck flowers and buds. A serious infestation in soil is best dealt with after obtaining advice from the Ministry of Agriculture.

Leaf hoppers are also sap-sucking insects. The adults do little harm but the larvae cause leaf mottling and weaken the shoots of plants. There are one or two types of hopper. The frog hopper forms the familiar cuckoo-spit to protect itself. Remove the cuckoo spit first with hose water. The roseleaf hopper moults 'ghost-fly' skins under the rose leaf. A spray with derris, pyrethrum or malathion will help plants under seige.

Scale insects produce a horrid clustering of six-legged insects on stems, which look like barnacles. Scales stay in the same place for a large part of their lives, when young, sheltering under the dead husks of the females. A winter wash of tar oil or some malathion works well but check that the plant is not sensitive to the cure. Some gardeners remove the scales and then sponge with an insecticide. Fruit trees, cotoneaster, gooseberry, peach and pyracantha and yew are likely plants to be attacked. A sign can be a sticky 'honeydew' excretion and sooty mould.

Red spider mites feed on leaves which they discolour bronze. Eventually the leaves shrivel and the plant is defoliated. They are one of several mites that damage plants. On the underside of leaves you might see with a hand lens moult skins, empty eggshells or a mat of silk threads. They like dry, hot weather and so in the normal English climate they are seldom at plague level. They are often a serious pest in the greenhouse. Outside use a derris spray or malathion, sprayed hard under leaves and repeated every few days for about a fortnight to catch all generations of mites.

Nymphs and adults of the **capsid bug** cause withered young flower buds and punctured and distorted foliage, sometimes with brown areas around the punctures. They are active pests and drop to the soil or hide under leaves. Early in the growing season the foliage of the plant and the soil beneath should be dusted with pyrethrum extract.

Eelworms are of various kinds, sometimes attacking stem and bulbs or the leaves and bulbs of flowers like chrysanthemums, strawberries, phlox and violets. They can survive for long periods in dried leaves and in the soil. Recognizable symptoms vary and the creatures are microscopic. Root-knot eelworms cause swellings on roots of plants such as tomatoes, lettuce and begonias. Like so many pests they produce large numbers of eggs. Root eelworms attack potatoes, tomatoes, beet and peas—the female cysts, pinhead size, can just be seen attached to roots and tubers. They contain hundreds of young in eggs. The best method for the gardener is to destroy the diseased plants and keep susceptible plants away from the infected soil for some years. There are elaborate hot water bath treatments for bulbs and stools which are only really worthwhile for professional growers.

Club root and finger and toe are names for trouble in the brassica patch, particularly for cabbages, Brussels sprouts, swedes and turnips. The roots swell and distort into long tuberous shapes or a gall-like mass. The plant becomes dwarfed or crippled. The cause is a parasite which contaminates the soil but does not thrive in limed soil. Control measures include regular liming except for potatoes and the use of 4 percent calomel dust. For example, you can get clean seedlings by growing them in a seed bed which has had 38g (approx 1½oz) of calomel dust per square metre raked into the soil. Also when planting make a creamy slurry of 4 percent calomel dust to approx 750ml (1pt) of water, plus some clay, and dip young plant roots in this as they are planted out. Rotation of vegetable crops is essential to keep down attacks by parasites such as the club root kind. It attacks all members of the *Cruciferae* family and this includes wallflowers, stocks, shepherd's purse (a weed) as well as brassicas.

Galls are irritations and distortions set up by larvae of some insects and mites, who inject poisons into the plant. A gall is sometimes tenanted by one grub only, sometimes by many. Oak is subject to galls, and the wild rose sometimes shows the bedeguar or robin's pincushion—a large soft gall that is rather attractive. The sawfly leaves unattractive galls on willow leaves, and you can find galls on black currants, pears and raspberry canes. Pick affected parts off and burn them.

The **earwig** attacks at night and is fond of carnations, chrysanthemums, dahlias and clematis in which it leaves very neat little holes and bitten areas. Earwigs tend their young, which is rare in insects, dislike the wet but love warm, dry places. If you want to trap them, fill flower pots or rolls of cardboard with straw and fix upturned on stakes among their favourite flowers. These traps must be emptied over a bowl of hot water daily.

Above: *Powdery mildew of roses causes unsightly marking easy to recognize.*

Below: *Black spot is a rose disease. All diseased leaves must be raked up and burnt.*

Above: *The disease rose rust can effect leaves and stems, showing orange pustules.*

Below: *The cockchafer or May bug larva. Right, an adult rose chafer. These pests are a gleaming golden-green colour. They feed chiefly on rose and sweet william flowers.*

The **slug** Slugs attack potatoes and tulip bulbs, among other plants. Slugs have plenty of predators after them—birds, toads, some worms, hedgehogs and centipedes—and you can best assist the chase by turning the earth over to expose them to their enemies. Liming and soot discourage slugs. If you want to kill them and cannot face crushing them, drop them in salt water. Slug bait works well but harms birds and pets, so use with great care.

Having dealt with most of the insects and their larvae whose healthy appetites for leaves, stems and flowers can cause disaster, let us now turn to the attacks of fungi and viruses. It is useful to remember here that if you give plants the conditions they need to grow strong and vigorous the less likely it is that they will become diseased. The rotation of vegetable crops, the removal of rubbish and weeds which harbour disease organisms, the sealing of any large pruning cuts and the choice of plants bred for resistance are all important for disease control.

For the beginner gardener the best way to deal with a diseased plant is to pull it out and burn it.

Mildew need not be too serious a disease but it is fairly common. It is caused by fungi. Powdery mildew spreads over the surface of leaves with microscopic white threads, and the spores spread from leaf to leaf. Many roses, gooseberries, strawberries, delphiniums and chrysanthemums are inclined to get powdery mildew. Spray the leaves well to prevent it spreading with Karathane, Dinocap, or a copper-based fungicide such as Bordeaux mixture. Your nurseryman might suggest a good proprietary spray, but no spray has certain results. You will need to spray at intervals but follow closely any instructions given with the spray you use.

Downy mildews, which you can get on onions, peas, spinach and lettuces, are rather worse but are controlled by spraying too, but take all precautions advised when dealing with edible crops. Downy mildews show as greyish patches of furry growth.

Black spot is another disease caused by fungi and many roses, including hybrids, are susceptible. The trouble shows as black spotting on the leaves which eventually shrivel and drop. As sulphur is a good fungicide, black spot is less common in large industrial towns with sulphurous smoke pollution. Except for weakening from leaf loss, plants will survive and flourish the next year although they are invariably attacked again. The disease spreads fairly slowly through a bed of roses. Affected leaves and prunings must be burnt—it sometimes helps to prune back affected bushes a little and feed and water them well. You can spray with a fungicide or Zineb or Captan if you feel impelled to.

Rust is also a fungus, betraying its presence on the leaves and stems of plants by rust-coloured pustules. The fungus is working from inside the plant, not on the surface of it, and is therefore difficult to treat and often fatal. You can spray against the spread of the disease but existing infections have to be destroyed. Sometimes in a garden rust has more than one host. For example, junipers can harbour rust infections which affect hawthorn, pears and rowan. For the same reason do not grow anemones near plums. You can buy rust-resistant cultivars of some plants, for example, antirrhinums. When you first see pustules, spray with Zineb to prevent the disease from spreading.

Damping off of young seedlings is seen when they begin to collapse and die. It is the work of several fungi and can cause either wilting of the seedling or rotting of the seed below ground level (pre-emergence damping). It is helpful to use sterilized compost for young seedlings as the fungi live in the soil. Avoid overcrowding and over-watering. Captan or Cheshunt compound can be used.

Virus diseases Only the effects of the minute organisms called viruses can be seen in plants—and sometimes not even that. Signs of virus diseases, however, are yellowing along the leaf veins, distortions, various outgrowths, misshapen fruits and general stunting. There is just about nothing that you can do about it except destroy the plants and plant nothing else susceptible there. Potatoes, fruit, roses and bulbs among many others can be attacked. Your best insurance against virus problems is good plant hygiene—removal of weeds, spraying against insects that carry the infections, burning the remains of previous year's crops, and, best insurance of all, buying plants that are certified free of specified viruses. Among certified stock you can buy strawberries, raspberries, blackcurrants, potatoes and loganberries.

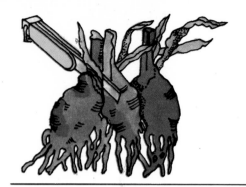

Simple multiplication

In a new garden you will probably stock up with quite a few beautiful nursery-grown plants, but to fill a whole garden with them would be very expensive. Most new gardens also start with a great many gifts of plants from friends; plants which they have produced quite simply from their own plants.

Once you have plants in your own garden, you can increase your stock of them to plant in other places, or exchange some with friends in return for plants you still have not got.

In an old garden you can take cuttings from old shrubs and produce young, vigorous shrubs.

With seeds you can pursue the sometimes slow but rewarding course of seeing a tree grow from a seedling smaller than a fingernail. You will also want to grow seeds of perennials and annuals. Seeds are produced by cross pollination, a sexual process. All the other ways to increase the number of plants you have are called vegetative propagation.

Seeds that are made by cross pollination of two plants of the same species will produce a plant just like them, but with hybrid plants this is not necessarily so—and many garden plants are hybrids. The only way to get other plants exactly like the plant you have is to grow cuttings, take layers, bud or graft. Budding and grafting are used widely by professional growers and nurserymen but they are not really necessary skills for the beginner.

Taking divisions of roots, making cuttings, layering and growing from seed are things you might want to do at any time.

Division
Some plants multiply by themselves by growing runners or little plantlets that root and can then be detached and potted up; or they develop little bulbs alongside the main bulb, or increase their underground growing stems or roots from which new shoots come, as in the case of mint.

Many clumps of perennials can just have their roots teased gently apart by hand, when they become too overgrown in their clumps. Then the outside shoots are young and vigorous and are replanted; the old,

Above: *Increase lilies by planting the individual scales upright in sand-peat compost.*

Below: *Cuttings of dwarf and evergreen azaleas can be taken towards the end of summer.*

Above: *Gladiolus cormlets are removed and stored in trays of peat in the winter.*

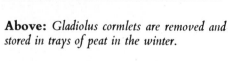

Right: *Azalea cuttings are inserted singly into pots with a sand and leafmould compost.*

Bearded irises need to be lifted and divided every few years after flowering. Old parts of the rhizomatous stock are discarded and the best pieces, usually from the outside, are used. Trim into pieces, each with one fan of leaves. Plant new pieces all in the same direction, with rhizomes facing towards sunny side of bed.

Below: *Division of perennials is simple. Clear soil from roots and separate by hand.*

woody central part is discarded.

Division of perennial clumps is done in early spring just as growth begins. You can also do it when plants are dormant.

Pyrethrum, *Chrysanthemum maximum*, ie shasta daisies, aubrieta, mimulus and one group of asters, *Aster amellus*, should be divided in the spring but other plants such as Michaelmas daises, heleniums, solidago, potentillas, phlox, geraniums, geums, armeria (thrift), campanula can be divided in the spring or autumn.

Hostas, agapanthus and peonies and other plants can be hard to pull apart. Use two forks to separate them as shown and cut the unseparable ones with a sharp knife or spade.

Trollius or globe flower, pulmonaria and others that flower early can benefit by being divided in autumn so that they can develop good roots before the spring.

Some gardeners pot up divisions or put them in a special protected bed until they are growing and rooting well, transferring spring-divided plants to the main garden bed the following autumn, and the autumn-divided plants the following spring. Whether you do this or plant straight into the garden bed, keep the divisions well-watered in dry periods until they become established.

Some plants that can be divided to increase your stock of them can also be grown from cuttings (described later). If you have a plant that you are uncertain how to propagate, check a gardening encyclopedia. It will give you a suggested method and the season to do it in, or obtain advice from the nurseryman where you bought the original plant. Tap-rooted plants grow better from cuttings than from division, whereas division suits fibrous-rooted plants.

The rhizomes of bearded, or flag iris should be divided after flowering. All rhizomes are best divided when the rhizome or food store is full, not when the plant is flowering. You will have to cut the fleshy rhizome with a sharp knife, bruising it will encourage infection. Cut back the iris leaves to about 15–20cm (6–8in).

Whenever dividing, it is a good idea to cut back any top growth to give the plant roots less to support until they are well-established.

Suckers

These are underground shoots that form and can be cut away with a sharp spade, with the roots, to form new plants. Remove suckers in autumn or spring for growing. You can increase your plants of raspberries, bamboos, some roses and lilacs in this way.

Suckers from any plant grafted onto a rootstock are no good for increasing the grafted plant as they are simply the rootstock trying to assert itself. Tear them out and throw them away. Tearing discourages growth better than cutting the suckers off.

Cuttings

Cuttings are pieces of a plant taken and planted in a suitable rooting soil where they make roots of their own and become new plants.

You can take cuttings from stems, roots, buds, or even single leaves, depending on the plant you are dealing with. Not all will grow for you the first time but such a simple cheap method of increasing plants can be tried again.

You can take stem cuttings of cistus, hydrangeas, fuchsias, chrysanthemums and many others. Some plants grow well from softwood cuttings and others from semi-hardwood or hardwood cuttings.

Cuttings like an aerated soil and must never dry out. Softwood cuttings like warm moist rooting compost for their roots to develop in and cool shady conditions above the soil. You can root cuttings in a John Innes cutting compost which you can buy ready-made. It is made of one part of medium loam, two parts of peat and one part of coarse sand.

If the weather is still cold, shelter the cuttings in a frame, cloche, greenhouse or indoors but never put them in the sun where they will lose moisture from the stem and die. Keep the soil moist but not too wet and wait until the roots are well-developed before you move a cutting. Even when the cutting sprouts it could still have a small root system so leave it until the middle of the following spring, for example, before you move an autumn cutting.

A rather curious thing about plants is that from any stem cutting the roots will always come from the end that was nearest the roots of the original plant. This means you must plant a stem cutting the right way up—to make sure you know which end is which if there is no bud on the cutting, cut the top end of the stem straight across and the lower end of the stem with a slanted cut. You are then less likely to plant it upside down.

You can buy hormone rooting compounds to help the cutting develop roots. Dip the root end of the cutting in the rooting powder and then plant it in the soil. You do not have to use a hormone rooting powder but it does help the formation of roots. However, it does not help the further growth of roots so there is no point in sprinkling it around the hole the cutting goes in. Follow the manufacturer's instructions carefully.

Softwood cuttings are made with soft young stems. With a very sharp knife, cut

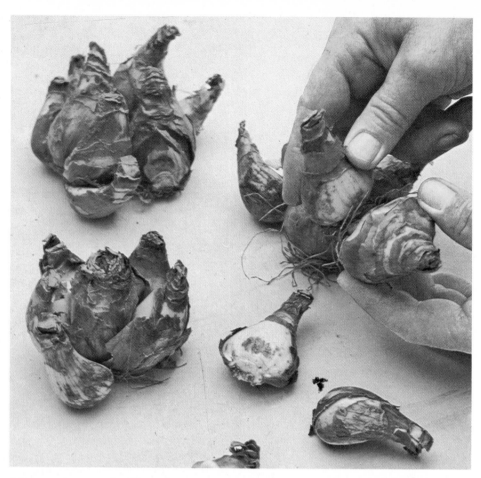

Above: *Removing the offsets of narcissi bulbs is one method of division. The new bulbs are then grown on as individual plants. Cymbidium orchids, cattleyas and miltonias can also be increased by careful division.*

Below: *Large clumps of perennials that cannot be handled easily can be pulled apart by placing two forks back-to-back between crowns, and levering handles until clump is broken. Separate clumps can then be planted.*

Above: *A delphinium crown showing the emergence of basal shoots. You can take cuttings from these basal shoots.*

Below: *Shoot is carefully removed with a very sharp knife. Cut below a leaf joint and remove any lower leaves.*

Above: *As many as six cuttings can be taken from one strong crown, which makes plants like this well worth propagating.*

Below: *The cuttings are planted firmly in a sandy compost in a cold frame or deep, glass-covered box.*

a piece of stem about 7·5cm (3in) long from a soft young shoot with plenty of nodes, that is, leaf joints, on it. If it has a bud at the end of the shoot leave it on. Trim the cutting just below a node or leaf joint—this is called a nodal cutting. The cut will seal and heal more quickly. Cut or nip off the leaves from the portion of the stem that will be below the soil and see that some nodes are below ground. Reduce the number of above ground leaves and any leaves near the soil. Dip the bottom end of the stem into a hormone rooting powder and stick it into the pot of John

Innes cutting compost or a similar compost. Softwood cuttings are made early in the growing season. Once there are good roots on the cutting, move it onto a new pot filled with a potting compost which will feed the young plant. Soft cuttings can be taken from chrysanthemums, dahlias, delphiniums, phlox, lupins, heleniums in early spring.

Semi-hardwood cuttings are stems on plants that are well-advanced in their first season's growth and firmer than a soft new shoot. Cut a piece of stem which is not flower-bearing and pot it up in the

same way as for softwood cuttings, using first a cutting compost until roots develop.

Sometimes a cutting is taken with a heel; the small shoot is gently pulled down and off, taking with it a sliver of the old wood attached. Trim the long strip at the bottom and then treat the cutting like any other. It is usually on plants that have shoots coming from relatively hard branches (shrubs such as camellia and some subshrubs and trees) that heel cuttings are made.

Hardwood cuttings are taken from mature wood at the end of the growing

Above: *Instead of a sandy compost, you could use vermiculite which is a good rooting medium because of its porous qualities.*

Above: *Once the cuttings have rooted, they are planted out under a cloche or in a protected place until they are established.*

Above: *Hardwood cuttings are taken during the autumn. A grip, or slit, is made in cleared and firmed ground in a sheltered place.*

Below: *Second step is for cuttings to be placed in slit and silver sand trickled in. Cuttings 25cm long are planted to about 12cm depth.*

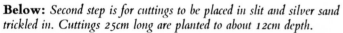

Above: *You can propagate more than one cutting at a time. Make a row of various cuttings—honeysuckle, climbing roses, shrubs.*

Below: *The grip or slit is closed and the earth firmed hard with the foot. Leave from autumn planting to the following spring.*

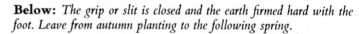

Leaf cuttings can be made from several plants such as streptocarpus. Slit across leaf veins.

Peg leaf down onto sandy compost. New plants will grow where the incisions were made.

The new plants are small but healthy and have their own roots.

Pot up new plant. Leaf cuttings should be shaded from direct sunlight while developing.

Soft cuttings can be taken of plants like coleus. Cut off a non-flowering shoot cleanly.

Trim cutting just below a joint and remove any lower leaves.

The cuttings are dibbled in. Set them around the edge of the pot in a sandy compost.

Below: *A beautiful collection of coleus showing their coloured and variegated leaves.*

season just before the dormant period of the plant about October or November. You can root hardwood cuttings out-of-doors. Currants, hedging plants, honeysuckle, gooseberries, climbing roses can be increased by hardwood cuttings. The cuttings are longer, about 22·5–30cm (9–12 in), pencil thick, with a clean cut made just below a bud eye. Remove all the leaves except for a few at the top and insert cuttings in sandy soil in a sheltered bed in the garden. You could use a cold frame or cloche. Keep the cuttings moist. They should have rooted by the following spring, but do not move them for about a year.

Leaf cuttings are used for plants like African violets, gloxinias and begonias. Remove a leaf, make sharp incisions with a knife across the underside of the leaf and lay it on the surface of moist compost. Peg leaf gently down with hairpins, or you can insert the leaf upright.

Bud cuttings are made with some plants like camellias. Take a soft, half mature stem carrying a bud between the leaf and the stem. Cut the stem just above the leaf joint carrying the bud and just below. Bury the cutting in a rooting compost until just the tip of the bud shows above the surface. Leave until roots form.

Root cuttings You can take root cuttings from dicentra, oriental poppies, Japanese anemones, gypsophilas, verbascums, romneyas, seakale, acanthus and horseradish among others.

Take root cuttings in autumn or early winter. Cut pieces of root about 5cm (2in) long and about pencil thickness. Cut a clean straight cut across the top and a slanting cut at the base and then you will remember to plant the roots the right way up, which is vital. Root them in seed compost or sandy soil. The top of the cuttings should be just below the surface. You can winter them in a cold frame, harden them and stand them in the open in spring.

Layering

You can try layering with rhododendrons, magnolias, carnations, lilacs, heathers and loganberries. Do it during the autumn or dormant season. Carnations and pinks though, should be layered in July, after plants have flowered and the layers will root in a few weeks in the warm soil. Some shrubs however will take months to develop roots from layering, so it is not the quickest method although it is fairly foolproof for the beginner.

Make a good fertile soil beneath the branch you are going to layer, adding plenty of sand and peat. Choose a young healthy branch or stem that can easily be pulled down to ground level. Cut the stem on the underside where it will touch the

A leaf-bud cutting of ficus is made by cutting between nodes leaving a bud at base.

Take a leaf and bud at the base to make a leaf-bud cutting of a camellia.

Placing hardwood cuttings on sphagnum moss for rooting in polythene.

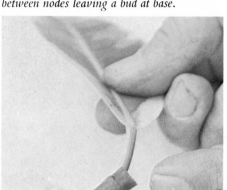

Small section of stem is left. Variegated plants are increased vegetatively to keep colour.

A single leaf-bud cutting, taken from the current year's growth, with plump, dormant bud.

The polythene is folded over lengthways so that moss and cuttings are held in place.

Cuttings are potted up singly. Compost in tray is used for firming plant.

The cutting is potted up singly in sharp, moist sand and kept in a warm place.

Roll the strip of polythene and cuttings up from one end to the other.

Rubber bands hold leaves in position. Cuttings will soon take root.

For quick rooting of many camellia cuttings, mist propagation is used.

Rubber bands make a neat parcel of the cuttings. Leave until cuttings root.

Above: *Border carnations and pinks can be increased by layering in summer after flowering. The layers will root in a matter of weeks.*

Above: *Sandy compost can be added at this stage to encourage rooting, the slit stems are pushed into the soil and compost and pegged down.*

Below: *A cut is made with a sharp knife on the underside of the stem to slit it horizontally through a node or joint.*

Below: *More sandy compost is added and soil surface levelled. The ground in the area should be kept moist.*

Above: *To increase strawberries, the runners can sometimes be pushed into the ground.*

Above: *The runners are pegged down so that the roots will grow behind the bud.*

Above: *Another method is to trim excess leaves and then peg runners down.*

prepared earth, cutting through a leaf joint or node if possible and making a lengthwise cut to form a tongue of wood. This cut node and tongue of wood is the part that must be pegged down or anchored with a stone into the soil. The cut interrupts the flow of sap and helps roots to form.

Air layering is a similar job except you make a little bag of rooting medium for the cut stem in the air. Use it for plants that have no convenient stems to weigh down in the soil. Prunus, camellias, liquidambars can be air layered. Make the cut through a young, year-old stem, forming the tongue. Dust the cut with a rooting powder. Wrap wet sphagnum moss into the tongued cut and wrap it all around the stem, then wrap over this and right around it a double layer of black polythene. Seal the polythene at both ends to make it watertight. April is a good month for air layering.

When roots are seen in the moss, cut the layer from the parent plant and carefully pot it up taking care not to damage roots. Cosset the new plant for a short while.

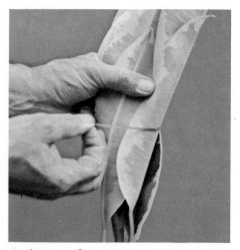

Air layering of Ficus elastica. Leaves are tied to keep them out of the way.

Second, leaves are removed on a section of stem. A healthy young stem must be chosen.

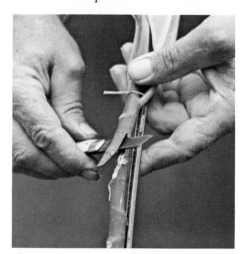

Third, a slanting cut is made behind a bud, as shown. Be careful not to cut right through.

Fourth, damp sphagnum moss is slipped into the slit. This is to be the rooting medium.

Fifth, more moss is wrapped around the cut part of the stem and tied securely.

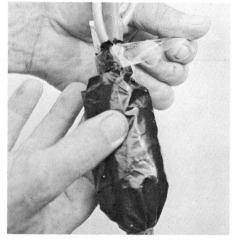

Sixth, the moss and stem is now wrapped in polythene which protects and seals it.

Seventh, the top leaves are released and the air layer is complete.

Right: *Weigela florida can be grown from cuttings but shrubs are also often layered.*

GLOSSARY

Bulb underground bud surrounded by fleshy leaf scales which is a food storage organ. It remains from year to year where a corm is renewed annually.

Compost term for all kinds of soil mixtures used for raising seedlings or growing pot plants.

Corm food storage organ which is a swollen underground stem, lasting a year. A new corm then forms to replace the old.

Cultivar a special name given to the cultivated variety to distinguish it from other varieties in the same genus.

Cutting a piece of a plant taken from stem, leaf, bud or root planted so that it will put out roots and grow into a new plant. It is one method of vegetative propagation.

Derris a vegetable-based insecticide effective against raspberry beetles, caterpillars, wasps and red spider mites. Is poisonous to fish so must be kept away from pools. Of short persistence.

Dibber small tool as thin as a pencil. Can be made from a cut-down handle. Used for making planting holes. Ideal for making holes for small plants but not bulbs or potatoes.

Drill shallow furrow made in the soil in which seeds are sown.

Glaucous used to describe leaves of blue-green or grey-blue which have a silvery blue or green bloom over them.

Grafting to grow one type of plant on the root or base stem of another plant. The lower stem and roots are called the rootstock, and the plant grafted on to the roots is called the scion.

Harden off gradually accustoming plants raised in protected conditions to outside temperatures and ventilation. If the process is too hurried, growth is checked and leaves can show signs of bad health.

Herbaceous adjective to describe those perennial plants whose growth begins from ground level each year. The herbaceous border was originally planned with only these plants but now has many other perennials and some shrubs.

Lateral a side growth, either a branch or a shoot. When pruning, make sure you distinguish between laterals and leading or terminal shoots, often known as the leader which is at the end of the branch. Laterals are usually cut back harder than leaders.

Layering pegging a long healthy shoot to the ground after making a short cut through joint (or node), so that plant will root from this area into earth. Air layering means that damp sphagnum moss is wrapped around cut branch if it cannot be bent down to the ground.

Malathion an organophosphorus insecticide useful in the control of aphids, scale insects, thrips, beetles and fruit tree red spider mites. Sweet peas, ferns and zinnias are plants that can be damaged by use of the spray. Of short persistence.

Mulch insulating layer of various materials put over soil to prevent loss of water by evaporation. Some mulches also feed the soil slowly.

Nicotine a vegetable-based poison useful as an insecticide against aphids, capsids, sawflies and leaf-miners. It is extremely poisonous to humans when in the concentrated state. Mark POISON; store under lock and key and never decant into harmless-looking containers. Of short persistence.

Node point in stem from which a leaf grows.

Organic derived from decaying natural (ie once-living) substances.

Prick out to lever seedlings out of their seed box as soon as they can be handled and to transplant into deeper seed boxes with slightly richer soil.

Pyrethrum flower heads of species of *Pyrethrum* (now botanically classified under Chrysanthemums) produce this insecticide which has a paralysing effect on insects. Decomposes rapidly particularly in bright sunshine. Sometimes combined with other insecticides in commercial products. Useful and safe when combined with derris to produce an insecticide of short persistence.

Rhizome underground stem or creeping rootstock usually growing horizontally from which shoots or flowers come.

Rootstock word with two meanings, either used as with the above term, or used to describe (more frequently) the root system on which a cultivated variety of plant has been budded or grafted.

Strike to strike a cutting is to get the cutting to form roots and grow.

Terminal at the end of branch or leaf.

Tilth the texture of the cultivated soil surface. Good tilth comes from good cultivation.

Tuber enlarged part of a root or underground stem lasting a year only.

Variety plant varying from typical form of a species, in colour, shape or habit. Used commonly about any plant differing from the typical form.

Picture credits:
Alpine Gardening Society 26BR
Amateur Gardening 20BC, 42T
H. Angel 138B
D. Arminson 27T, 45C, 56BL, 56/7, 80BL,
85T, 96BR, 102TC, TR, 103TR, 104T,
110C, 112B, 132BR
P. Ayres 18T, 44TC, BL, 98/9 (2 pics), 100B,
101BC, 102RC, 103BL
P. Becker 136C, 137TR, CR, BR
C. Bevilacqua 127TL
S. Bicknall 127TR
T. Birks 28B
P. Booth 36B, 44TL, 59B
M. Boys 129
J. Burras 140T
M. Chiswick 56TL
R. J. Corbin 22B, 23B, 25T, CL, CR, B,
26TL, 31BR, 32BL, 49TL, TR, C, 62T,
68CL, BL, BR, 71T, 73L, R, 74T, C, B, 75BL,
BR, 76T, C, B, 77TL, TR, BL, BR, 78T, C,
BL, BR, 79 (6 pics), 80BC, BR, 81TL, TC,
CL, CR, CC, 83TL, TR, CL, CR, BL, BR,
84T, 85BL, 86TL, TC, TR, BL, BC, BR,
87T, B, 88TL, R, 89TL, TR, BL, BR, 94TR,
97, 107TL, TC, TR, CL, CC, CR, BL, BC,
BR, 113BL, 119TL, 120L, BC, BR, 128TL,
TR, CR, 131L, R, 132TL, CL, CR, BL,
133TR, TL, BL, BR, 134BL, T, BR, 140BL,
CR, BR, 142T, 144CL, CR, BL, BR,
145TL, TR, TCL, TCR, BCL, BCR, BL
J. Cowley 88BL, 130TL, TR, BL, BR
C. Dawkins 102BL
C. Dawson 95T
A. Derrick 93CR

G. Douglas 59TL
J. Downward 21TL, 31TL, 37TR, 42BL,
43TR, 51TL, 117BL, 121TR, 128BR
V. Finnis 11T, 20TR, 21TR, 26BC, 38B,
53B, 54BC, 60BR, 100T, 102CL, 103TC,
BR, 108TL, 109TR, TL, 110R, 119TR
B. Furner 112T, 117TR
P. Genereux 17, 26BL
S. Grubb 108BR
M. Hadfield 61T
B. Halliwell 103BL
I. Hardwick 9T, 24BL, 91B
R. Hatfield 71B
J. Hovell 14C, 93BL, 94CL
J. Howden 139T
P. Hunt 14BR, 20BC, 21BL, 29T, BR, 30TR,
31TR, CR, 32T, 36T, 37TL, 57C, 63TR,
64BR, 94/5, 101CL, 104BR, 105BR, 124CL,
128BL
A. J. Huxley 14TR, 49BL, 109BL
G. Hyde 18BL, 20BR, 37BL, 39T, 42C,
44BR, 57BR, 139BR, BL, 93TL, TR,
95BL, BR, 101TR, 103TL, 105T, 124BR,
125B, 126B, 135T, BL, BR, 136TL, TR,
BR, 137CL, BL,139
L. Johns 24T, 55BR, 64T, 94TL, 106T, B,
111, 127B
R. Kaye 9BL, 109BR
J. Markham 4, 39BL, 56CL, 61B, 108TR,
BR, 124TR
E. Megson 55BL, 90, 101TL
Ministry of Agriculture & Fisheries 115T
A. Mitchel 53T, 102BR
Murphy Chemical Co. 138T
Natural History Photographic Agency 135C,

137TL
M. Nimmo 54T, 56TR, BC, 105BL, 128CL
S. J. Orme 19B, 57TL
K. Paisley 70
R. Parrett 29BL, 143TL, TR, BL, BR,
144TL, TR
Picturepoint 11BL, 45BR, 91T, 114T, 117TR
N. Procter 141B, 142B, 147
R. Procter 118, 123TL
J. Roberts 66, 67TL, TC, TR, CL, CC, CR
R. Rutter 81BR, 85BR, 92BR
J. T. Salmon 60BL
Shell 136BL
D. Smith 38T, 80T, C, 120T, 122, 123TR,
CL
H. Smith 2/3, 8, 9BR, 10, 11BR, 15T, B, 19T,
20TL, 21BR, 22T, 24CL, BR, 27BL, BR,
28T, 30TL, CR, BR, BL, 31BL, 32BR, 33L,
39, 40, 41, 42BR, 43TL, BL, BR, 44TR, C,
45TL, TC, TR, BL, 47T, B, 49BR, 50T, B,
51BL, BR, 52, 54BL, BR, 55T, 57TC, TR,
58T, B, 59TR, 60T, 62BR, 63TL, B, 64BL,
65, 66T, 67BL, BR, 82, 92T, BL, 93BR,
94BL,96BL,101BL,104T,113T,BR,117BR,
121TL,125T,126T,148
Suttons Seeds Ltd 84B
Tourist Photo. Library 33R, 124TL
Colin Watmough 16
C. Williams 29C
D. Woodland 96T
ZEFA 145BR

Designer: Carol Collins

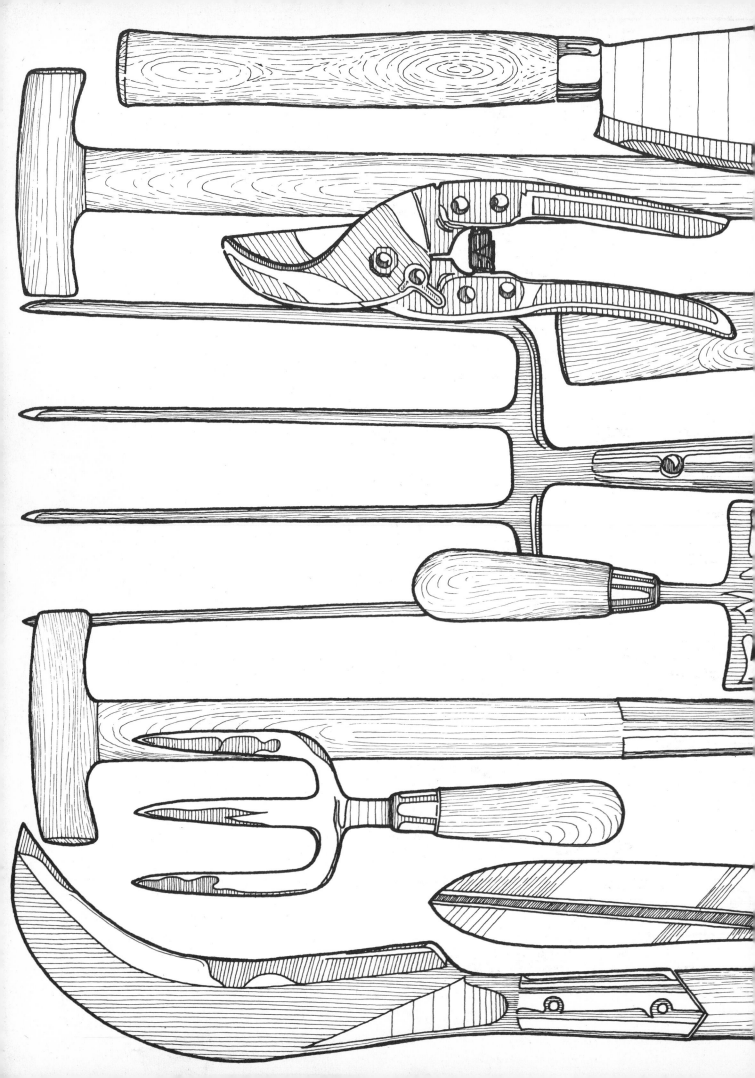